THOMAS SPEAR

KENYA'S PAST
AN INTRODUCTION TO HISTORICAL METHOD IN AFRICA

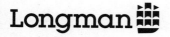

LONGMAN GROUP LIMITED
LONDON

© Longman Group Ltd 1981

Longman Group Limited,
Longman House,
Burnt Mill, Harlow, Essex
U.K.

First published 1981

British Library Cataloguing in Publication Data

Spear, T
  Kenya's past.
  1. Kenya – History – To 1895
  I. Title
  967.6'201   DT433.565

  ISBN 0-582-64695-2 Pbk
  ISBN 0-582-64696-0 Csd

Printed and bound in Great Britain by
William Clowes (Beccles) Limited,
Beccles and London

CONTENTS

LIST OF MAPS

LIST OF FIGURES

LIST OF PHOTOGRAPHS

ACKNOWLEDGEMENTS

The author and publisher would like to acknowledge the use of the following works in drawing a number of the maps in this book: B. A. Ogot (ed.), *Zamani*, Longman, 1974 (Map II); D. Nurse and G. Philippson, 'Historical Implications of the Language Map of East Africa', in E. Pokome (ed.), *Language in Tanzania*, International Africa Institute, London, 1980 (Maps 2.1, 2.2, 2.6); R. Burger, *Islamization among the Upper Pokomo*, Syracuse: Program in Eastern African Studies, 1973 (Map 4.1); G.S.P. Freeman Grenville, *The East African Coast*, Clarendon Press, Oxford, 1962 (Map 4.3); A. Frontera, *Persistence and Change*, Crossroads Press, Waltham., Mass., 1978 *and* E. H. Merritt, 'A History of the Taita of Kenya to 1900', Ph.D, Indiana, University Microfilms (Map 4.4); H. E. Lambert, *Kikuyu Social and Political Institutions*, OUP for IAI, Oxford, 1956 (Map 4.5).

The publishers are grateful to the following to reproduce photographs in the text: David Keith-Jones, p. 139; Royal Commonwealth Society Library, pp. 95, 98, 115, 135, 144; T. Spear, pp. 72, 73, 87. The photograph on p. 4 is taken from Leakey, *Olduvai Gorge*, Volume III, Cambridge University Press, 1971; p. 7 from D. W. Phillipson, *The Later Prehistory of Eastern and Southeastern Africa*, Heinemann, London, 1971; p. 9 from Phillipson in *Azania*, Volume XII, 1977; p. 13 from R. Soper in *Azania*, Volume II, 1967; p. 65 from R. Meinertzhagen, *Kenya Diary*, Oliver and Boyd, 1957; p. 77 from Leakey, *The Southern Kikuyu before 1903*, Volume III, Academic Press, New York, 1977; p. 103 from B. Bernardi, *The Mugwe*, OUP, 1959. The cover photograph was kindly supplied by T. Spear.

PREFACE

Over the past two decades African history has come of age. Working in the archives and the field, with documents and tape recorders, historians have patiently collected the traditions of hundreds of African peoples and written their histories. These local histories now constitute the foundations upon which we must think about the African past. This book could not have been written without them.

But I also hope that it represents a departure from them. My focus here is on a region; my aim to explore the dynamic of change in African societies through time. The emphasis to date has been to write African history as much within the Western academic historical tradition as possible in a chronologically sequenced progression of dates, events, and peoples. But these are precisely the areas where African historical sources are weakest, and so the exercise has proved to be a frustrating one at best. Where the African data excels is the way in which it reveals general processes of change. I have thus sought to capture a view rooted in African conceptions of the past that the elders of earlier generations would themselves appreciate, while, at the same time, contributing to the developing theory of the field.

As such this book represents a synthesis of my thinking about African history over the years. In the process of coming to these ideas I have encountered and learned from a number of other people struggling with similar problems. Many of these encounters have been the impersonal ones that come from reading books; I hope that I have made my manifold debts clear on that score, particularly to the oral historians who have done so much recently to explore Kenya's past, in the acknowledgements which follow each chapter. Luckily, many of my encounters have also been intensely personal ones. Jan Vansina and Stephen Feierman initiated me into African history and their ideas continue to challenge me today. I am also deeply indebted to Joseph Miller for his uncanny combination of imaginative thinking and meticulous criticism. This book would have been much the poorer without his insistent voice. Many of my greatest challenges and deepest insights have come from the different perspectives brought to my thinking by Sheila Spear. Finally, work on this book has initiated an extremely rewarding relationship with Derek Nurse, as linguistic advisor, critic, and enthusiast.

This book ranges far beyond my own particular expertise and I am particularly grateful to a number of specialists in other areas who have patiently endured my naivite and instructed me in the subtleties of their crafts. Glynn Isaac and Neville Chittick were very helpful in their criticisms relating to archaeology, as were Derek Nurse and Christopher Ehret on linguistics, and

David Parkin on anthropology. John Berntsen and Richard Waller gave me valuable insights into the traditional histories of the Maasai from their unpublished work, while Waller and Mary Ireland provided valuable critiques of the whole manuscript.

There are, of course, numerous other debts: to my students at Vwawa Upper Primary School who first stirred my interest in African history, to my fellow students at the University of Wisconsin who stimulated my early thoughts on the subject, to the Mijikenda elders who patiently entrusted me with their traditions, and to my students at La Trobe University who have challenged me to articulate my ideas clearly and simply and to extend my thinking in new directions. But most of all, I would like to dedicate this book to my fellow African historians, who through their commitment, enthusiasm, hard work, and sharing have accomplished so much in such a brief time and made African history such a joyful, creative, and rewarding enterprise, in the hope that you the reader will be persuaded, however briefly, to join with us in seeking a greater understanding of the African past.

Tom Spear, Williamstown, Mass., U.S.A.
January 1981

INTRODUCTION
HISTORY IN EASTERN AND CENTRAL KENYA

This book is intended for both beginning and advanced readers of African history and has three aims. The first is to introduce the reader to the history of Africa through a case study of eastern and central Kenya. This area was chosen because we know more about it than we do about any other on the continent. History from the earliest days of mankind through to the Iron Age is being mapped out in impressive detail from the archaeological sites at Olduvai Gorge, Koobi Fora east of Lake Turkana, and numerous early Iron Age sites scattered throughout the area. Linguistic studies are proceeding apace, with detailed classification of the Bantu languages of central and southeastern Kenya completed and work proceeding on the Cushitic and Nilotic languages of the north. This is also an area containing some of the earliest ethnographic reporting, as European missionaries and explorers traversed the area from the mid-19th century, well before the imposition of colonial rule in the 1890s, and wrote extensive descriptions of conditions at the time. Finally, local histories, based on oral traditions collected in the field, have now been written for almost all of the peoples of the area. For the first time anywhere in Africa, we are now in a position to combine these particular sources and histories into a comprehensive regional history, while at the same time, providing the reader with insights into some of the patterns that characterize the history (or histories) of Africa generally.

The second aim is to introduce the reader to the diverse methods used in our exploration of African history. Few historians discuss the methods of the historian and the logic of his or her explanation of events as explicitly as I do here. The reason is simple. African societies have transmitted their history, literature, and general knowledge orally from one generation to the next. As historians schooled in the analysis of written documents we have had to devise new methods to collect, validate, and analyse oral data and to rely heavily on additional data provided by archaeology, linguistics, ethnography, and anthropology. The data provided by these various methods and disciplines is not always comparable, and each type carries its own implications for the complex task of historical interpretation and explanation. Thus history written from an archaeological perspective stresses the development of material culture, while that written from linguistic data concerns the history of languages. To understand the African past, then, it is essential to understand both how these unusual sources are used in its reconstruction and how they influence our explanation of events.

The third aim is to develop a systematic approach to processes of change and cultural development in Africa. Change is, of course, the essential element in all of our study of history, but most historians content themselves with explaining specific changes in the past and are wary of generalized theories of social change. In Africa, however, we have no choice. Oral traditions rarely mention specific events, but talk about general processes in the past. Nor do the other methods employed – archaeology, linguistics, ethnography, and anthropology – provide the detailed day-to-day succession of events which the historians of literate societies use to analyse why and how certain events happened when they did. The nature of our data thus forces us to talk about general patterns and processes of change, using the more specific instances which we know about to test and validate the general theories.

Having discussed the aims in general, let us now turn to examine each of them in greater detail.

EASTERN AND CENTRAL KENYA AS AN HISTORICAL REGION

Although eastern and central Kenya is a diverse area and has never formed a single nation or state, it does form a cohesive region for historical study. As individual people have wandered over this area throughout history, they have inevitably come into contact with others with whom they settled, traded,

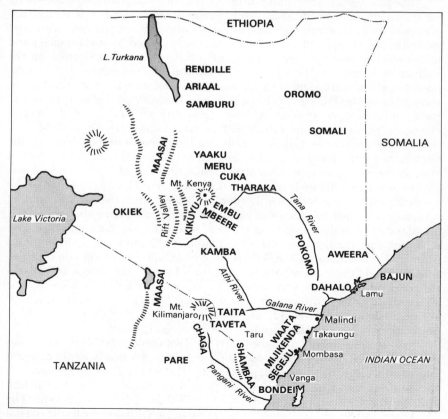

Map I *Peoples of eastern and central Kenya today*

married, fought, or exchanged ideas. The spread of major influences and developments among different peoples reveals the intensity of such interactions in the past. This interactive dimension has been missing from the local histories to date because of their focus on what is distinctive about individual peoples, not on what is general among many. But interaction has frequently been a major cause of change. A group of people living in isolation from others normally changed more slowly than different peoples who interacted with one another, each constantly offering cultural alternatives to the other. Histories which ignore interaction thus neglect one of the main factors in historical change.

Local histories may not have painted the whole historical picture, but they have taken the essential first step in sketching in the outlines of the individual elements. It is only through understanding the development of each people that we can begin to see the parallels between them and the areas where their development has been linked with that of others in the past. It is thus only now, when a rich lode of local data has been mined, that it is possible for us to extend our scope to examine the more dynamic patterns of shared interactions among the peoples of eastern Kenya.

The peoples of eastern and central Kenya have also shared its challenging environment. The fertile coast and highlands of southeastern Kenya are occupied today by mixed farmers, growing various grain and root crops and raising cattle, sheep, and goats. All speak closely related Bantu languages and follow similar decentralized patterns of social organization centred on the individual homestead or village. The natural environments of this area, however, show marked local variations as the land rises from sea level at the coast to over 5 000 metres at the peak of Mt. Kenya. Peoples' adaptations to these individual environments have produced a number of distinctive ecological zones, each one subdivided by more subtle variations within it.

The first is the coastal zone, including the narrow coastal plain and the slightly broader inland ridge. The coastal plain, less than eight kilometres wide in the south, receives an average annual rainfall of 1 300 mm and was covered by forest before it was cleared for farming. This is the home of the Swahili peoples, coastal town dwellers who built their fishing and trading settlements on offshore islands or coastal inlets, farming adjacent areas of the mainland. The main areas, from north to south, are the Lamu archipelago, including the island towns of Lamu, Pate, Manda, and Siyu; Malindi and Mambrui at the mouth of the Galana River; Kilifi and Takaungu on opposite sides of Kilifi Creek; Mombasa on Mombasa Island; and Vanga and Wasin clustered on the islands and inlets at the mouth of the Umba River on the Tanzanian border. Intervening coastal forests have long been occupied by Waata, Dahalo, and Aweera hunter-gatherers who lived off the local elephant population and frequently supplied ivory to Swahili traders.

As one moves inland from the central and southern coast, the land rises to a ridge 150–250 metres high before it flattens out on a slowly rising plateau. The coastal ridge, from the Galana River to south of the Tanzanian border, is the home of the nine Mijikenda peoples – the Kauma, Chonyi, Jibana, Kambe, Ribe, Rabai, Giriama, Duruma, and Digo – and of the Segeju. The Mijikenda and Segeju are mixed farmers who today cultivate the fertile coastal ridge and drier inland plateau.

Rainfall decreases markedly inland of the ridge until 40–50 km from the coast it drops below 600 mm, agriculture becomes impossible, and permanent human habitation ceases. This is the vast expanse of dry savanna woodland stretching 250 km into the interior known as Taru and is unoccupied except for two fertile pockets in its midst. The Tana River basin in the north forms a flood plain, 5–30 km wide and 400 km long, that provides a fertile agricultural environment for the riverine Pokomo peoples settled along its banks. In the south the Taita hills rise starkly above the plains to over 2 000 metres, the relief bringing increased rainfall as one ascends the hills. The Taita peoples are mixed farmers who intensively farm the steep hill sides between 750 and 1 350 metres, using irrigation to supplement the 900–1 300 mm of annual rainfall,

Fig. I *Peoples of eastern and central Kenya today*

People	Other Names	Language	Area
Hunter-Gatherers			
Aweera	Boni	Boni(?)	E. of Lower Tana R.
Dahalo	Sanye	Dahalo(?)	E. of Lower Tana R.
Okiek	Dorobo, Thi, Si	Kalenjin and Maa	Central Highlands
Waata	Langulo, Sanye	Oromo	Galana R. and Taru
Yaaku	Mogogodo	Yaaku(?)	N. of Mt. Kenya
Agriculturalists			
Cuka		Cuka	E. slopes of Mt. Kenya
Embu		Embu/Mbeere	S.E. slopes of Mt. Kenya
Gicugu		Gicugu	S. slopes of Mt. Kenya
Kamba		Kamba	Machakos and Kitui
Kikuyu		Kikuyu	E. slopes of Nyandarua Ranges
Mbeere		Embu/Mbeere	Lower S.E. slopes of Mt. Kenya
Meru		Meru	N. and E. of Mt. Kenya
Mijikenda	Nyika	Mijikenda	Coastal hinterland
Ndia		Ndia	S. slopes of Mt. Kenya
Pokomo		Pokomo	Tana R. flood plains
Segeju	Thagicu/Daiso	Daiso, Digo	S. Coast and S.E. Usambara Mts.
Swahili		Swahili	Coastal towns and islands
Taita		Saghala and Dawida	Taita Hills
Taveta		Pare	S.E. of Mt. Kilimanjaro
Tharaka	Thagicu(?)	Tharaka	E. of Mt. Kenya–Tana R.
Pastoralists			
Ariaal		Rendille and Maa	E. of L. Turkana
Maasai		Maa	Rift Valley
Oromo	Galla	Oromo	N. of Tana R.
Rendille		Rendille	E. of L. Turkana
Samburu		Maa	S.E. of L. Turkana
Somali		Somali	E. of Tana R.

and graze cattle in the colder montane areas above and drier plains below. East of the Taita, the Taveta exploit a fertile forested foothill of Mt. Kilimanjaro, where they grow bananas and yams along the banks of forest streams.

As the plateau rises above 600 metres along the Athi River rainfall begins to increase. West of the river the land rises further to 2 400 metres in Mbooni and rainfall approaches 1 500 mm annually, while east of the river the Yaata Plateau remains between 600 and 900 metres and the annual rainfall is limited to 250–750 mm. Kamba today occupy both sides of the river and practice a

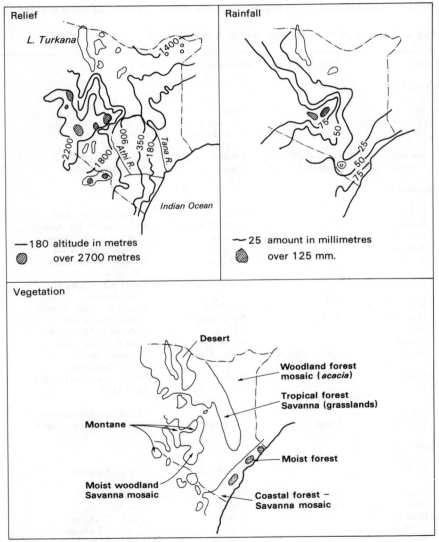

Map II *Eastern and central Kenya: environment*

wide range of agricultural and pastoral pursuits to suit the varying environments. In Mbooni, for example, Kamba raise maize and finger millet in the area between 1 500 and 2 000 metres and bananas and rootcrops above this, while south and east of Mbooni they raise drought-resistant millets, sorghum, and cassava in the wetter areas and graze cattle in the drier ones.

Proceeding further inland, the land continues to rise into the Central Highlands surrounding the Nyandarua Range and Mt. Kenya. The environments of this area vary enormously with altitude. The lower reaches of the mountains are dry woodland and grassland savanna, the middle belt fertile Kikuyu and Star grass zones, while the upper altitudes are bracken, bamboo, and moorland montane environments. The Kikuyu, Gicugu, and Ndia peoples farm the middle belt on the Nyandarua Range, 1 800–2 100 metres high with an annual rainfall between 1 300 and 2 300 mm, using the grasslands on either side for grazing. Higher up in the mountains live the Okiek hunter-gatherers. The Embu, Cuka, and Meru (Igembe, Igoji, Imenti, Mwimbe, and Muthambe) peoples farm a parallel zone circling Mt. Kenya and nearby Nyambene, 1 200–1 500 metres above sea level, while the Mbeere, Tharaka, and Tigania Meru peoples live in the lower areas, 900–1 200 metres, where the lesser rainfall (500–750 mm) forces them to rely on drought resistant grains and herding.

The drier areas of northeastern Kenya and the floor of the Great Rift Valley bisecting Kenya west of the Central Highlands are predominantly dry savanna grasslands and woodlands. This zone is occupied by migratory herders, the Somali in the northeast; Boran and Orma Oromo north of the Tana River; Rendille, Ariaal, and Samburu east and south of Lake Turkana; and Maasai in the Rift Valley. Considerable variation exists within these areas. Rendille and Somali herd camels in the drier far north and east, while the others herd cattle, sheep, and goats in the wetter areas further south.

The geographic differences between and within these zones are further accentuated by annual climatic variations that occur. Rainfall can vary by over 50 per cent either side of the averages cited above, and serious drought afflicts eastern Kenya an average of one or two years every decade. Nor is rainfall evenly distributed throughout the year. In most areas there are two rainy seasons – the long rains from February to May and the short rains from October to December – punctuated by intervening dry seasons. The combination of great ecological differences and dramatic seasonal variations provided an eternal challenge to the peoples of eastern and central Kenya, but they were also one of the main factors integrating the region into an interactive whole. People producing different goods complemented one another, each exchanging its specialties with others for those that it lacked. Droughts, famines, or diseases rarely affected everyone equally. Those affected were thus able to obtain relief from their own misfortunes among their more fortunate neighbours.

While this region falls largely within the borders of modern Kenya east of the Rift Valley, it overlaps its borders at a number of points. Since the modern political borders were only imposed at the end of the period which this book covers, however, it is not surprising that they have little historical justification, and we will frequently follow historical threads into adjacent areas. In the southeast, for example, historical interaction frequently occurred over the past two thousand years with the closely related peoples of northeastern Tanzania, while in the north Bantu speakers once extended up the Somali coast to Mogadishu, Somali today extend into northern Kenya, and Oromo spread throughout Ethiopia.

RECONSTRUCTING THE AFRICAN PAST: SOURCES AND METHODS

The history of eastern and central Kenya stretches over more than two million years from the initial emergence of mankind itself to the present. Historians use a number of different kinds of data and methods to reconstruct this past. The earliest evidence that we have are the material remains of past cultures discovered by archaeologists painstakingly sifting through the living sites of earlier peoples to uncover their bones, tools, and religious artifacts. From this data they are able to reconstruct what the people themselves looked like, how they lived, their economy, their settlement patterns and social organization, and even on occasion their beliefs. Using modern scientific techniques, many of these items can also be generally dated and compared with similar items found elsewhere, enabling archaeologists to trace the main developments in the history of humanity from the emergence of mankind through the

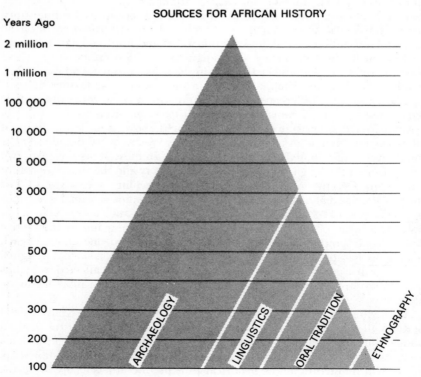

Fig. II *Sources for African history*

development of agriculture and iron working to the present. The view of the past which we get from archaeological data is thus one of general developments taking place over very long periods of time rather than a precise record of daily events.

A second method used to reconstruct the African past is comparative linguistics. Languages change over time. As people speaking a single language move away from one another, their speech slowly diverges, first into related dialects of the single language and eventually into separate languages. By comparing modern languages and classifying them by their degrees of similarity, linguists are able to place these past developments into a family tree of ancestrally related languages. From this data, historians can then infer that the speakers of two or more languages which share a common origin in the past must have lived together at one time and spoken a single language. By looking at the common elements among such closely related languages, linguists are also often able to reconstruct the main elements of the ancestral language itself. Vocabulary reconstructed in this way can tell us much about the culture of the speakers of the earlier language. If they had a number of words dealing with cattle they were probably pastoralists, but if they did not have a word for iron, it is unlikely that they were iron workers. Finally, linguists can discover which words in a language were borrowed from other languages. Since borrowing usually only occurs when there has been some interaction between peoples speaking different languages, the presence of loan-words in a language provides us with evidence for such interaction. All the languages in the world derive their word for tea from the Chinese *ch'a*, for example, indicating that tea originated in China. Comparative linguists can thus provide us with the history of language development, aspects of the cultures of speakers of earlier languages, and indications of interaction between speakers of different languages in the past. But, like archaeologists, they can only provide us with these within the context of general trends in the past.

Oral traditions provide a third perspective on the African past. Oral traditions are stories told about the past, but they are not history as we know it today. They are legendary accounts full of the exploits of heroic ancestors and rich in cultural imagery relating to the development of a people, much like the Old Testament. They abstract the main lessons from the past and compress these into a single elegant message for the present. African historians have developed a complex methodology over the past decade for decoding the rich cultural language of traditions to reveal their historical basis and now use them extensively in reconstructing the past. Like archaeology and linguistics, however, they are limited. Traditions do not extend more than four or five hundred years into the past and are concerned exclusively with the major themes in the development of a people rather than the minor digressions that may have occurred along the way.

The fourth major source for the African past are early ethnographies, or descriptions of African societies, written by the earliest European travellers, missionaries, and colonial administrators in Africa. These are detailed accounts of the way people lived prior to colonial conquest, including their economy, social structure, and beliefs. These are invaluable first-hand accounts of life in the later 19th century and early 20th century, but they are deeply flawed by the ethnocentrism, racism, and ignorance of their authors, who often showed a very limited understanding of the people among whom they were living. Nevertheless, they provide a valuable complement to the other sources, helping the historian to place them in their cultural context.

We have noted that each of the main sources for reconstructing the African past emphasizes general trends in the development of African cultures and societies rather than detailed trains of events. The composite picture which we get when we put these all together, then, is a social and cultural history of the peoples of Africa, quite different from the political history with which we are more familiar.

SOCIAL AND CULTURAL CHANGE IN HISTORY

History is the study of change. If African history is largely social and cultural history, then, we need to understand why social and cultural changes occurred and how these changes took place. Change was rarely simple. It could be brought about through any number of causes, some coming from within a society and others from without. And once initiated, changes could have unforeseen and widespread effects; change in one area of a society often sent shock waves throughout the society affecting numerous other areas in unpredictable ways. Change is also an exceedingly difficult subject to study. The actors in the historical drama were rarely aware of its occurrence at the time, so slow and imperceptible were its effects. It was thus largely an unconscious process as far as the participants were concerned. To study change we must therefore dig below the surface of human activity to discover the underlying causes of change and the processes by which it occurred. This is what we will now try to do.

Change came both from within and from outside the societies of eastern Kenya. External causes of change are often the easiest to identify. Changes often occurred in response to changes in the physical environment. The environment set certain limits on peoples' activities, depending on their ability to control and exploit it. The relationship between people and environment, known as ecology, could thus be altered either by changes in the environment itself or by changes in peoples' means of exploiting it. The drying up of the Sahara during the 3rd millenium BC, for example, transformed it from a prosperous hunting, fishing, and grazing area to a virtually useless desert, forcing the peoples who inhabited it to migrate elsewhere, while the domestication of plants and animals in Kenya in the last millenium BC allowed man to support large settled populations and led to the development of more complex social and political structures. Dramatic changes in the environment or in mankind's adaptation to it were few, however, and took place gradually over thousands of years. But individuals could effect major changes in their environment simply by moving from one area to another, forcing them to alter their technology, their herbal pharmaeopoeia, and even their descriptive language to accommodate to the new conditions. Periodic changes in the environment also occurred. Droughts, locusts, and diseases disturbed peoples' adaptations to their environments, and these occurred with disarming frequency in eastern Kenya. To some extent, people could adapt to such periodic occurrences by incorporating defences against them within their normal practices. Crop diversification, rain magic, and extended trade networks helped people to survive droughts, while healing techniques and natural immunities protected them from prevalent diseases. Each people thus developed their own unique cultural ecology suited to their own conditions; any change in those conditions forced them to re-examine and reformulate their adaptive mechanisms.

Interaction with other peoples and cultures was a second external cause of change. In small-scale societies where each village or area had its own customs and mores, one had to adapt one's behaviour to relate to strangers coming from outside the village world. A common language had to be found and common practices adopted in order to accommodate the stranger within one's own social universe. Other peoples also offered alternatives to one's own cultural practices. They grew different crops, used different methods of healing, and had different marriage customs. All of these offered the potential for adaptation to one's own way of life, particularly when they had an advantage over one's own ways or met a clearly perceived need. Finally, other peoples offered a wider experience of reality. One people might have had access to salt-pans, another to iron ore, while a third to a distinct plant or animal product. By exchanging separate resources, all could expand their own material bases. The same applied to ideas and social practices. The microcosm of the village world thus became expanded into the macrocosm of a wider cultural universe. Such interaction with others was a daily occurrence in African life. Because most men married women from other areas, there were always a number of women in a village who came from outside the village. And since women were usually responsible for gathering or raising the main food supplies and valued for their medicinal and healing knowledge, they had the opportunity to introduce new practices into significant areas of village life. Interaction was also frequent on the fringes of the village world, where people traded their own specialized products and resources for those from other areas. Finally, population growth, drought, or epidemics frequently forced people to migrate from one area to another, bringing them into intensive interaction with the people among whom they settled.

A third external cause of change was the spread, or diffusion, of cultural practices from one area to others. Different types of agriculture and herding, iron technology, and languages all spread over large areas of Africa. Diffusion sometimes occurred in conjunction with the migration of people from one area to another, but more often individuals or small groups of migrants, such as traders, ritual specialists, iron workers, or hunters, were able to spread new ideas over considerable distances in the course of their normal travels. Then too, ideas could and did spread on their own, as people freely borrowed practices they had observed elsewhere. Diffusion has, however, been an overwrought theme in African history, used to account for virtually any change which occurred. We now know that many innovations were made locally, and in any case, sweeping diffusion theories neglect the key processes of interaction by which new ideas were altered and adapted in the process of incorporation.

The other source of change was from within society itself. Probably the commonest internal cause of change was the continual tension that existed in any society between a people's norms and their actual behaviour. Behaviour rarely measured up to norms. For one thing, norms were practices evolved in the past and might not account for current conditions, while for another, norms were ideals, statements of perfect patterns of behaviour for imperfect human beings. Thus the two existed in continual tension, with people striving to adjust their behaviour to the ideals or to reinterpret the norms to suit their behaviour. In time, the gap between the two became too great to bridge and the ideals were modified to suit the reality. Thus there was always a delay, or 'cultural lag', before a people's ideals articulated in the past were adjusted to the daily reality of the present.

A second set of tensions existed among the ideals themselves, an ideal pattern of behaviour in one area conflicting with that in another. Murder was condemned in peacetime but glorified in war. Individuals within a society had to negotiate continually among conflicting norms, providing them with considerable latitude in their behaviour. Deliberate transgression of one norm could often be justified by appeal to another. And the opportunities for such negotiation were greatly increased in interactive situations where alternative norms were provided by other peoples. Like the conflict between norms and behaviour, if the conflict between different or alternative norms became too great, a belated adjustment of one or the other had to be made to bring them more into line. Such changes in ideals are the essence of cultural change. 'Culture' can be broadly defined as a meaning system by which individual societies seek collectively to understand, interpret, and structure their world. It is, on the one hand, made by people, part of the cumulative heritage passed on from one generation to the next; while on the other, it makes people by stating mandatory patterns of behaviour. Thus to revise normative patterns is to change the content of culture itself and to influence future behaviour.

A third internal cause of change was the unforeseen ripple effect of change in one area of culture or society upon other areas. The adoption of a new crop, for example, may inadvertently cause an alteration in the sexual differentiation of labour, and as we will see, the adoption of new trading patterns in the 19th century in Kenya had profound social and cultural ramifications.

Population increase also caused profound changes, putting a strain on resources and causing people either to seek more resources or to intensify their exploitation of existing ones. The first led to periodic outward migrations, as young people abandoned overcrowded areas to seek greater resources elsewhere, causing existing social groups to fragment and new social groups to form elsewhere. Dispersal could occur as long as there was land available elsewhere, but ceased to be a viable tactic when suitable land was limited, as it often has been in the restricted riverine, coastal, or montane environments of eastern and central Kenya. In this case people had to intensify their exploitation to produce more from the same resources. Such a need may well have underlaid a number of the more significant innovations in Kenya, such as the transition from hunting-gathering to farming and herding and the progressive intensification of farming practices from long-cycle bush fallow systems to shorter and shorter cycle systems involving crop rotation, intercropping, irrigation, and manuring. Each of these changes involved progressively greater labour inputs to produce a given amount of food and thus would not have been adopted had they not been required to feed increasing numbers of people in a given area. Such intensification had profound social and cultural effects. Hunter-gatherers had to remain mobile to exploit the shifting resources of large areas, and thus were organized in small shifting bands of people, while farmers were concentrated in more permanent and denser settlements and had to evolve more complex forms of social organization.

A fifth internal cause of change were the dynamic capabilities inherent within social and cultural institutions themselves. We will discuss a number of these in the chapters that follow, so a single example here will suffice. Most of the societies of Kenya were organized along the lines of kinship, all the descendants of a single man or woman belonging to the same descent group, or lineage. The members of a lineage lived together in the same village, held land in common, and conducted their own political affairs. But lineages were always expanding, getting both younger and older at the same time, as their members produced children and the number of generations in the lineage grew. This contradiction led to an ongoing lineage dynamic as older generations sought to maintain standards and power while younger generations sought to alter standards and gain power for themselves, causing lineages to split, or fission. But lineage members also had to seek their spouses from outside the lineage, creating an ongoing pattern of marriage alliances or fusions, between lineages. Thus lineages were constantly in the process of fragmenting and reforming in a variety of ways. The dynamics become ever more complex in interactive situations where one lineage was adopted by another, two fused on equal grounds or become interdependent, or one dominated another and become a royal or an aristocratic lineage. Thus, over time, lineage-based villages could develop into hierarchical chiefships or be amalgamated into kingdoms, while kingdoms could equally devolve into their component lineage villages.

There were thus numerous external and internal causes of change in African societies, but what was the impact of these forces on the society? How were new influences and new patterns incorporated into cultures so that they become part of the ongoing development of those cultures? These processes were even more complex than the causes of change and require a discussion of what I mean by 'development'.

Ironically, there is no suitable word in English to convey the processes by which societies have adapted to new circumstances in the context of their own cultural heritages. Each individual and, collectively, each society has its own ways of looking at the world, understanding how it works, accounting for mankind's role within it, and integrating new experiences with older ones. Thus when internal contradictions arise or new influences occur, each society will build on their past experience to perceive, understand, and come to terms with them. The first Europeans in Africa saw the contact experience in very different terms from the Africans who encountered them, and each incorporated the different lessons they learned in different ways into their different cultures. It was on such misunderstandings, for example, that the shaky foundations of colonial rule were laid. It is this process whereby people constantly modified their culture, building on their heritage to adapt and change it in the light of historical circumstances, that I have termed 'cultural development'. I do not mean to imply any evolutionary perspective here, such as that often conveyed by such usages as 'economic development'. New developments were not necessarily any better or any worse than the old; nor are they to be placed on any evolutionary continuum from less advanced to more advanced cultural forms. They were simply the normal changes people made to adapt their ways to their circumstances.

REFERENCES AND SUGGESTIONS FOR FURTHER READING

A work of this scope cannot hope to acknowledge all the intellectual debts incurred or the sources used. As a general policy, I have chosen to discuss only the most recent or important works on a subject at the end of each chapter. Readers are urged to consult these for greater detail, while the detailed lists of sources each contains provide ready avenues for the researcher to pursue individual topics.

The reader is referred to these discussions in the chapters that follow for specific references relating to the issues discussed in the introduction. References pertaining primarily to archaeology have been grouped in Chapter 1, to linguistics in Chapter 2, to oral traditions in Chapter 3, to ethnography and anthropology in Chapter 4, and to economics in Chapters 5 and 6.

CHAPTER ONE

EARLY MANKIND TO THE IRON AGE
THE ARCHAEOLOGICAL RECORD

The earliest view of Kenya's past is provided by archaeologists' studying the material remains of the past. For the distant past, such remains consist mostly of human and animal bones together with stone tools, pottery, and other things which are able to survive natural processes of decay. From these, archaeologists can often reconstruct the way of life followed by the people who used them. Tools are often the most frequently found items. By analysing the types of tools found and the method of their construction, archaeologists can tell much about the economy and ecology of the people who used the tools. Stone adzes and pounding stones, for example, are common tools used by gatherers in the forest, while choppers, cleavers, knives, or spear and arrow points are the tools of savanna hunters. Similarly, grinding stones, bowls, and digging implements indicate forms of wild grain gathering or agriculture. Animal bones are also a commonly found item. If these are the bones of wild animals, then the people must have been hunters, but if they are the bones of domestic animals, then they were herders.

It is also possible to reconstruct the social organization of prehistoric peoples. Archaeologists may be able to estimate the number of people occupying a site from the remains of hearths, the number and placement of hut poles, or simply the area of the site. The amount and type of material found on a site can indicate whether it was permanently occupied or only the temporary stopping place of nomadic hunters. A large and varied collection of tools together with the remains of a number of different animals indicate a permanent or semi-permanent settlement, whereas the bones of a single animal together with only the tools required to butcher it indicate a temporary camp at a kill.

It may also be possible to say something about the beliefs of the people who lived there if they buried their dead in ritually prescribed ways, if they left ritual objects, or if they portrayed their life and beliefs in their art. Cave paintings throughout Africa convey in considerable detail the lives and culture of the hunter-gatherers who painted them.

Finally, biologists can learn much about the physical capabilities of earlier forms of humanity and their place in mankind's evolutionary development from studying their fossils. Brain size can be measured and mental capabilities assessed. The arrangement of the pelvis and of the leg and foot bones reveal how well adapted people were to walking upright. The bones of the hand show how adept they were at manipulating objects in their hands. And the size of the jaw and type of teeth can tell us what kind of diet was eaten.

In addition to what we can learn about a single society living on a single site, we can also learn about the evolution of mankind through time by comparing different sites. One site may be on top of other sites, enabling archaeologists to work down through a succession of earlier sites, reconstructing the evolution of humanity from the earlier deeper layers to the higher later ones. Similarly, finds from different sites, but located in the same geological strata can often be compared and a relative sequence established. Archaeologists are also able to date some materials absolutely by one of a number of technical processes and so arrange them in a chronological sequence. Organic remains of once living things can be dated by the radiocarbon method. All living plants and animals absorb carbon 14 radiation while they are alive, but it decays at a fairly constant rate (one half its radioactivity approximately every 5 700 years) after they die. By measuring the amount of carbon 14 radioactivity still within a specimen, scientists can then calculate how long that specimen has been dead. Thus if there are any organic remains on a site, such as pieces of charcoal, these can be dated and the dates applied to other objects nearby which cannot be dated, such as iron or pottery. Similarly, the potassium–argon method can date volcanic ash, and then objects in, above, or below the ash can be related to the dates of the ash itself. Using these and other methods, archaeologists can assign a date to the level with which a find is associated and, by arranging a number of sites chronologically, can reconstruct the evolution of humanity through time.

In addition to the material remains found, scientists can also study the habitat in which they were found. The climate and ecology of the time can be assessed from the soil and rock surrounding the finds, and long departed lakes or forests can be reconstructed. Taken together, the evidence of an archaeological site can tell us much about the people who once inhabited it. We can reconstruct where they lived, what type of people they were, what kind of food they ate and how they acquired it, how they lived, and what the climate and environment of the time was like. By placing a number of such reconstructions in chronological sequence, archaeologists can then trace the physical evolution and cultural development of mankind through time.

THE EVOLUTION OF MANKIND AND THE DEVELOPMENT OF CULTURE

The archaeological record of mankind in Kenya is the oldest in the world, stretching back some four to five million years to the earliest men and women and their immediate forebears living on the shores of Lake Turkana. This arid area today may seem an unlikely site, but here surely was part of the Garden of Eden where humanity first emerged. The history of mankind is an exceedingly long one and painfully slow in its initial developments. If we were to make a movie of this history lasting twenty-four hours, the first 23 hours and 55 minutes would show stone tool using hunter-gatherers who slowly improved their tools from rocks they first chanced to pick up to the refined blades and chips still commonly used two thousand years ago. In the last five minutes of our film, however, the pace of change would begin to accelerate as people first domesticated animals and plants and then discovered metallurgy, enabling them to produce more food, to clear and settle forests more efficiently using iron tools, and thus to support a larger, settled population. Villages, towns, and cities would begin to emerge in which some people could pursue specialized crafts producing pottery, skilled metalwork, fine cloth, monumental buildings, and works of art. The images would start to flash across the screen faster now as states and empires developed, supported by surplus agricultural production and trade. One minute from the end Christ would appear, followed almost immediately by Mohammed. In the last nine seconds we would view the complete industrial revolution, from the first factories to the space age; in the last three seconds Africa would be colonized and regain its independence; while the last two seconds would encompass the lifetime of most of us watching.

If changes have come so rapidly in the modern world, why did it take people so long to develop simple stone tools or to domesticate the animals they hunted and the plants they gathered? To some extent the answer lies in the accumulation and exchange of knowledge. Each generation was able to build on the developments of previous generations and share its knowledge with its contemporaries. Knowledge thus accumulated at an increasing rate. Such an explanation only applies to the last 150 000 years – the last seventy-two minutes of our film – however, for up until that time the most crucial process was the evolution of mankind itself from small-brained human-like creatures to intelligent beings capable of speech, complex thought, and fine manipulation of its hands to produce better tools. Mankind's first task, then, was mankind. Nowhere is this demonstrated better than in Kenya.

It is difficult to know when to begin our story of people in Kenya. The ability to walk upright on two legs, known as bipedalism, probably started some five to six million years ago, slowly freeing the hands for carrying and allowing the thumb to develop in its opposed position, making the hands more adapted to gripping and manipulating objects. Similarly, brain capacity and mental skills increased only slowly over millions of years. No one event, not even the acquisition of culture, marked humanity's emergence. Rather it was a process of mankind's physical evolution and its cultural development interacting and developing together which slowly defined its unique position as intelligent, social, cultured beings.

The crucial interaction of physical evolution and cultural development is seen prominently in tool use. The more people used tools, the more their hands evolved a fine grip in order to manipulate them and the more their brains evolved to create them, both of which led to still greater tool use. To take another example, bipedalism freed the hands, but the evolution of a narrower pelvis to facilitate walking upright and of a larger head made it more difficult for women to give birth, so the human child came to be born in an undeveloped state with a brain only 25 per cent of adult size. Combined with the increasing complexity of the human organism, this increased the time it took the child to mature, leading to a prolonged period of immature and dependent childhood. Such dependency, in turn, brought about a division of labour in society to allow some to look after children while others obtained food. At the same time, it provided a long period during which adults could transmit learned behaviour, or culture, to their young. Those who were able to cooperate socially with others and to develop and transmit ideas increased their control over their environment and were more likely to survive and to reproduce than those who did not. Thus evolutionary processes ensured that the more

3

intelligent, adaptive, cultured social beings were selected. Human cultural development was thus an integral part of physical evolution.

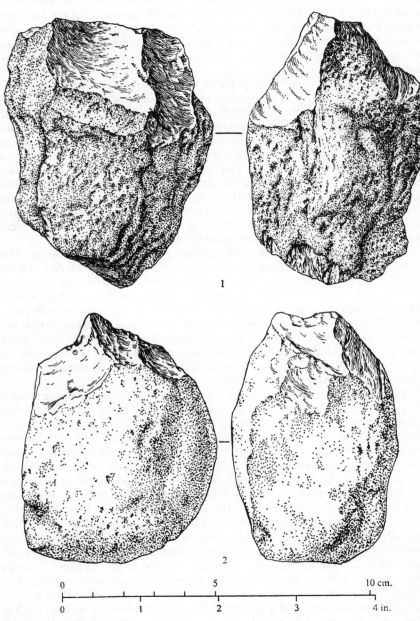

Photo 1.1 *Oldowan tools*

As difficult as it is to pinpoint the beginnings of mankind, the co-existence of at least two human-like beings as contemporaries at Olduvai and Lake Turkana offers dramatic evidence of the stages that were crucial to its evolution. First into the archaeological record is *Australopithecus*, an upright creature who first lived four to five million years ago. By two to three million years ago *Australopithecus* had a neighbour, *Homo habilis*, or Handy Man, so called because of its use of crude stone tools to butcher animals and break up their bones. Although by this time *Australopithecus* could also make and use tools, *Homo habilis* had already developed a larger brain (700 cc, compared to *Australopithecus's* 450–550 cc) and used tools extensively. By the process of evolution, the more *Homo habilis* used tools and its brain, the more its brain developed. By one to 1.5 million years ago humanity had evolved sufficiently to enable archaeologists to distinguish a new species, *Homo erectus*, or Upright Man, with a brain size of 775–1 225 cc, and by 150 000 years ago *Homo sapiens* (Intelligent Man), with a brain size of 1 300–1 500 cc, was fully evolved. It would thus appear that a critical point in human evolution came somewhere in

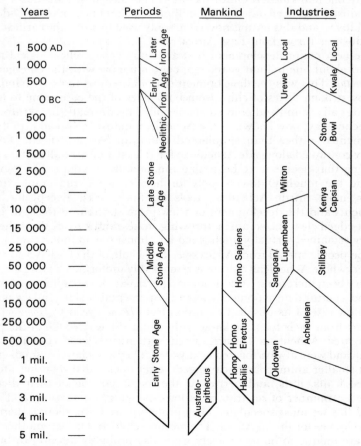

Fig. 1.1 *Chronological sequence of mankind in eastern and central Kenya*

the region of two to three million years ago with the evolution of a larger brain and a more upright posture, and the development of culture, culminating in the emergence of modern mankind 150 000 years ago.

THE EARLY STONE AGE (c. 3 million–50 000 years ago)

The initial period of human development is known as the early Stone Age. The earliest examples come from Koobi Fora at Lake Turkana, where numerous core and flake stone tools mixed with associated animal bones have been found on one occupation site, while a few tools and the bones of a single hippo have been located on a nearby butchery site. Both have been dated to 2.5 to 3 million years ago. From the evidence of the occupation site, it is clear that these people manufactured simple tools, hunted, and brought back their kills to a semi-permanent settlement where there was probably some cooperative division of labour and sharing of food. Such a complex of factors is commonly used to define mankind. At Olduvai Gorge in northeastern Tanzania a similar stone industry has been dated to 1.9 million years and been named Oldowan, after Olduvai, and this term is now commonly used to name the earliest Stone Age industries throughout East Africa.

The next major development that appears in the archaeological record occurred about one million years ago, contemporary with the emergence of *Homo erectus*. This was the development of double-edged tools, or hand axes, made by striking flakes of chips from both sides of the core stone to form a sharp edge all around and pointed at one end. This dramatic breakthrough in stone technology, now known as the Acheulean industry, spread rapidly, but supplemented rather than supplanted Oldowan. An advanced Oldowan industry continued alongside Acheulean for at least another half million years, indicating that people were beginning functionally to adapt their tool kits, retaining the tough Oldowan tools for heavier work and employing the sharper, more brittle Acheulean tools for finer tasks. Except for minor refinements and the development of a few more specialized tools, including straight-edged cleavers, scrapers, throwing stones, and knives, the Acheulean industry remained virtually unchanged for almost one million years. During this time people spread from Africa over the whole of the Old World tropics and everywhere Acheulean culture is remarkably uniform. The rate of change may have been increasing – Oldowan had persisted for two million years – but mankind's cultural development was still imperceptably slow, linked as it was to the slow rate of its physical evolution from *Homo erectus* to *Homo sapiens*.

Apart from their tools we know little about the way of life of the people who created Acheulean culture. Their settlements were confined to the savanna and were always located near water. They associated in small groups, hunted smaller animals and scavenged larger ones killed by other animals, gathered fruits, nuts, and berries as the major portion of their diet, and occupied a number of separate sites for quarrying, butchering, and living. Beyond this we must speculate. They probably used fire, though there is no direct evidence for this in Africa. The mother–child and father–mother bonds which are unique to human society were also probably developed, but it is unlikely that these had yet been extended into the wider structures of kinship.

Finally, their language was probably rudimentary at best. *Homo erectus* was unable to make more than a few basic sounds of speech as its tongue and pharynx (the area of the throat where sounds are first formed before being further modified in the mouth) were not yet well enough developed to make the numerous sound distinctions required for fully articulated speech and its brain was insufficiently developed to codify and control language. Thus, for the duration of the early Stone Age humanity remained incompletely evolved and its means of adaptation to the environment remained crude and unspecialized. Both of these were to change in the succeeding era.

THE MIDDLE STONE AGE (c. 180 000–10 000 years ago)

Once humanity had 'made itself' with the evolution of *Homo sapiens* by 150 000 years ago, cultural development became increasingly specialized to exploit different environments in the middle Stone Age. Oldowan and Acheulean had been savanna-oriented industries, initiated when *Australopithecus* had first

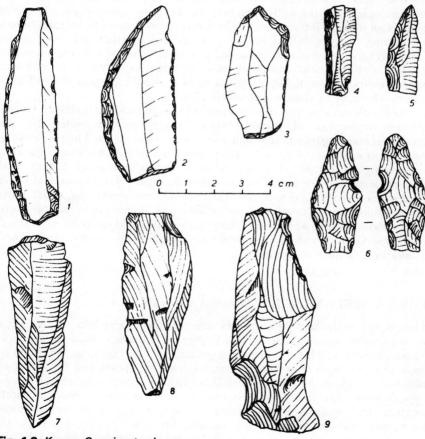

Fig. 1.2 *Kenya Capsian tools*

ventured out of a forest habitat rich in vegetable diet and started eating meat to supplement the more meagre yields of fruits and berries in the drier savanna. The end of Acheulean times, between 180 000 and 50 000 years ago, occurred during the beginnings of the last Ice Age as temperatures in East Africa fell, rainfall increased, and the forest expanded to cover more of the countryside.

As conditions slowly changed, people were forced to devise new tools better suited to a forest environment. Adzes and chisels were developed for woodworking and pounding stones adopted to mash roots gathered from the forest. Tool making techniques also became more sophisticated as people learned to strike off thin slivers of stone and to haft these to wood with natural gums and sinews to make lightweight lances. Fire was used more extensively in hunting, in cooking poisonous roots to neutralize the poison, and in extracting poisons for hunting. Today these forest industries are termed Sangoan or Lupemban after the areas where they were first discovered.

Acheulean industries continued to persist in the savanna long after the development of Sangoan industries in the forest areas, probably because they continued to provide an efficient means of hunting and gathering in the savanna. Nevertheless, change came eventually to the grasslands as well with the development of the Stillbay industries. This development paralleled the earlier tool making innovations in the forest to produce light hunting lances and cutting tools as well as throwing stones tied together to hobble game. These savanna peoples also expanded during this period into the semi-arid regions of the Horn. Mankind now occupied a number of different environments in eastern Africa and made increasingly specialized tool-kits to match. The pace of change was accelerating.

As people became more efficient in their hunting and gathering and made different ecological adaptations, they became less restricted by the environmental constraints that had affected their ancestors. Their way of life changed in other ways as well. They now occupied rock shelters for long periods of time. Ritual beliefs and practices began to develop. Finally, and most critically, people began to use symbolic representations and abstract thought, as revealed in ornamentation, painting, and engraving, which must have entailed a fully developed use of language. People now had far more potent tools for the acquisition, innovation, and transmission of learned behaviour. Culture had become dominant over physical evolution in peoples' adaptations to their environments.

THE LATE STONE AGE (c. 20 000–1 500 years ago)

The opening millenia of the late Stone Age were cooler and drier, followed by a warmer, more humid phase leading to present climatic conditions. Areas in eastern Kenya which had been characterized by open savanna inhabited by large gregarious animals became more thickly vegetated and inhabited by smaller animals which were more difficult to hunt. Some archaeologists have hypothesized that this prompted man to develop lighter, more accurate weapons, but these were probably also the result of ongoing developments and the local availability of obsidian, a volcanic glass which produces particularly fine tools. In any case, it was during this period that people developed the first

8

microlith industry, now known as Kenya Capsian, in central Kenya. Microlithic technology was the culmination of the stone tool maker's art and began in different areas at different times as local craftsmen successively refined their techniques. It consisted of small, thin blades struck with considerable precision and combined into composite tools, such as barbed spears and arrow heads, sickles, and saw blades. These tools, and others, were used in a variety of activities. Bows and arrows, combined with poison, were used for hunting, nets and bone harpoons for fishing, sickles for wild grain

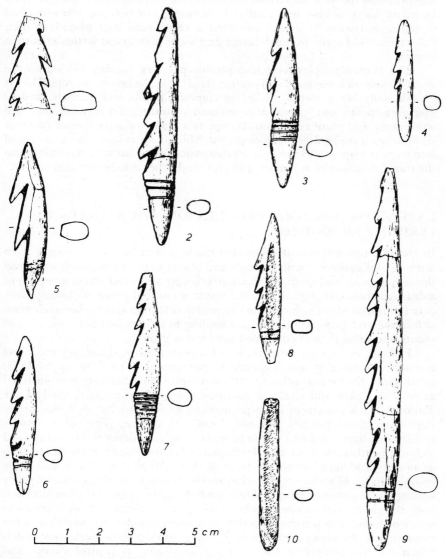

Photo 1.3 *Bone harpoon-heads (Capsian)*

gathering, and digging sticks weighted with bored stone weights for root gathering. Capsian peoples probably engaged in a number of these different activities on a seasonal basis, occupying a series of favoured rock shelters and settlement sites as they moved in groups of eight to twenty-five people from hunting to gathering to fishing.

By 5 000 BC a second microlithic culture had developed in central and western Kenya. Known as Wilton, its tools were also adapted to a variety of activities, including hunting, root and grain gathering, and fishing. Fishing was probably the most important advance of the Capsian and Wilton peoples. In many ways, fishing was similar to hunting, but because fish remained within a restricted area and provided a continuous and abundant diet, fishermen could settle in much larger and more permanent settlements than hunters.

The Wilton peoples were also prolific painters, leaving behind on the walls of their rock shelters vivid portrayals of life in the late Stone Age. The art reveals daily life in detail, including common plants and animals; animal disguises, spears, and bows and arrows used in hunting; fights and dances; and wild honey and plant collection. It depicts a stone industry hunter-gatherer civilization at the peak of its development. Mankind was now poised for takeoff into its next major development: the domestication of animals and plants and the transformation from hunter, gatherer, and fisher into herder and farmer.

LATE STONE AGE FOOD PRODUCTION: THE NEOLITHIC PERIOD (2 500 BC–AD 500)

In the last two millenia BC Kenyans made a shift in their economy from hunting and gathering wild animals and plants to producing their own food through farming and herding. Although this appears in retrospect to represent a dramatic breakthrough, it was the result of gradual processes taking place over thousands of years, including the growth of fishing and the intensification of hunting and gathering techniques leading to the gradual domestication of plants and animals and continued population growth.

Fishing, as we have seen, exploited a permanent and concentrated food resource, enabling people to settle in permanent villages of up to 1 000 inhabitants. By the 3rd millenium BC communities of fishermen were clustered around the lakes and rivers of northern central Kenya, particularly Lake Turkana. This growth of large permanent settlements led to a number of important developments. People began to make permanent houses constructed from mud and wattle to replace the temporary shelters they used as hunter-gatherers. They also developed bulky and fragile implements, such as pottery and large stone bowls. And they had to devise new and more complex forms of social organization and leadership to maintain social order among larger groups of people. These probably developed along kinship lines, with people related to one another through their descent from a common ancestor living and working together as a lineage under the direction of the most elderly members of the group. People also developed religious beliefs based on the powers of their lineage ancestors to control events and supernatural sanctions for social behaviour based on the ability of certain individuals to affect others through witchcraft and sorcery. In short, fishing provided people with the opportunity to begin to develop the institutions of village life that would become crucial with the development of agriculture. It may also have provided one of the main impetuses for the development of agriculture when, from the 3rd millenium BC, the lakes and rivers of central Kenya began to dry out, forcing the dense populations of fishermen to seek alternative food supplies. Such populations could not hope to survive through hunting and gathering. They had to rely on the increasing availability of domestic plants and animals brought about through the intensification of hunting-gathering techniques.

We have already seen how the late Stone Age peoples were able to intensify their hunting and gathering using more efficient microlithic sickles, spears, and bows and arrows. At the same time, their more intensive gathering led to subtle genetic adaptations in the plants gathered that effectively transformed them over time from wild to domestic varieties. The seed pods of wild grains commonly shatter, the seeds mature at different times, and once scattered, they lie dormant on the ground for long periods before germinating. These characteristics all help to ensure the survival of wild plant varieties by spreading their seeds far and wide and extending their reseeding over a long time. But gatherers tended to collect only those seeds that had matured simultaneously from plants that had grown at the same time. By thus selecting non-shattering seeds which matured and germinated at the same time, gatherers began the process of transforming wild plant varieties into domestic ones. They influenced selection in other ways as well, by choosing seeds on the basis of their colour, size, taste, or storability. Over time people also began to replace a few of the seeds or tubers they had gathered. This may have started quite accidentally when people dropped seeds around their settlements on their way home in the evenings or when they dropped the unwanted part of a tuber back into the hole where they had dug it up, but the effect was to promote potentially desirable domestic varieties at the expense of wild ones. Such casual planting, or vegeculture, may have been practised by gatherers for some time before people moved more fully into agriculture. The reason is simple. Agriculture requires more work to produce the same amount of food as gathering, and so people were not likely to adopt it until forced to do so. This is just what happened slightly earlier in the Sahara.

Prior to 3 000 BC the Sahara had been a well-watered area inhabited by large numbers of late Stone Age hunters, gatherers, and fishermen. Over the next two thousand years, however, the Sahara slowly became drier, its lakes and rivers evaporated and desert sand spread south, forcing its inhabitants into the savanna. The Sahara had also been rich in potentially domesticable wild plants, such as sorghums, millet, fonio, rice, and eleusine, all of which became domesticated as people were forced to seek alternatives to fishing in farming. Once people started deliberately to plant certain varieties of grains, the process of selection of desirable domestic characteristics rapidly completed the transformation of wild varieties into domestic ones. Conditions in Kenya, the Sudan, and Ethiopia were similar to the Sahara as lakes dried up or became too salty for fish. Wild varieties of finger millet (*Eleusine coracana*), sorghum (*Sorghum bicolor*), and pearl millet (*Pennisetum americanum*) were all potential domesticates. We do not know if these were actually domesticated in central Kenya or further north in Ethiopia or the Sudan, but everywhere people had to develop local varieties to suit their own conditions.

The first East African agriculturalists were probably the 'Stone Bowl' peoples of the Central Highlands and Rift Valley of Kenya and northern Tanzania. The culture is named after the distinctive carved stone bowls which they used and are found in abundance on their sites together with earthenware pots, ground stone axes, grindstones, mortars and pestles, and animal bones. We know from the animal bones that they herded domestic cattle and sheep or goats and from the grindstones and mortars and pestles that they either gathered wild grains in abundance or, more likely, cultivated millets and sorghums. The Stone Bowl peoples lived in large settlements, and there is evidence at one site that they built mud and wattle houses. Some also cremated their dead along with their main possessions. One such cremation occurred at the Njoro River Cave in western Kenya, where a large number of normally perishable items were burned and carbonized, and thus preserved for posterity, including basketry, cords, carved and decorated wooden vessels, and pendants and beads made from bone, shell, nuts, sedge seeds, and semi-precious stones.

The Stone Bowl culture thus reveals a number of changes that accompanied the transition to mixed agriculture. Like fishermen, farmers could stay in one place, build permanent houses, support large populations, and collect bulky and heavy artifacts. They also probably continued to develop social and religious institutions based on kinship and certainly practised ritual burials. But the further extension of agriculture and the settled life it brought was limited by their stone and wooden tools, a limitation Kenyans would soon overcome with the adoption of iron.

THE EARLY IRON AGE (600 BC–900 AD)

Iron technology, by its very nature, represents a dramatic break from the stone technology which preceded it. Whereas stone technology developed through the increasing refinement of chipping techniques and materials to produce sharper and finer tools, iron technology involved the transformation of one substance into another through the combination of smelting the ore-bearing rock or sand at very high temperatures to extract the basic metal and forging the metal into the desired shape. These processes were first devised in eastern Turkey and spread from there throughout Asia, Africa, and Europe, reaching eastern Africa by the 6th century BC.

The earliest Iron Age sites in eastern Africa are found in the area around Lake Victoria – Buhaya, Rwanda, Kavirondo, and Chobi – and date from the 5th–6th century BC in Buhaya to the 3rd–4th century AD in the Kavirondo Gulf and northern Uganda. These sites are characterized by tall cylindrical smelting furnaces, a distinctive style of pottery termed Urewe-ware, dense village settlements, and agriculture.

A second series of sites is found in southeastern Kenya and northeastern Tanzania – at Kwale, Kilimanjaro, Pare, and Usambara – dating from the 2nd–3rd century AD. These have their own distinctive pottery style, termed Kwale-ware, and also show evidence for permanent settlements and

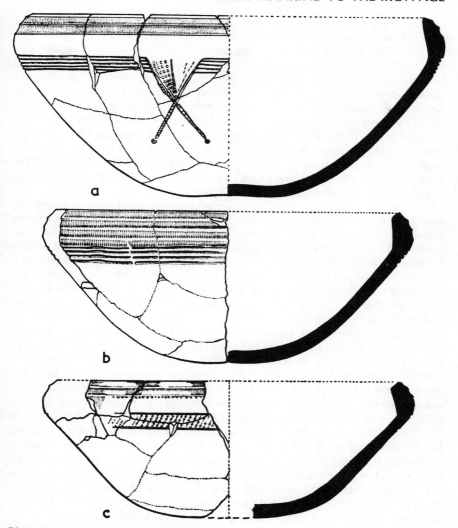

Photo 1.4 *Kwale-ware pottery bowls*

agriculture. Similar sites to these, dating from the 4th century AD, occur further south in Malawi, Zimbabwe, the Transvaal, and eastern Zambia. The earliest site in this group, and the one whose pottery has come to type the whole group, is at Kwale in the Shimba Hills of southeastern Kenya and date from 120 to 270 AD.* Kwale is a particularly valuable site, both because of its

---

*It should be noted here that all dates established by the radiocarbon method contain a standard error to account for possible statistical errors in the measurement process and the rate of decay of carbon 14 radiation. Thus the earliest date for Kwale is given correctly as AD 120±115, indicating that the true date probably falls between 5 AD and 235 AD. I have generally omitted the standard error for the sake of convenience, but the full dates can be found in Figure 1.2. I have also omitted several dates generally considered to be too early or too late.

antiquity and because many of the elements commonly associated together with the early Iron Age have been found there. These include stone flakes, a flat sandstone grinding stone, an iron arrow-head, iron slag, a clay tuyere or pipe used at the bottom of smelting furnaces for draught, burnt clay, and over two thousand fragments of pottery. There is thus evidence of a contemporary stone industry, agriculture, an iron industry, and pottery manufacture. The pottery itself consists of a number of differently shaped bowls and pots, all with thickened rims and flat or concave bases, decorated with hatched or grooved bands. Pottery is one of the main diagnostic tools for studying the early Iron Age because distinctive types of pottery are commonly associated with iron working, pottery is often the most prevalent material found in early Iron Age sites, and the style of pottery found in one area can be compared with that found in other areas to see if they are possibly related.

Kwale-type pottery is also found in abundance in northeastern Tanzania, where it has been dated from early in the 3rd century AD. What is fascinating about the Tanzanian sites, however, is how rapidly the common tradition developed into a number of regional and local traditions. Kwale-ware itself is found only in South Pare and in the foothills of the Usambaras, whereas a number of local styles, mostly unrelated to one another, follow throughout the area from the 4th century, indicating a common process of initial diffusion of ideas from Kwale followed by the localization and synthesis of these ideas with local cultural traditions. We cannot be sure exactly what forms this process took, but a number of possibilities are suggested by the northeastern Tanzanian evidence. In the case of South Pare, Kwale-ware is dated from 220 AD and is located on the eastern slopes of the mountains. Slightly higher up the eastern slopes and along the western fringe and dated from 870 AD, Maore-ware is found, while Pare Type B-ware is located exclusively along the eastern fringes of the mountains and on the adjacent plains and dated from 890 AD. Given that different ecological systems prevail in each of these areas, it is possible that these three types could either represent a single tradition locally adapted to the three areas, three separate traditions, possibly borrowing from one another, or a combination of the two. Another alternative is suggested by the presence at the Maore site of numerous shell beads and at the Type B sites of shells, beads, cowries with their backs removed, and double glass beads, all trade items obtained from the coast. Perhaps the different traditions were related to the influence of traders. We do not know.

Similar variations occur at the other sites. On Kilimanjaro both Kwale and Maore types are found on the same sites, dated from 250 AD, with purely local types from the 13th century. In North Pare Kwale-ware and Maore-ware are found on the same sites and even combined on the same pots from the 6th to the 10th centuries, and Pare Type B is found on other sites from the 10th century. In the Usambaras Kwale-ware is found around the fringes of the mountains, while three local types are found in different upland areas. Finally, around Mt. Kenya Kwale-ware does not appear until the 12th century, with a local tradition following from the 16th century.

Obviously no clear conclusions can yet be drawn from this data. But it does seem that the initial impetus for the development of iron working did come from a common fund of ideas which were then locally adapted by people in each of the areas to which they spread. To see how this might have occurred, it is first necessary to discuss some of the more general issues of change raised by the archaeological data. We will then return to the early Iron Age to conclude our discussion.

CULTURE AND CHANGE

As we have reviewed the archaeological record, we have seen the main causes of change in eastern Kenya over more than three million years. The first was the interaction between mankind's biological evolution and its cultural development, a process which dominated the history of humanity throughout

Area	Type	Date	Distribution
Kwale	Kwale	AD 120 ± 151 – 270±110	Shimba Hills
Usambara	Kwale	?	All around fringes of mountain zone.
	Usambara C	AD 360±130	Northwest mountains (Mlalo) and southeast fringes (Lwengera Valley). All sites found in valleys near streams.
	Usambara D	?	Southwest Usambara (Vuga, Bungu, Lwengera Valley) and north Usambara (Mnzai). Most sites on hilltops.
	Recent	AD 1900	On defensible hilltops.
South Pare	Kwale	AD 220 ±115	Eastern fringes of Pare mountains
	Maore	AD 870±115	Higher in eastern mountains and along western fringe.
	Pare B	AD 890±110	Eastern plains
North Pare	Kwale/Maore	AD 520±270 – 920±130	
	Pare B	AD 960±105	
Kilimanjaro	Kwale & Maore	AD 250±330	
	Kilimanjaro C	AD 1225±190 – AD 1445±200	On slopes of mountains.
	Kilimanjaro D	AD 1445±200	On plains
	Kilimanjaro E	Present	
Mt. Kenya	Kwale	AD 1140 ± 130 – AD 1350± 80	
	Phase B	AD 1515±105	

Fig. 1.2 *Pottery styles in northeastern Tanzania and eastern Kenya*

the early Stone Age, and, as we will see, continues to influence history. We have also seen how the development of culture was cumulative, painfully slow in its early stages, but accelerating in the later ones as fishing, food production, and iron working were progressively added to peoples' knowledge and exploited to support larger populations, establish permanent settlements, and elaborate material culture. We have also seen the effect of changes in the environment on mankind's development and his increasing ability to overcome environmental limitations by adapting to different environments and by exploiting the differences between them by combining hunting, gathering, and fishing in seasonal cycles or by adopting mixed agriculture. Finally, we have seen how ideas developed in one area could spread to other areas where they interacted with local cultures and were adapted to them. As individual peoples became more specialized from the late Stone Age, the opportunities for social interaction and the diffusion of ideas increased in the exchange of different products and ideas. Forest hunter-gatherers could exchange animal and forest products with savanna farmers for food, pottery, or iron wares. Salt, pottery clay, copper, and iron were each restricted to a few areas, facilitating trade between these areas as people exchanged commodities they had for those that they needed. As specialization and complementarity among different peoples increased, the total fund of resources and knowledge also increased, and change accordingly became more rapid in the interchange of these goods and ideas. By the early Iron Age new ideas and technologies could diffuse rapidly and be adapted to a number of different environmental and cultural conditions.

This view of change, with its emphasis on local development and adaptation, contrasts with an earlier view which saw individual peoples and cultures as largely static. Change in this view was largely the result of migrations, as new peoples brought new technolgies with them from elsewhere and imposed them locally. Each new technology, then, was associated with a different group of people, often assumed to be a different race. Thus the hunter-gatherers of the middle and late Stone Ages were assumed to be 'Khoisan' and ancestral to the Khoisan-speaking hunter-gatherers of southwest Africa today. These were then pushed south by successive waves of tall thin 'Caucasoid' invaders bringing the microlithic Capsian and neolithic Stone Bowl cultures from North Africa, and surviving in Kenya as the ancestors of the nomadic Maasai, Turkana, Galla, and Somali pastoralists of today. Finally, there was the migration of 'Negroid' farmers, who were thought to have brought agriculture and iron working from the western Sudan and spread them throughout central, eastern, and southern Africa.

These 'racial' types were determined largely on appearance, but the only scientific way to study the differences between human populations is through the study of genes. Genes determine hereditary characteristics and thus can be expected to vary for different human types. When we compare genetically the hunter-gatherer peoples of Kenya with the Khoisan-speaking peoples of southwest Africa, for example, we find that they have very little in common. Each people, in fact, is more similar to its agricultural and pastoral neighbours than it is to the other. Similarly, the so-called 'Caucasoid' peoples are genetically less like the caucasians of northern Africa than they are like their heavier-set agricultural neighbours. In short, Kenyans are genetically more similar to one another than they are to any outside group. Whatever strangers have migrated into the area in the past have intermarried with local peoples and been absorbed within the general population.

There are, of course, differences between the peoples of Kenya today, but these are primarily due to environmental adaptation and restricted marriage patterns. The tall thin stature characteristic of the pastoralists, for example, is adapted to the hot dry climate typical of the pastoral areas of Kenya, while a shorter, heavier-set stature is adapted to the cooler moister areas inhabited by agriculturalists. Such adaptations become accentuated by restricted marriage patterns. If a group splits from its parent group and thereafter only marries within itself, significant differences from the parent stock can occur within as little as twenty generations, or five hundred years.

Migration should thus not be assumed to be the only explanation for physical differences between different peoples. Nor should it be taken as the only way to explain cultural innovations. The Kenya Capsian peoples were assumed to be caucasian because of their tall thin stature and because of the similarity between Kenya Capsian microliths and those of the northern African Capsian industry after which it was named. But physically the Kenya Capsian peoples fall well within the range of physical variation of the present population of Kenya, and, as we have already seen, the tall thin pastoralists today are genetically more like the rest of the peoples of Kenya than they are like caucasians. Kenya Capsian industries were probably developed locally. The variations between different sites, are related to previous industries and the availability of local materials such as obsidian. It is thus probable that Kenya Capsian was primarily a local development as people progressively refined their stone technology. Some ideas may have originated elsewhere, particularly in the Kenyan–Sudanese–Ethiopian borderlands, but these soon became incorporated within local styles and absorbed by them.

The Stone Bowl peoples were also assumed to be caucasian, both because of their stature and because it was assumed that farming and herding had northern African origins. But we have already seen that the essential preconditions for food production, more intensive grain gathering, fishing, wild plant varieties suitable for domestication, and population increase, were all present in Kenya before the beginnings of agriculture in the area. People were thus ready for agriculture. We cannot, of course, say for certain that domestication actually occurred in Kenya, but even if domestic varieties were introduced from the Sudan or Ethiopia, Kenyans would have had to breed local varieties and to develop agricultural methods suitable for local conditions. Domestic cattle, sheep, and goats, which may well have been introduced from the north, also had to be bred to local conditions to obtain varieties adapted to the local environments and resistant to local diseases.

The beginnings of mixed agriculture in Kenya may thus have involved a combination of locally developed items and ideas with borrowed elements. But this does not mean that a mass migration of Stone Bowl people had to occur. Individual elements may have been introduced on their own and adapted to local conditions. As with trade goods, cultural items and ideas can travel considerable distances by being passed from neighbour to neighbour without necessarily involving the movement of people at all. We know, for example, that the Khoikhoi of southern Africa were once hunter-gatherers, but became converted to herding by first hunting the cattle of their neighbours and then herding them. We must thus be very careful when studying processes of diffusion to isolate just which items were borrowed and how these were adapted by local peoples.

A more complex combination of diffusion and local developments took place during the early Iron Age. The similarity of early Iron Age industries throughout eastern and southern Africa, characterized by Urewe and Kwale pottery, iron working, mixed agriculture, and dense settlement patterns, have led archaeologists to conclude that there must have been a single interrelated cultural tradition, called the Early Iron Age Industrial Complex, which spread from Lake Victoria to eastern Kenya and thence to southern Africa in the 2nd to 4th centuries AD. This tradition is seen as a dramatic break from the Wilton and Stone Bowl past and thus must have resulted from the rapid migration of a new people who brought a wholly new set of related industries to eastern and southern Africa and displaced the earlier hunter-gatherers. The hypothesis is a simple and logical one: agriculture and iron were both such complex technologies that they were probably not developed in a number of different areas at the same time. Further, both were such a break from the eastern African past that they must have been developed elsewhere and combined in the Western Sudan. Once introduced, this combination represented a formidable advance on mankind's exploitation of the environment, enabling people to clear forests and plant them in high-yielding domestic crops. Such high yields would support much larger populations than hunting and gathering, and so led to steady population increase and the development of larger social groups residing in permanent village settlements. With an exploding population and the technological means to conquer virgin lands, Sudanic Iron Age agriculturalists burst across Africa during the last millenium BC and within a few centuries cleared and settled the whole of central, eastern, and southern Africa, usurping prime hunting land and forcing the earlier hunter-gatherers into remote ecological niches or out of the area altogether.

The hypothesis makes sense logically, but when we look at the individual components of the Early Iron Age Industrial Complex, we find that many of them were developed separately and only became associated with one another within different areas of eastern Africa. We have already seen that mixed agriculture preceded iron working in Kenya by at least one to two thousand years and that large settlements had been developed even earlier among fishing people. Thus, by the opening of the Iron Age, there already existed developed neolithic industries and village societies in Kenya.

Pottery also preceded the Iron Age by at least a millennium. Archaeologists argue, however, that the early Iron Age was characterized by distinctive styles of pottery, Urewe in the west, Kwale in the east, and a series of styles related to Kwale in the south. The classification and comparison of pottery is extremely difficult, however; where one archaeologist sees two styles related, another sees them as distinctive and unrelated. There is little doubt that Urewe is the distinctive style associated with the early Iron Age in the Lake Victoria region, nor that Kwale is the local style for southeastern Kenya and northeastern Tanzania, but the relationship between these two styles is still conjectural. Similarly, there are at least nine other local styles in Malawi,

Zimbabwe, Zambia, and South Africa whose relationships to one another and to Kwale are debatable. The most that we can say about these styles is that they typify a number of Iron Age industries which share a number of aspects in common, but which are also distinctive in a number of others.

Iron, the fourth component of the Early Iron Age Industrial Complex hypothesis, was initially developed in eastern Turkey and spread from there to the rest of the Old World. Precisely how it arrived in eastern Africa is, however, unknown. The earliest Iron Age sites in Sudanic Africa are Nok in Nigeria, dated to the 3rd century BC, Meroe in the Sudan, dated to the 3rd to 4th century BC, and Axum in Ethiopia, dated to the 4th to 5th century BC, but, as we have seen, iron working in Buhaya was at least as old or older than any of these sites. Nor have any other sites been found in either Uganda or Zaire that could have been intermediaries between the Sudan and Buhaya. The ultimate origins of iron in east Africa, then, must remain conjectural, though a spread from Meroe up the Nile to the Lake Victoria region is the most plausable route at the moment, and Meroic furnaces and tool styles are similar to those in East Africa.

What is clear, however, is that iron spread into East Africa subsequent to the other components of the Early Iron Age Industrial Complex and must have been fused with them by local peoples within East Africa itself to form the Urewe and Kwale cultures. Once developed, these ideas then spread to nearby areas, either passed from neighbour to neighbour by themselves or carried by itinerant smiths and potters. Until recently smiths were frequently a separate group within society, feared for their ritual powers in transforming one substance into another, but widely respected for their skills. Once adopted, these ideas were rapidly adapted to local cultural and environmental conditions, as we saw earlier in the case of Kwale-ware in eastern Kenya and northeastern Tanzania. Once established in East Africa, the combination of iron working, agriculture, and pottery spread south into Malawi, Zambia, Zimbabwe, and South Africa where they were all new industries to the hunting and gathering inhabitants.

The way that iron working spread gives us some indications of the processes which must have been involved. One of the most striking aspects of the Zambian evidence is that late Stone Age rock shelters and early Iron Age settlements were located quite near one another, indicating that Stone Age hunters must have coexisted for some time with Iron Age farmers in the same areas. Archaeologists have also found Iron Age pottery in addition to stone tools in the rock shelters of hunter-gatherers, showing that the two peoples conducted some trade with one another. The eclipsing of Stone Age hunter-gatherers by Iron Age farmers and herders must have been a lengthy process as hunter-gatherers persist in some areas into the present. In the meantime, the two have coexisted in a mutually interdependent relationship in which each provided the goods that the other lacked. Such a relationship is typical of the relations today between Okiek hunter-gathers and Kikuyu farmers around Mt. Kenya or between Waata hunters and Giriama farmers at the coast, as we will see in later chapters. Relationships such as these are one of the main ways that new ideas spread. The availability of cultural alternatives allowed individuals, or a whole people, to adopt new methods and even new identities if they assimilated to their neighbour's way of life. Local trade networks in salt, pottery, clay, iron, copper, cowries, and beads provided other potential avenues of cultural exchange.

The Zambian Iron Age sites were only occupied for a generation or two before their inhabitants moved to other areas. This pattern is typical of shifting agriculturalists and would have caused the savanna woodland to be cleared rapidly, thus denying its use to hunter-gatherers. As their area shrank, those still following a hunting-gathering way of life were probably persuaded to take up farming or herding. If Stone Age hunter-gatherers seem to have disappeared, then, they did so by being converted into Iron Age farmers and herders.

In the process, however, the spread of Iron Age cultures was uneven, as ideas which did filter south were adapted to local circumstances and cultures. Such localization became even more prominent in succeeding centuries, just as it did in Pare, Usambara, and Kilimanjaro. Thus, even if it is assumed that the Early Iron Age Industrial Complex diffused initially as a unified entity, its components rapidly broke down as people adapted them to their previous cultures and local conditions.

Processes of change are very complex and only rarely will a single explanation for them suffice. On the purely local level, people must constantly apply the wisdom of the ancestors to new problems and so add new knowledge to the ancestral store. Regionally, they are presented with alternative ways of doing things by their neighbours with whom they trade, fight, marry, and exchange ideas. Some even cross social and cultural borders and assimilate to their neighbours' way of life. Finally, they are occasionally confronted with conquerors seeking to impose their culture on them, but as often as not, it is the conquerors – like the 19th century Ngoni – who assimilate to the cultures of the people they have conquered. In all of these cases, however, people confront new ideas and ways of doing things in the context of their own past, their own values, their own cultural perceptions of the world, and in deciding whether or not to adopt the new ideas, are guided by their own logic. If the new idea is a local development, it is generated naturally out of the wisdom of the past interacting with the needs of the present. If it is borrowed from someone else, it interacts with both past ideals and present needs. Change is thus a constant process of interaction between ideals established in the past and the needs of the present, creating an ongoing synthesis as new ideas interact with old and the results are integrated into the culture.

REFERENCES AND SUGGESTIONS FOR FURTHER READING

Much of the basic data and interpretation for the Stone Age is summarized in J. D. Clark, *The Prehistory of Africa* (London, 1970) and, specifically for East Africa, in M. Posnansky, 'The Prehistory of East Africa' in B. A. Ogot (ed.), *Zamani* (2nd ed.), pp. 52–69 (Nairobi, 1973), while the standard work for the biology of human populations in Africa is J. Hiernaux, *The Peoples of Africa* (London, 1974). A technical summary and assessment of work to 1973 at Lake Turkana and the Omo River Valley on the origins of man is contained in Y. Coppens, F. C. Howell, G. Ll. Isaac, and R. E. F. Leakey (eds.), *Earliest Man and the Environments in the Lake Rudolf Basin* (Chicago, 1976), while the standard works for Olduvai are L. S. B. Leakey, *Olduvai Gorge* (Cambridge, 1951) and L. S. B. and M. D. Leakey and P. Tobias, *Olduvai Gorge* (Cambridge, 1965–71).

The process of plant domestication is ably summarized in J. M. J. de Wet, 'Domestication of African Cereals', *African Economic History*, 3 (1977), pp. 15–32, and is discussed in greater detail in J. R. Harlan, J. de Wet, and A. Stemler (eds.), *Origins of African Plant Domestication* (The Hague, 1976).

A valuable collection of data concerning the early Iron Age is D. W. Phillipson, *The Later Prehistory of Eastern and Southern Africa* (London, 1977). Specific site reports convey more detailed pictures for eastern Kenya and northeastern Tanzania. Kwale is described in R. Soper, 'Kwale: An Early Iron Age Site in South-Eastern Kenya', *Azania*, 2 (1967), pp. 1–18, and a number of reports are collected in a symposium published in Vol. 6 (1971) of *Azania*, including articles by R. Soper, K. Odner, and A. Siiriäinen on Pare, Kilimanjaro, Usambara, and Mt. Kenya. A major breakthrough in combining early Iron Age archaeology with oral traditions is reported in P. R. Schmidt, 'A New Look at Interpretations of the Early Iron Age in East Africa', *History in Africa*, 2 (1975), pp. 127–136, and his *Historical Archaeology: A Structural Approach to an African Culture* (Westport, 1978).

Recent radiocarbon dates appear periodically in the *Journal of African History* and those for 1970 (pp. 1–15), 1972 (pp. 1–24), 1974 (pp. 175–192), 1976 (pp. 161–195), and 1977 (pp. 171–191) have been used here to update earlier reports.

CHAPTER TWO

LANGUAGES AND PEOPLES
THE LINGUISTIC RECORD

Languages like people have ancestors. Daughter languages commonly develop after people speaking a common language become separated from one another for some reason. In time the speech of the two separate communities tends to diverge, initially into mutually understandable dialects of the common parent language and eventually into separate daughter languages. Over time a whole 'family tree' of descendant languages can develop genetically from the one language, as shown today by the over 400 languages all descended from a single original Bantu language. Through studying the relationships of present languages to one another, linguists are often able to reconstruct such family trees and even a general description of the ancestral, or proto, language itself.

Linguists compare selected parts of present languages to make such reconstructions. This is frequently done with vocabulary. If two or more languages share a large number of words having the same meanings, known as cognates, they are usually closely related while those with lower percentages of cognates are more distantly related. This is because once people speaking a common language have become separated each group slowly adopts new words to replace the common words of the original language. Thus the fewer words two descendant languages share, the longer the people speaking them have been separated. People adopt new words into their language either by deriving them from other words in the language or by borrowing them from another language. Derivation normally proceeds at a fairly slow and constant rate, while borrowing can be very uneven, depending on the amount of contact people who speak the language have with others. Linguists have discovered, however, that some words are less prone to borrowing than others, and thus can be assumed to change at the more constant rate. These words, including such items as numbers and parts of the body, have been collected into basic vocabulary lists which linguists can then use to assess the relationship of different languages with one another.

By collecting lists of basic vocabulary from two or more languages and comparing them, linguists can calculate how many words they share in common as a percentage showing how closely related they are to one another. It is then possible to reconstruct the genetic development of those languages by gathering the most closely related languages together into sub-groups, closely related sub-groups into larger sub-groups, and so on until a whole family tree has been reconstructed. An example will show how this is done. If languages C and D share 70 per cent of their basic vocabulary in common, but the two together share only 60 per cent with language E, we can say that C and D share a more recent origin with each other than either does with E, a relationship commonly sketched in a family tree diagram as follows:

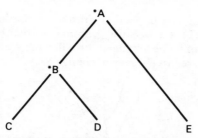

in which *A represents the hypothetical proto-language from which C, D, and E all descend and *B the hypothetical intermediate proto-language from which C and D developed. Initially, then, two languages developed, *B and E, with *B subsequently splitting to form C and D.

While vocabulary is an important basis for comparison, the main grounds used by linguists are sound changes that have occurred during the development of related languages. Just as people may adopt new words, they may also change the way they say a certain sound. Thus the speakers of *A above may have said *moja*, a pronunciation retained in E but changed by *B speakers to *moya*, so that both C and D speakers today say *moya*. Alternatively, *A and *B speakers may have said *tatu*, a form retained by D and E speakers today, while C speakers have changed the 't' to 'ch', giving *chachu*. In our first example, the linguist studying the present languages C, D, and E sees that C and D speakers say *moya* while E speakers say *moja*, and from this infers that *B speakers were the ones responsible for changing the 'j' sound to 'y'. He or she can then sub-group the languages as follows:

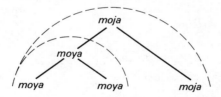

In our second example, using *tatu/chachu*, the sub-grouping would look like this:

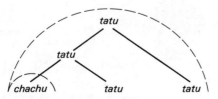

Sound shifts are important for classifying related languages because they are more resistant to the effects of borrowing than vocabulary; they can be arranged sequentially in the order in which they occurred, thus enabling linguists to group the languages into related sub-groups; and they enable linguists to establish cognates even when words are pronounced differently if the differences are the result of known and predictable sound changes between the two languages.

A third basis for comparison is grammar, commonly the most stable aspect of language. This is because grammar forms the basic structure of a language and can only be changed by effecting changes throughout the language. While it is relatively easy to change a single word, it is much harder

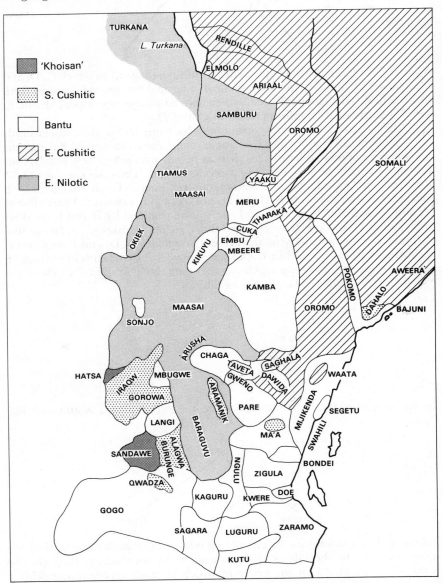

Map 2.1 *Languages of eastern and central Kenya and northeastern Tanzania*

to change rules for forming the past tense, or the patterns of agreement along the subject, predicate, objects, and modifiers in a sentence. The historical development of structural changes can be reconstructed in much the same way as the development of sound changes described above. All three of these methods, then, employ comparison of present languages to reconstruct earlier ones, much as we might interview living people to reconstruct their genealogies. They are thus well suited to tracing the genetic development of languages.

If linguists wish to trace external influences on language development they use a fourth approach. This is the study of borrowing, or loan-words, in which they look at the words and other components of language that a people speaking one language have borrowed from others. Since borrowing normally occurs when people speaking two languages interact with one another, evidence of borrowing between two languages can be used to posit historical interaction between the speakers of the two languages. Usually this occurs with select cultural items. If a people borrow the technology for working iron from their neighbours, they are also likely to borrow such words as 'iron', 'forge', or 'to smelt' from the same source. Any language usually has a number of different sets of loan-words, indicating that its speakers have interacted with different peoples at different times. By identifying these sets, and arranging them sequentially when possible, linguists can reconstruct these patterns of historical interaction.

Such complex methods obviously entail a number of problems, but most of these are technical and are best considered by trained linguists. A major problem of interpretation for the historian, however, is to relate languages and patterns of linguistic development to historical peoples and events. In the preceding chapter, for example, I refrained from attaching the linguistic labels commonly applied to the peoples being discussed for one simple reason: we can never know purely from the archaeological record of preliterate peoples what language they spoke. Similarly, it is often difficult to know what people may have spoken a given historical language. People may adopt another language in close interaction with others, such as occurs frequently in intermarriage. The Segeju, for example, now speak Digo, but originally they lived in the highlands and spoke Daiso, a language related to Kikuyu and Kamba. They only adopted Digo after they had migrated to the coast and settled among Digo speakers, but they continue to call themselves Daiso, or its cognate Segeju. We must be very careful, therefore, to distinguish between a people as a social community with its own history and peoples speaking a certain language as a language community with its quite distinct history. Frequently the two are not the same.* When discussing the history of the development of languages in the present chapter we will usually be referring to hypothetical communities of language speakers and will only attempt to identify these with historical peoples when there is sufficient evidence to do so.

Nearly fifty different languages are found in eastern and central Kenya

---

*Confusion between a social community and a language community is common in English because, unlike the Bantu languages where the language (e.g., *Kiswahili*) is distinguished from the people (*Waswahili*), English makes no distinction between the two. Few would assume, however, that all people who speak the English language are English or that all Swahili speakers are Swahili.

and northeastern Tanzania today, representing five major families of languages. Their distribution can be seen on Map 2.1 and Figure 2.1. The first of these families which we will discuss is the 'Khoisan'.

Fig. 2.1 *Languages of eastern and central Kenya and northeastern Tanzania*

Family		Local Sub-groups		Languages	Dialects
'Khoisan'				Sandawe	
				Hatsa	
Southern	Mbuguan			Ma'a	
Cushitic	Dahaloan			Dahalo	
	Rift	East		Aramanik	
				Qwadza	
		West		Iraqw/Gorowa	Iraqw, Gorowa
				Alagwa	
				Burunge	
		South		?	
		Nyanza		?	
Bantu	Northeast	Coast	Saghala/Pare	Saghala	
				Pare/Taveta	North and South Pare/Taveta
			Sabaki	Swahili	
				Mijikenda	Digo, Giriama, R Chonyi, Jibana Kambe, Kaun Rabai, Durum
				Pokomo	North and South Pokomo, Elwa
		Ruvu	West Ruvu	Gogo	
				Kaguru	
				Sagara	
			East Ruvu	Zaramo	
				Kuti	
				Kami	
				Kwere	
				Doe	
			Seuta	Shambaa/Bondei	Shambaa, Bonde
				Zigula/Ngulu	Zigula, Ngulu
			Luguru	Luguru	
	Chaga/Taita	Dawida		Dawida	
		Chaga/Gweno	Gweno	Gweno	
			Chaga	W. Kilimanjaro	
				C. Kilimanjaro	
				Rombo	
	Thagicu	Sonjo		Sonjo	
		West		Kikuyu	
				Embu/Mbeere	Embu, Mbeere
				Cuka	
		Central		Meru	Imenti, Mutham Tigania, Igoji, Mwimbi, Igen
				Tharaka	
		East	Daiso	Daiso	
			Kamba	Kamba	

Family	Local sub-groups			Languages	Dialects
Eastern Cushitic	Lowland	Oromo		Oromo	Boran, Orma, Waata
		Omo-Tana	Western	Arbore Dassenech Elmolo	
			Baiso	Baiso	
			Eastern	Rendille Somali Aweera	
		Yaaku		Yaaku	
Eastern Nilotic	Ongamo/Maa			Maa	Maa, Samburu Arusha
	Teso/Turkana			Turkana	

'KHOISAN'

Among the oldest languages for which there is any evidence of having once been spoken in Kenya are languages superficially similar to the Khoisan languages now spoken in southwestern Africa, though there is no evidence definitely linking the two. This is because these East African 'Khoisan' languages are now extinct and have left few loan-words in other languages from which we can infer their existence. Sandawe and Hatsa, both now spoken in northern Tanzania, show some similarities to Khoisan languages, however, and a few other languages retain Khoisan-like elements. Both the Dahalo and the Yaaku, for example, still retain some of the click sounds and vocabulary characteristic of Khoisan languages though both today speak other languages. It thus seems reasonable to infer that Khoisan languages, or languages like them, were widely spoken in Wilton times prior to the arrival of peoples speaking Southern Cushitic languages. A variety of cultural syntheses resulted from interaction of 'Khoisan' speakers with southern Cushitic speakers and subsequent migrants. A few retained 'Khoisan' speech, but most eventually adopted Southern Cushitic or other languages after centuries of interaction with their speakers. It is thus by looking at other language groups that we can discover more of the 'Khoisan' heritage.

SOUTHERN CUSHITIC

Southern Cushitic languages are only spoken today by a few groups of isolated hunting-gathering peoples (see Map 2.2), but the influence of Southern Cushitic speakers was once sufficiently great to cause others to borrow vocabulary extensively from them. Loan-words from Southern Cushitic are found in many of the present languages of eastern Africa. Thus, even if no Southern Cushitic languages were spoken today, we would still have to infer their former existence and wide distribution over eastern Africa from the prevalence of existing loans. What is more, the words that were borrowed fall into particular cultural sets which enable us to say something about the contribution of Southern Cushitic speakers to eastern Kenyan history. One set of loans widely borrowed from Southern Cushitic includes terminology for cattle, goats, sheep, and the herding, milking, and bleeding of cattle, indicating that at least some Cushitic speakers were pastoralists and that others subsequently adopted pastoralism from them. Another loan-word set includes agricultural terms for cultivating, harvesting, sorghum, and eleusine, while a third set of words borrowed from Southern Cushitic includes terms for circumcision, clitoridectomy, and some aspects of age-set organization. It would thus appear that Southern Cushitic speakers practised both farming and herding and had organizations based on age. Southern Cushitic is one

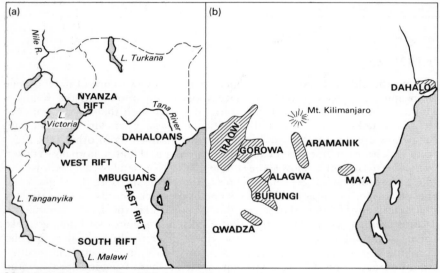

Map 2.2 *Southern Cushitic languages*

branch of the Cushitic languages, almost all of which are now located in or around Ethiopia. The great diversity of the Southern Cushitic languages in southwestern Ethiopia indicates that this was probably the homeland of ancestral, or proto, Southern Cushitic itself, since such diversity indicates the area where the descendant languages have developed over the longest period. It is thus logical to assume that the Southern Cushitic languages originated in southwestern Ethiopia and spread from there into Kenya and Tanzania. By comparing the present Southern Cushitic languages, it is also obvious that they have been separated from one another for a considerable period of time. Christopher Ehret, the linguist and historian who is primarily responsible for the imaginative reconstruction of the Southern Cushitic presence and influence in eastern Africa, has estimated that the initial differentiation of proto-Southern Cushitic, and the subsequent settlement of Southern Cushitic speakers in Kenya and Tanzania, must have occurred at least 3000–4000 years ago for these languages to have become as differentiated from one another as they are today.

Languages only spread and become differentiated as people speaking them move away from their ancestral homelands. It appears, then, that people speaking Southern Cushitic languages spead from southern Ethiopia into central Kenya 3–4000 years ago. Further, these people were either already herders and farmers, with a social organization based on age-sets, or they developed these practices soon after their arrival. The parallels with the Stone Bowl cultures of the eastern Rift which we have seen in the archaeological record are obvious. The Stone Bowl peoples were also food producers living in central Kenya 3–4000 years ago. Though neither the linguistic nor the archaeological record can establish certain links between these two, it seems likely that the Stone Bowl peoples were Southern Cushitic speakers who drifted from the Ethiopian borderlands down the Rift Valley into Kenya and central Tanzania in the 2nd millenium BC. One group (Dahaloan speakers) expanded into eastern Kenya, another (Mbuguan speakers) into northeastern Tanzania, and a third (Rift speakers) throughout Tanzania and around Lake Victoria.

These Southern Cushitic-speaking peoples must have made considerable impact on the pre-existing Wilton, possibly 'Khoisan'-speaking, hunters and gatherers. Occupying the most fertile savanna lands, the farmers and herders would have absorbed many hunter-gatherers and pushed others into remote forest or desert niches where they were free from continued competition over land. Under constant ecological and cultural pressure over more than 1000 years, many hunter-gatherers must have adopted farming or herding. In this early period of mixed agriculture, however, the distinction between a hunting-gathering and a food-producing way of life was probably not great, with many people passing back and forth between the two. Herders and farmers continued to hunt extensively, while hunters and gatherers could easily learn to herd or farm. Many people must have learned new languages as well. As Southern Cushitic-speaking peoples grew in numbers and became preponderant in the savanna, others adopted their way of life and language. Remote hunter-gatherers would have been the last to convert, but they eventually did as well because when Bantu speakers later supplanted Southern Cushitic speakers in the savanna, Southern Cushitic languages continued to be spoken by remote hunter-gatherers until the present.

BANTU

The great majority of peoples of eastern, central and southern Africa today speak one of the more than four hundred different Bantu languages. The Bantu languages are not only numerous and widespread, they are also closely related to one another, indicating their rapid spread over this vast area within the last two or three thousand years. By looking at the classification of the Bantu languages, it is possible to see how this occurred.

The greatest differentiation among the Bantu languages occurs in the northwestern corner of their distribution – in southeastern Nigeria, Cameroon, Gabon, and Zaire – where seven of the eight primary sub-groups of Bantu are found, according to the most detailed classification of the languages to date made by Bernd Heine (see Map 2.3). The Bantu languages are also part of a larger family of languages, known as Benue-Congo, most of which are centred around the Benue–Cross rivers area of southeastern Nigeria. It is thus clear that the earliest Bantu speakers lived in this area where their closest relatives are, and that they spread throughout the forest zone of equatorial Africa where the initial differentiation of Bantu into its eight constituent sub-groups occurred. Eventually the speakers of one of these sub-groups emerged from the southern fringes of the forest zone onto the savanna along the lower Congo River and slowly expanded south down the west coast into present-day Angola and Namibia and east towards the Great Lakes. This too

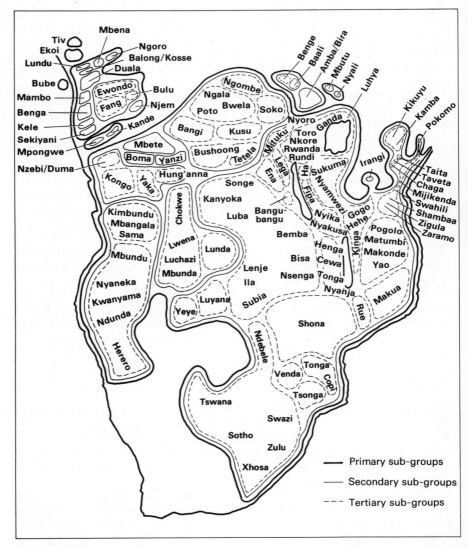

Map 2.3 *Bantu classification*

must have been a slow process, because seven of the eight sub-groups of savanna Bantu developed along the forest fringe. On reaching the area of the Great Lakes, however, the spread of Bantu speakers must have quickened as all the Bantu languages from eastern to southern Africa are closely related languages belonging to a single eastern highlands sub-group of savanna Bantu, as we can see on the map. While it is not possible to say precisely when these various movements occurred, the differentiation among the Bantu languages indicates that the initial spread of Bantu speakers through the equatorial forest must have occurred during the 2nd millennium BC, while that

Initial diffusion of Bantu languages   Diffusion of Bantu languages in the Savanna
c. 2nd millennium BC   c. 1st millennium BC

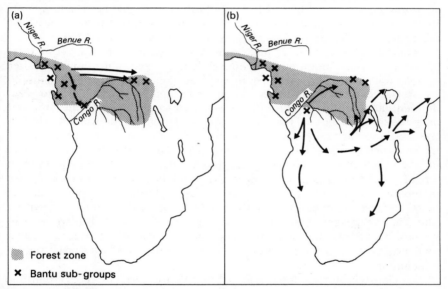

Map 2.4 *Diffusion of the Bantu languages*

of the savanna Bantu took place from early in the 1st millennium BC, and of the eastern highlands Bantu during the later 1st millennium BC and early 1st millennium AD.

By comparing the common words, or cognates, widely spread in the present Bantu languages, linguists have also been able to reconstruct substantial portions of proto-Bantu as it may have been spoken prior to the expansion of the Bantu-speaking peoples. From this reconstructed vocabulary it is obvious that the earliest Bantu speakers in the Congo basin were fishermen and root crop cultivators, for they had words for fishing with a hook and line, fish-hooks, fishtraps, dugout canoes, paddles, yams, oil palms, and goats, but they did not have words for grains or bananas, cattle-herding, iron working, or pottery, making it improbable that they practised any of these activities. Iron working is a good example. The present Bantu languages have at least fifty roots for the word 'iron', some borrowed from other languages and some derived from their own words, such as 'white' or 'stone'. It is thus obvious that

Bantu speakers acquired the skills of iron working after significant differentiation had already occurred among the various Bantu languages. With no common root to draw on, all had to devise their own words for the new process. Bantu speakers must thus have been present in the savanna before the beginnings of iron working in this area in the last centuries BC.

Nor are there words in proto-Bantu relating to grain cultivation or herding cattle. Forest-dwelling Bantu speakers were root cultivators. Since grains were unsuited to a forest ecology and tsetse prevented herding cattle, Bantu speakers could only have adopted those practices after they had emerged on to the savanna. Sorghum, millet, and cattle had already been domesticated in eastern Africa at this time, and the Bantu speakers of the area generally borrowed Southern Cushitic terminology for irrigation, fertilization, sorghum, eleusine, and livestock. It would thus seem that eastern highlands Bantu speakers adopted iron working and mixed agriculture within East Africa from earlier peoples speaking Southern Cushitic languages.

The first Bantu speakers must thus have expanded into the equatorial forest as fishermen and root cultivators early in the 2nd millennium BC. After nearly a millennium, during which they spread along the rivers throughout the equatorial forest zone and their language became differentiated into eight different languages or sub-groups of closely related languages, some emerged on to the savanna south of the Congo Basin. Over the next millennium, the last one BC, these Bantu speakers spread throughout the savanna zone, adopting mixed agriculture and, later, iron working. We cannot be sure precisely where or when these innovations took place, but grain cultivation and herding had already been long established in East Africa and the earliest iron-working sites in sub-Saharan Africa are those associated with Urewe-ware pottery in the Lake Victoria region dating from the 5th–6th century BC. It thus seems likely that Bantus speakers first adopted mixed agriculture and iron working in western East Africa and then introduced those industries into eastern Kenya and subsequently into the rest of eastern and southern Africa during the 1st millennium AD.

Previously historians have assumed that Bantu speakers were responsible for the spread of mixed agriculture and iron working throughout sub-Saharan Africa. If West African Bantu-speaking Negroes practised agriculture and iron working, so the reasoning went, their population would have grown, forcing them to expand, and they would have been able to clear and cultivate the savanna easily and quickly, enabling them to spread rapidly. As we have seen, however, the earliest examples of mixed agriculture and of iron working were both in eastern Africa, and Bantu speakers did not adopt these until the later stages of their expansion from West Africa. The diffusion of these industries and of Bantu-speaking peoples was thus far from even. This can be seen further in the physical types of present Bantu speakers. Coming as they did initially from West Africa, Bantu speakers are usually assumed to be Negroid, like other West Africans, but today they vary quite considerably, reflecting the influence on them of the peoples among whom they settled. These included the Pygmies of the Congo forest, who themselves speak Bantu languages today, the tall, thin Africans of the East African savanna and the Sudan, and the Khoikhoi and San of southwestern Africa. Negroes thus did not displace earlier peoples, but assimilated many and converted others to

Bantu speech. Such assimilation not only explains the differences among the Bantu-speaking peoples today, it also helps account for their spectacular population increase and expansion. Just as the Ngoni assimilated thousands of people as they moved north from South Africa in the early 19th century, the present Bantu-speaking populations of eastern Africa are probably largely the descendants of the earlier inhabitants of the area who have adopted Bantu speech. In summary, then, the so-called 'Bantu migration' should not be seen as a single migration of cultivating, iron-using, Bantu-speaking Negroes sweeping across Africa from west to east displacing all in their wake, but as a series of inter-related diffusions and syntheses as small groups of Bantu speakers interacted with pre-existing peoples and new technical developments to produce a range of distinct cultural syntheses across the southern half of Africa. The variety of these syntheses is pronounced in eastern Kenya where the earliest Bantu speakers encountered Southern Cushitic, 'Khoisan', and probably Sudanic speakers and still mix with Eastern Cushitic and Eastern Nilotic speakers today along the northern borders of Bantu speech. This complex and fascinating area can thus tell us more about the history and development of the Bantu languages.

The northeast Bantu languages

Our evidence for the expansion of Bantu-speaking peoples within East Africa itself comes largely from the detailed lexicostatistical analysis and classification of the East African Bantu languages by Derek Nurse and Gerard Philippson. Their sub-grouping reveals the outlines of the development of these languages over the past two thousand years. As we have seen, Heine classifies all the languages of eastern and southern Africa into a single eastern highlands sub-group of the savanna Bantu languages. Sub-dividng this eastern highlands sub-group further, Nurse and Philippson have divided the Bantu languages of Kenya, Uganda, and northern Tanzania into five sub-groups: Lacustrine, West Tanzania, Northeast Coast, Chaga/Taita, and Thagicu.* Lacustrine includes those languages presently spoken around Lake Victoria that are closely related to languages in adjacent Zaire. The other four sub-groups, however, form part of a continuum of related languages stretching diagonally from southern Tanzania to eastern Kenya, with three of these sub-groups clustered around the Kenyan–Tanzanian border: Northeast Coast includes those languages presently spoken in coastal Kenya and Tanzania, Chaga/Taita those spoken in the highland areas of Mt. Kilimanjaro, the Pare Mountains, and the Taita Hills, and Thagicu, those spoken in the central Kenyan highlands around Mt. Kenya and the Nyandarua range. This distributional pattern indicates that northeastern Bantu speakers probably spread from Zaire around the southern tip of Lake Tanganyika and then moved across East Africa from southwest to northeast, finally settling in the eastern Kenya–Tanzania borderland. The borderland area, then, must have been the centre of the earliest Bantu-speaking settlement in the area, from

---

* While in general agreement with Heine's classification, Nurse and Philippson differ with Heine in the details of their sub-grouping. This is to be expected, given that Heine's work involved the broad classification of all the Bantu languages, while Nurse and Philippson were concerned with the detailed classification of only the East African Bantu languages.

which Bantu speakers later dispersed north and south along the Kenyan and Tanzanian coasts.

By looking at the percentages of words the northeastern Bantu languages share in common, it is also obvious that they have been in the borderland area for a fairly long time. The languages of the Northeast Coast sub-group share only 41 per cent of their basic vocabulary in common, while those of Chaga/Taita share 44 per cent, placing the origins of both these sub-groups early in the 1st millennium AD, as we shall see. Thagicu, by contrast, is much younger. The languages of this sub-group share 63 per cent of their basic

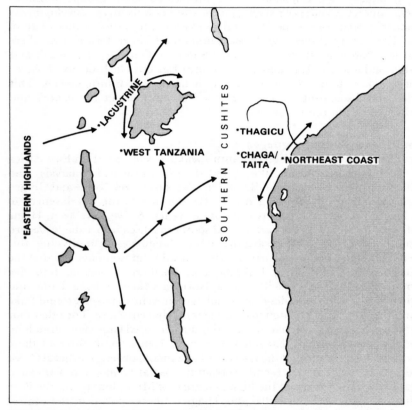

Map 2.5 *Diffusion of Bantu into East Africa, c. 500 BC—c. 1000 AD*

vocabulary in common, indicating its origins lie early in the 2nd millennium AD. We can thus conclude that the earliest Bantu speakers in the northeast probably settled in the area between Mt. Kilimanjaro, the Taita Hills and the coast early in the 1st millennium AD.

These conclusions place the earliest Bantu speakers in the same areas and contemporary with the earliest iron workers in the area. The earliest iron-working site is Kwale, just north of the borderland, dating from the 2nd century AD, and other sites dating from the 3rd to 4th centuries are in Pare,

Kilimanjaro, and Usambara. All of these are located in the central northeastern zone, and no other Kwale-ware sites have been found for this period outside of this zone. Later, Bantu speakers moved into the central highlands of Kenya, where Kwale-ware has been found dating from the 12th century, contemporary with the development of the Thagicu languages. It would thus appear that the earliest Bantu speakers in eastern Kenya and northeastern Tanzania introduced iron-working skills into this area. Coming from the west, they may have acquired these in either eastern Zaire or western Tanzania in the closing centuries BC before they expanded further east in the 1st century AD. Once settled in the northeast, they quickly became differentiated into their constituent sub-groups. It is to the development of these sub-groups that we now turn.

Northeast Coast Bantu

The largest, most widely distributed, and apparently oldest of the three northeastern sub-groups is Northeast Coast, including all the languages of the Kenyan and northern Tanzanian coasts and immediate hinterland areas (see

Fig. 2.2 *Northeast Coastal Bantu*

Northeast Coastal Bantu (41 per cent)
  Saghala/Pare (46 per cent)
    Saghala
    Pare/Taveta
      South Pare
      North Pare/Taveta
  Sabaki (60 per cent)
    Mijikenda/Swahili (65 per cent)
      Mijikenda (71 per cent)
      Swahili (79 per cent)
    Pokomo
  Ruvu (47 per cent)
    West Ruvu (58 per cent)
      Gogo
      Kaguru
      Sagara
    East Ruvu (66 per cent)
      Zaramo
      Kutu
      Kami
      Kwere
      Doe
    Seuta (71 per cent)
      Shambaa/Bondei (76 per cent)
        Shambaa
        Bondei
      Zigula/Ngulu (83 per cent)
        Zigula
        Ngulu
    Luguru

Map 2.6). The languages of the Northeast Coast group are sub-grouped as shown in Fig. 2.2, which reveals that the ancestral language, proto-Northeast Coast, initially sub-divided into three: proto-Ruvu, proto-Saghala/Pare, and proto-Sabaki. With time each of these three slowly expanded and became further differentiated into the present languages of the area, as can be seen from the chart. A graphic picture of this development can be seen by plotting the development of the Northeast Coast family tree against the relative chronology obtained from the percentages of shared cognates of the various sub-groups (Fig. 2.3). Such a relative chronology is not always accurate as languages can vary in their rates of development. Peoples speaking related languages and living next to one another, for example, may mutually reinforce

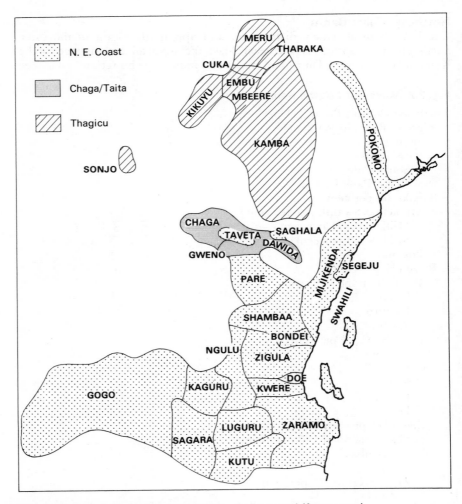

Map 2.6 *Bantu languages of eastern and central Kenya and northeastern Tanzania*

one another and their languages will diverge more slowly than languages whose speakers are further away from one another. But the chart does convey a general picture of the relative development of the various sub-groups. And, since we think that two sub-groups, Sabaki and Mijikenda, developed late in the 1st millennium and early in the 2nd millennium respectively, we can also estimate the chronological periods over which this took place.*

From the pattern of sub-group development and the present distribution of the languages which comprise Northeast Coast, we can also reconstruct a likely pattern of diffusion. This is because language development normally occurs when the speakers of a single language move apart from one another and settle separately. The normal rule of logic imposed on such reconstructions is the 'rule of least moves': that is, the reconstructed movements have to account for the present distribution of the languages in the least number of moves by ancestral speakers away from their homeland. Thus, if related languages A, B, and C were all contiguous and D separate, we would postulate that speakers of D split from speakers of A, B, and C (one move), rather than that speakers of A, B, and C each moved away separately from D speakers (three moves). A-B-C is, accordingly, the homeland. On this basis, the likeliest homeland for the Northeast Coast sub-group as a whole lies at the juncture of the three sub-groups, Saghala/Pare, Sabaki, and Ruvu, on the Kenya–Tanzania border between the Taita Hills and the coast. The earliest move was probably of proto-Saghala/Pare speakers to the Taita Hills early in the 1st millennium, closely followed by proto-Ruvu speakers to the south and later by proto-Sabaki speakers to the north. Then, as speakers of each of these languages expanded, they became further differentiated into the languages presently spoken in these areas today. Thus, late in the 1st millennium proto-Sabaki became differentiated into Mijikenda, Swahili, and Pokomo. Later during the 2nd millennium, each of these languages in turn became differentiated into the different dialects spoken today. Thus Pokomo speakers, settled along the lower Tana River, developed regional northern and southern dialects; Swahili speakers, dispersed into coastal towns the length of the coast, developed local dialects along the Somali–Kenya coast, the northern Tanzania coast, and the southern Tanzanian coast; while the nine Mijikenda peoples, settled in their separate hilltop *kayas*, or villages, each developed their own dialect.

The differentiation of these languages and dialects was also facilitated by the fact that as speakers of each moved away from their fellow speakers they came into contact with speakers of other languages from whom they borrowed new words, replacing common roots in their original language. The presence of these loan-words also tells us what languages they came into contact with and the nature of the interaction between the speakers of the two languages. One of the clearest cases of intensive interaction and borrowing in the northeast concerns Saghala and Dawida. Both are Bantu languages, but related to each other only very remotely: Dawida is a member of the

---

* The dating for Sabaki and Mijikenda comes from the traditional and documentary evidence discussed in the following chapter and is only approximate. These dates do indicate, however, that the Northeast Coastal languages have retained approximately 80 per cent of their common basic vocabulary per millennium, placing the origins of the sub-group as a whole at the beginning of the 1st millennium AD.

Chaga/Taita sub-group while Saghala is a member of the Northeast Coast sub-group. Once speakers of the two languages had settled together in the Taita Hills, however, each borrowed intensively from the language of the other, so that today both languages include a substantial number of

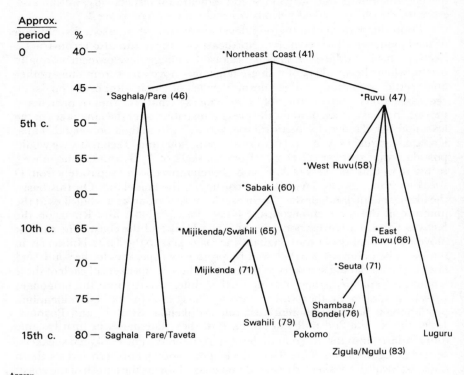

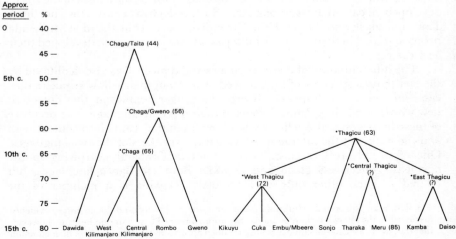

Fig. 2.3 *Classification of the northeastern Bantu languages*

loan-words from the other. Both also contain a number of words borrowed from Southern Cushitic, indicating early interaction with Southern Cushitic speakers who must have occupied the area before them, as well as words later borrowed from Southern Nilotic and Eastern Nilotic languages. Similarly, the Sabaki languages as a group share a set of loan-words from the Dahaloan branch of Southern Cushitic, while Dahalo contains a reciprocal Sabaki set, indicating there was interaction between the speakers of these two languages before proto-Sabaki split up into its present languages, Mijikenda, Swahili, and Pokomo.

We have thus seen how Northeast Coast speakers first settled in the northeast early in the 1st millennium AD. The initial differentiation within this group occurred as proto-Saghala/Pare speakers moved into the Taita Hills, proto-Ruvu speakers moved south along the Tanzanian coast, and proto-Sabaki speakers moved north along the Kenyan coast. In each of these areas they settled amongst the earlier Southern Cushitic-speaking inhabitants. Eventually most of these Southern Cushitic speakers were absorbed by the Bantu speakers, but not before they contributed a number of words and concepts to the Bantu languages. As the Bantu speakers continued their expansion over the northeast, their languages continued to diverge from one another, producing the present languages and dialects of the area.

Chaga/Taita
We can trace the development of proto-Chaga/Taita into its present constituent languages directly from the chart (Fig. 2.3). Proto-Chaga/Taita began its development early in the 1st millennium AD, probably from the slopes of Mt. Kilimanjaro, where the Chaga still live today. Subsequent differentiation occurred as some people moved north to settle in the Taita Hills while others moved south to North Pare. Loan-words in Chaga, Dawida, and Gweno indicate that there was considerable interaction between speakers of these languages and earlier Southern Cushitic and 'Khoisan' speakers in all of these areas, while Dawida speakers also came into close contact and interacted with Saghala speakers, as we have seen.

Thagicu
The successive differentiation of proto-Thagicu is also shown on the chart (Fig. 2.3), from which it is apparent that this language initially developed from the beginning of the 2nd millennium as its speakers fanned out over the central highlands from a probable origin in Thagicu, between the upper reaches of the Athi and Tana rivers. Four sub-groups subsequently developed. Proto-West Thagicu emerged as proto-Thagicu speakers moved north and west along the mountain ridges and subsequently it became differentiated into Cuku, Embu/Mbeere, and Kikuyu as its speakers spread further along the mountain ridges in the first half of the 2nd millennium. Proto-East Thagicu speakers were probably moving south in this same period to settle the Machakos area, from which Kamba speakers subsequently spread into the Ulu–Kitui areas and Daiso speakers moved into Pare, Usambara, and the coast. Daiso speakers are still present in eastern Usambara today, but the Segeju of the coast have subsequently adopted the Digo language of their neighbours. In the meantime, Central Thagicu speakers were fanning out around Mt. Kenya,

where the Meru dialects and Tharaka developed, and Sonjo speakers moved west of the Rift Valley to settle in their present location. With the dispersal of Thagicu speakers in the central highlands, northeastern Bantu speakers had achieved their current distribution throughout southeastern Kenya. The focus of activity then shifted to the north, where people speaking another group of languages had already started to infiltrate the area.

EASTERN CUSHITIC

After the 16th century the expansion of Bantu-speaking peoples to the north was brought to an abrupt halt and in some cases reversed by another major expansion of Cushitic-speaking peoples from the Ethiopian borderland as Eastern Cushitic speakers started to expand into Kenya in large numbers. Eastern Cushitic is a second major division of Cushitic and is divided into Highlands and Lowlands sub-groups (see Fig. 2.4). The majority of the Lowlands sub-group are today clustered in the area north of Lake Turkana, making this the probable homeland for the sub-group as a whole. Judging from the much lower percentages of cognates that exist between the sub-groups and individual languages of Lowland Eastern Cushitic than those for the northeastern Bantu languages, these languages are much older and must date from at least the 2nd millennium BC. By the 1st millennium BC the first Eastern Cushitic-speaking peoples were pushing into eastern Kenya, but the only remnant of them which still exists is the Yaaku people who live north of Mt. Kenya. The Yaaku today are Maa-speaking hunting-gatherers, but earlier in this century they still spoke an Eastern Cushitic language which also contained some remnants of 'Khoisan'. Thus, they may originally have been 'Khoisan' speakers, who subsequently adopted an Eastern Cushitic language just as they have recently adopted the language of their Maasai neighbours. They represent what must have been a common pattern of language change throughout eastern Kenya over the past 3–4000 years.

Other Eastern Cushitic speakers were slower to expand south. Western Omo/Tana speakers have apparently been moving south along the Omo River and eastern shores of Lake Turkana since the 1st millennium AD and once must have extended as far south as the southern tip of Lake Turkana, where the Elmolo fishermen once spoke their language. Similarly, Eastern Omo/Tana-speaking peoples must have also pushed south about this time, Rendille into Kenya and Somali into the Horn. But it was the Oromo- (or Galla-) speaking peoples who were able to make the most dramatic impact. Oromo is a language spoken today from northern Ethiopia to central Kenya. Its origin lies in southern Ethiopia, where it was spoken in only a small area as late as the 15th century. Early in the 16th century, however, Oromo speakers started to expand from this area, rapidly conquering and settling vast areas to the north, east, and south over the following three centuries, before their expansion was halted and reversed by the Somali and Maasai in the 19th century.* It was only then that a somewhat stable border between Bantu expansion from the south and Oromo and Somali from the north was achieved. Prior to the 16th

---

* The dates here come from the documentary evidence discussed in the following chapters.

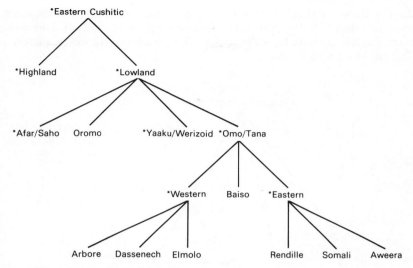

Fig. 2.4 *Eastern Cushitic languages*

century, Sabaki-speaking peoples had settled along the Somali coast as far as Brava and Mogadishu. They were pushed back into Kenya by the Oromo who, at one point, extended as far south as Mombasa. By the late 19th century, however, the Oromo were in retreat, and the present border between Bantu speakers in the south and Eastern Cushitic speakers in the north of eastern Kenya was established.

EASTERN NILOTIC

The fifth major language group in eastern and central Kenya today is Eastern (or Plains) Nilotic, including the Turkana and Maa languages (see Fig. 2.5). Maa speakers comprise a number of different peoples, including the Samburu, Camus, Arusha, Baraguyu, and Maasai, but all speak closely related dialects of the single Maa language. While the Turkana and Maasai between them stretch from the northern borders of central Kenya right through Kenya and into central Tanzania, the majority of Eastern Nilotic languages are spoken in the Kenya–Uganda–Sudan border area, making this the probable centre of ancestral versions of these languages. But the present languages are fairly young. There are only small differences between the southern Maa and northern Maa dialects, resulting from their wide dispersal from the 17th century to the present. The Maasai, then, are relative newcomers to the eastern Kenya scene. During their spread into Kenya, however, Maa speakers interacted with a number of other peoples, as indicated by the prevalence of loan-words in their language. Maa itself contains a number of loan-words from Southern (or Highlands) Nilotic languages, such as Kalenjin, while Eastern Nilotic as a whole contains a number of loan-words from Eastern and Southern Cushitic languages, indicating earlier patterns of interaction between the speakers of these languages in southern Sudan and Ethiopia. Maa speakers continue to interact today with other language speakers, including eastern Cushites (Oromo, Somali, Rendille, and Yaaku), Southern Nilotes (Kalenjin), and Bantu, in eastern Kenya.

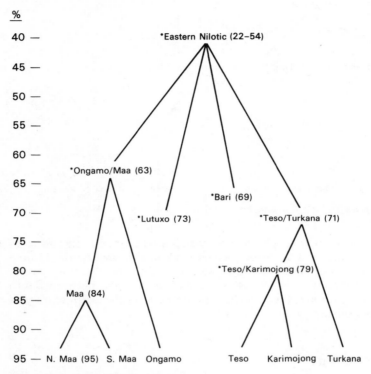

Fig. 2.5 *Eastern Nilotic languages*

LANGUAGE AND CULTURE

The linguistic history of eastern and central Kenya was a busy one over the last 3000–4000 years, with the intermingling of peoples speaking languages from at least five different language families. As peoples speaking new languages spread from adjacent areas, they interacted with the peoples already there. Usually these groups coexisted for long periods, and representatives of most of these language families can still be found today. Most, however, eventually became assimilated by others, but the peoples and their cultures remained, absorbed into the developing cultures of Kenya. We have traced many of these earlier peoples through the patterns of internal growth and the development of their languages and others through the evidence of loan-words they have left in each other's languages.

The 1st millennium and early 2nd millennium AD were obviously a time of cultural growth, as the main components of present cultures coalesced into their modern forms. In the south, 'Khoisan', Southern Cushitic, and Bantu speakers intermingled and interacted to produce a range of local syntheses. While Bantu speakers and their languages eventually became dominant in this area, their cultures were heavily influenced by those of the pre-existing peoples. The interaction between peoples speaking different languages and the internal development of these languages were thus part of the larger historical drama taking place as immigrant and local populations intermarried and grew to produce the present peoples of the area. Technology developed as people blended hunting and gathering techniques with farming and herding practices and stone skills with iron-working ones. Social organization increased in scale as disparate peoples were assimilated and integrated into agricultural village settlements united by kinship and age sets binding age mates of different kin groups together. Similar developments occurred in religious and ritual practices, patterns of power and authority, and design of housing and of dress.

While the cultural horizons of individual peoples were expanding, they were also becoming more specialized as different cultural strategies were adopted to cope with different ecologies. From the earliest differentiation of the northeastern Bantu-speaking peoples, for example, they developed specialized cultural ecologies. Thus Northeast Coast speakers remained largely along the coastal lowlands and developed agricultural practices, herbal medicines, immunities from prevalent diseases, and culture appropriate to their environment. Such specialization can readily be seen in vocabulary, where the Mijikenda, for example, have a highly elaborated vocabulary embracing every part and use of the all important coconut palm. Chaga/Taita speakers, by contrast, remained exclusively in a highlands environment and have up to twenty different words for bananas. When they migrated from Mt. Kilimanjaro, they sought similar montane environments in Pare and Taita rather than settling in the intervening lowlands. The same was true of the highlands Thagicu speakers. Subsequent migrations re-enforced this pattern, as individual Pare, Shambaa, Chaga, Taita, and Kamba travelled from one highland area to another, while lowlands Mijikenda, Pokomo, and Swahili remained in the lowlands. Only very occasionally was an alternative environment chosen, usually out of dire need for land, as when Kamba moved down from Ulu into Kitui, for to do so required a dramatic shift in culture as well as ecology.

At the same time as these developments were taking place in southern Kenya, similar processes were occurring to the north. Where the patterns in the north differed from those further south was in the peculiar nature of the arid expansive environment. Except for the Tana River Basin, the coastal strip and the central highlands, all previously occupied by Bantu-speaking farmers, the northeast is only suitable for extensive pastoralism requiring constant movements of men and stock between available grasslands and water to maintain subsistance. Thus a far more mobile pattern developed, with conflict among 'Khoisan', Eastern Cushitic, and Maa speakers engendered by competition for scarce resources. The cultural ecology of this area is not uniform, however. The extreme dryness of Rendille country favours camels, while further south in Samburu country cattle are more advantageous. Thus specialization developed here as well, with hunters, fishermen, cattle herders, and camel herders all making their own distinctive responses to the challenges of the environment. These processes have taken place over a shorter term than in the south, however, and the area is still in a state of flux. Boran Oromo and Laikipiak Maasai have been driven from the area within living memory, while Yaaku and Elmolo are still in the process of adopting the Maa language today. Waata hunters who earlier adopted Oromo are today settling among Mijikenda agriculturalists and adopting their language.

Language is only one aspect of culture, but through looking at the processes of language development and the evidence of wider aspects of ecology, social and political organization, and ritual contained in vocabulary, we have been able to trace a number of processes in the cultural development of eastern and central Kenya to supplement the earlier archaeological evidence. We now turn to examine these same processes in the immediate past as they come to us through the traditional records and early accounts of the present peoples of the area.

REFERENCES AND SUGGESTIONS FOR FURTHER READING

The linguistic history of eastern Kenya is only now beginning to be studied and written. Thus no comprehensive synthesis is yet available, but comments on method can be found in many of the following studies.

The classic study of African language classification is Joseph Greenberg, *The Languages of Africa* (3rd ed.) (Bloomington, 1970). Very little exists yet on the Khoisan languages, but a major study of Southern Cushitic influence is Christopher Ehret, *Ethiopians and East Africans* (Nairobi, 1974), following his now classic study *Southern Nilotic History* (Evanston, 1971). Both are based on the analysis of loan-word evidence and are summarized in a number of places, including 'Cushites and the Highlands and Plains Nilotes to AD 1800' in B.A. Ogot (ed.,) *Zamani* (2nd ed.), pp. 150–169 (Nairobi, 1973).

The argument for a West African homeland of the Bantu languages is decisively made by Joseph Greenberg, 'Linguistic Evidence Regarding Bantu Origins', *JAH*, 13/2 (1972), pp. 189–216 and Christopher Ehret, 'Bantu Origins and History: Critique and Interpretation', *Transafrican Journal of History*, 2/1 (1972), pp. 1–9, while the most complete classification of the Bantu languages is B. Heine, 'Zur genetischen gliederung die Bantu-Sprachen', *Afrika und Übersee*, 56 (1972–73), pp. 164–185, as revised by B. Heine, H. Hoff, and R. Vossen, 'Neuere Ergebnisse zur Territorialgeschischte der Bantu' in W. Möhlig, F. Rottland, and B. Heine (eds.), *Zur Sprachgeschichte und Ethnohistorie in Africa*, pp. 57–72 (Berlin, 1977). The linguistic evidence regarding Bantu iron working is carefully analysed in P. de Maret and F. Nsuka, 'History of Bantu Metallurgy: Some Linguistic Aspects', *History in Africa*, 4 (1977), pp. 43–65, and proto-Bantu cultural vocabulary can be found in M. Guthrie, *Comparative Bantu* (London, 1967–70).

Over the past few years linguists Derek Nurse and Gerard Philippson have been engaged in the formidable task of classifying all the Bantu languages of East Africa. Their work, still in progress, can be seen in D. Nurse and G. Philippson, 'The Northeastern Bantu Languages of Tanzania and Kenya: A Classification', *Kiswahili*, 45/2 (1975), pp. 1–28; D. Nurse, *Classification of the Chaga-Dialects: Language and History on Kilimanjaro, the Taita Hills, and the Pare*

Mountains (Hamburg, 1979); and D. Nurse and G. Philippson, 'Historical Implications of the Language Map of East Africa' in E. Polome (ed.), *Language in Tanzania* (London, forthcoming).

The Sabaki languages are discussed in Thomas Hinnebusch, 'Prefixes, Sound Changes, and Sub-grouping in the Coastal Kenyan Bantu Languages' (Ph.D. thesis, University of California at Los Angeles, 1973); T. Hinnebusch, 'Swahili: Genetic Affiliations and Evidence', *Studies in African Linguistics*, Supl. 6 (1976), pp. 95–108; and Philip Sedlak, 'Sociocultural Determinants of Language Maintenance and Language Shift in a Rural Coastal Kenyan Community' (Ph.D. thesis, Stanford University, 1975). Thagicu is analysed in Patrick Bennett, 'Dahl's Law and Thagicu', *African Language Studies*, 8 (1967), pp. 127–159.

A detailed classification of Eastern Cushitic is not yet available, but see Christopher Ehret, 'Cushitic Prehistory' in M. Bender (ed.), *The Non-Semitic Languages of Ethiopia*, pp. 85–96 (East Lansing, 1976); M. L. Bender, 'The Languages of Ethiopia: A New Lexicostatistic Classification', *Anthropological Linguistics*, 13 (1971), pp. 165–288; Joseph Greenberg, 'The Mogogodo: A Forgotten Cushitic People', *Journal of African Languages*, 2/1 (1963), pp. 29–43; Bernt Heine, 'Notes on the Yaaku Language (Kenya)', *Africa und Übersee*, 58 (1974–75), pp. 27–61, 119–138; B. Heine. 'Notes on the Rendille Language', *Africa und Übersee*, 59 (1976), pp. 176–233; B. Heine, 'Bemerkungen zur Boni-Sprache (Kenia)', *Africa und Übersee*, 60 (1977), pp. 242–295; and Harold Flemming, 'Baiso and Rendille: Somali Outliers', *Rassegna di Studi Etiopici*, 20 (1964), pp. 35–96.

Eastern Nilotic and the Maa dialects are discussed in R. Vossen, 'Linguistic Evidence Regarding the Territorial History of the Maa-Speaking Peoples', *Kenya Historical Review* (forthcoming).

CHAPTER THREE

TALES OF ORIGINS
THE TRADITIONAL RECORD

As we move into the study of the earliest history of the present peoples and cultures of eastern Kenya starting between AD 1000 and 1500 , we also move into their own accounts of these events as related in their traditions. Oral traditions are stories told about the past and served in preliterate societies as the main vehicle for remembering history. Old men would gather around the fire at night and recount the legends of ancestral heroes, of migrations, or of the origins of present practices. Professional singers and narrators would relate the epic poems of royal dynasties at great ceremonial occasions. Elders might reveal the secrets of the past in formal initiation ceremonies of the young, or herbalists, diviners, and smiths might convey the specialist knowledge of their crafts to their apprentices. An occasion rarely passed without some acknowledgement of the lessons learned from the past in proverb, song, story, music, or dance. Each society and group within society had its own distinctive forms, but in all history was a living reality more immediate than the school books of modern societies.

Oral traditions differ in a number of important respects from conventional history based on written documents. Unlike a document which is usually contemporary with the events it describes and survives unchanged into the present, oral traditions are only preserved by being remembered and retold by successive generations from the time of the event to the present. They are thus subject to lapses in memory and manipulation by successive tellers in the process of transmission.

This is readily seen in the way traditions treat different time periods. Historians divide traditions into three time periods. The earliest period usually tells of the origins of mankind and of a people, often in mythical or allegorical form. The tradition of Genesis in the Old Testament is a classic origin tradition, relating the beginnings of the universe, man, the peoples of Israel, and their culture in a compact and abstract statement in which thousands of years of history are encapsulated in a timeless mythical moment. Origin traditions frequently unite a whole people in a single genealogy in which the earliest ancestors are represented as supra-human cultural heroes who established orderly human society out of the chaos of the universe and who bequeathed to future generations the proper social conventions for civilized human discourse. The Kikuyu legend of Gikuyu and Mumbi is typical of African origin legends: God created the first man and woman and gave them sheep, goats, and land. The two had nine daughters, among whom the land was divided. These were the ancestresses of the present Kikuyu clans and these clans still farm the land that was initially allocated to them by God. The lesson is simple. Mankind did not evolve, but emerged fully developed as a cultured, Kikuyu-speaking member of the Kikuyu people with rights in land. Origin traditions thus cannot be taken literally as they are highly abstract statements defining a people and their culture. As Joseph Miller has put it, they provide a model, much like scientific models, for explaining things as they are and how they came to be.

Following the richly elaborated period of cultural origins, the middle period of traditions is often a much abbreviated account of events from earlier beginnings to the recent past. Genealogies for this period are sharply telescoped as only those ancestors who gave rise to significant sub-clans and lineages are remembered, while those of intervening generations are unceremoniously forgotten. Dramatic changes which may have occurred in this period are usually grafted on to the earlier period of origins, giving the impression that the timeless values expressed in the origin legends have continued to the present. Usurpation of authority or assimilation of foreigners are hidden in fictionalized genealogical links to the original clan. The middle period of traditions thus stresses recurrent processes which have continued from the time of creation to the present. The remembered past is seen as a reflection in the present of an idealized heritage in such a way as to support the maintenance of current institutions and values as a timeless historical heritage.

The most recent period of traditions stems from living or recent memory and is concerned with daily life and politics. Homesteads and local lineages are descended from old or recently deceased men and define the bounds of everyday social discourse. Random historical events are remembered because they happened to known individuals. It is a vibrant living period where changes have been known to occur, even if they are regretted as deviations from the classical model. Such changes as survive will later be abstracted and assimilated to that classical model, but now the ambiguities of the present and recent past are a daily source of anxiety. Since people usually prefer the proven verities of the past to the uncertainty of the changing present regardless of changes which may have rendered those past values irrelevant, it is in the present period that we see the dysfunctions between a people's ideals and their practice that are hidden from our view in the idealized norms of the past. Thus traditions are always in the process of becoming, accounting for the present in the past at the same time as abstracting the present into the past to account for changes as they occur.

It is for these reasons that many anthropologists and historians have doubted the usefulness of traditions as historical sources which accurately convey a picture of the past as it really was. Functionalist anthropologists, following Malinowski, have stressed that the traditional past is merely a cultural charter for the present, constantly manipulated to reflect changing circumstances and current political interests. Thus genealogies are frequently manipulated to reflect the adoption of strangers or to support one or another faction in a dispute. Traditions might tell us something of the present, therefore, but little of the past. Structuralist anthropologists in the school of Claude Lévi-Strauss have chosen to emphasize the symbolic aspect of traditional myths. According to Lévi-Strauss, all myths are composed of symbols which arise not out of present historical circumstance but out of universal patterns of human thought that transcend specific cultures and historical circumstances. Myths therefore tell us nothing of specific men but only make universal generalizations about mankind.

Historians, following the pioneering work of Jan Vansina, have sought to establish a third interpretation of traditions which seeks to identify the various roles played by traditions and to examine these roles individually and in interaction with one another. Two of the roles are those of charter and of symbol already examined. A third concerns the historical framework in which legends are narrated. Ancestors led their people from place to place, interacting with various other peoples en route. Lévi-Strauss himself speaks of the myth maker as *bricoleur*, assembling his stories out of the historical debris of the past. Real events thus become the framework for symbolic statements and for cultural charters. The three roles are frequently complementary: a symbolic statement can act as a cultural charter for an institution created in the past. In this light a legend becomes an elegant and highly symbolic abstraction of a people's deepest values placed in an historical context; it is thus a source for both narrative events and the value systems of the people who shaped those events.

While such complementarity means that we can extract the values and perspectives of the people involved and obtain an inside view of their culture as well as an historical narrative, it also means that the various levels are likely to interact with each other and with reality. As institutions change, legends are slowly updated to reflect the current reality. Conversely, a legend may play a conservative role in supporting outdated institutions. A legend arising out of one set of historical circumstances becomes a part of future reality for, once created, it assumes an independent existence affecting adaptation to future conditions. Traditions thus play a series of multi-faceted and dynamic historical roles which are all potential historical sources once the traditions are correctly decoded.

Decoding is an arduous job that requires extensive knowledge of the local linguistic and cultural idiom. Traditions frequently personalize whole peoples, clans, or lineages, and cultural statements have a reality equal to that of historical events. The Mijikenda origin myth starts with Muyeye and his two wives, Mbodze and Matsetse, who between them had nine sons, Mdigo, Mribe, Mgiriama, etc. – the fathers of the nine Mijikenda peoples today. All lived at a place called Singwaya in Somalia and migrated down the coast to Kenya in response to attacks on them by the Oromo. We know from other evidence, however, that only six of the Mijikenda peoples came from Singwaya and, of these, numerous sub-clans and lineages came from other places. Mijikenda acknowledge this, but see no conflict between the origin of the people at Singwaya and the diffuse origins of individuals. The Singwaya legend is a story of cultural origin – the birth of a people, a language, and a culture – which all Mijikenda share, while the diverse origins of individuals are of little consequence. The legend defines the essence of Mijikenda-ness which all Mijikenda, regardless of origin, share. Individual lineage traditions are merely eddies within a dominant cultural current.

The traditions of nearly all of the peoples of eastern and central Kenya, like those of the Kikuyu and Mijikenda, start with the origins of mankind and of the people. These traditions do not relate to the evolution of early man which we have seen revealed in the archaeological record, however, but to the much more recent cultural origins of the present peoples. We have already seen that a number of important historical developments have taken place over the past two–three thousand years, including the development and spread of farming and herding, the adoption of iron working, and the absorption of earlier 'Khoisan' and Southern Cushitic-speaking peoples by immigrant Bantu, Eastern Cushitic, and Eastern Nilotic-speaking ones. This was a period of great historical ferment, as new peoples and ideas interacted with older ones to produce a wide range of new cultural syntheses. During the later stages of this process over the past four–five centuries these peoples and ideas eventually coalesced into the present peoples and cultures of eastern Kenya, and it is this process of cultural formation to which the traditions refer. We have seen that each emergent people had their roots in the past peoples and cultures of the area, but the traditions are rarely concerned with this earlier history. What concerns them is that moment when a distinctive cultural identity emerged which we call Kikuyu or Mijikenda today. From the generalized story of mankind and his languages, then, we turn now to the specific histories of the present peoples of eastern Kenya.

HUNTER-GATHERER TRADITIONS

After the usual preface regarding the origins of the universe and of mankind, most traditions open with the origins of the people. Most of the peoples of eastern Kenya claim to have migrated from somewhere else to their present location, but a few claim always to have resided where they live today. These are the hunting-gathering peoples, including the Waata (or Sanye) of the Galana River and Taru Desert, the Dahalo (Sanye) and Aweera (Boni) east of the Tana River, and the Okiek (Dorobo) and Yaaku (Mogogodo) of the central highlands (see Fig. 3.1 for other popular variants of these names).

Okiek traditions collected by R. Blackburn are a good example. There are dozens of small, widely scattered Okiek peoples living today throughout the Mau Escarpment, the Nyandarua Ranges, and Mt. Kenya, all of whom share a common culture and identity linked to the highlands over 2 000 m which most inhabit. The Okiek speak the Southern Nilotic (Kalenjin) languages of their northern and western neighbours, but they deny any further affinity with the Kalenjin-speaking peoples and do not share their traditions of origin to the northwest. Okiek recall instead series of local migrations within the highlands they inhabit today. In general, they say they have always lived in the area, and this statement is re-enforced by the traditions of their neighbours, all of whom recall the Okiek (or people like them) as present in the area when they arrived and often credit Okiek with granting them land and facilitating their settlement. The Kikuyu claim they obtained land from Okiek (called Athi or Asi in their traditions) and that many of the earliest Kikuyu clans were founded by assimilated Okiek. Similarly, the Waata today recall no other homeland than Taru and both Waata and Mijikenda acknowledge that the Waata were the earlier inhabitants of the area. The Giriama relate that the Waata (called Laa in the traditions) showed them to a refuge from continued Oromo raids and taught them tactics which enabled them eventually to overcome the Oromo. The two have been firm friends ever since. While it is not always possible to identify early hunter-gatherer groups positively because of their number and the different names attributed to them by others, the following list of hunter-gatherer traditions (Fig. 3.1) provides convincing evidence of their presence prior to the occupation of eastern Kenya by herders and cultivators.

All of these peoples followed a specialized hunter-gatherer mode of subsistence until recently and many still do. The Okiek gathered honey and hunted in central highlands areas over 2 000 m. Waata hunted elephant in the forests along the Galana River and on the plains of Taru until they were

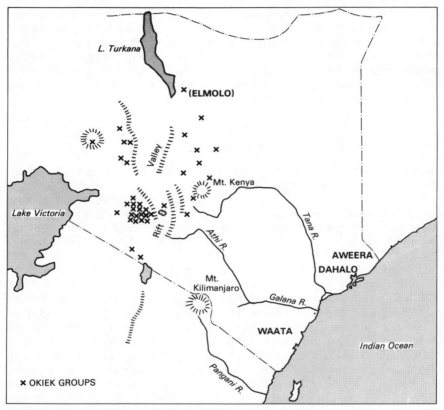

Map 3.1 *Hunter-gatherers of eastern and central Kenya*

expelled from this area by the wardens of Tsavo National Park. Both interacted closely with their neighbours. Waata gave meat (and formerly ivory and rhino horn) to Giriama in exchange for grain, livestock, and palm wine. Waata maintained close personal partners among the Giriama with whom they conducted this gift exchange. If a Waata killed an elephant, he delivered some of the meat or a tusk to his Giriama partner. Later, the Giriama reciprocated with a gift of palm wine, grain, or a goat. Both frequently partook in the rituals of the other, and Waata performed an important role in Giriama

50

ritual as the first owners of the land. Okiek played similar roles in Maasai society by providing honey for ritual beer, shields, sheaths, and necklaces, for which they were given livestock in return.

Fig. 3.1 *Hunter-gatherer traditions*

People	Names used by others	Traditions mentioning	Languages spoken	(PRESENT)
Aweera	Boni	Somali	'Khoisan'→	E. CUSHITIC
Dahalo	Sanye	Swahili, Pokomo	'Khoisan' →	S. CUSHITIC
Waata	Waata	Oromo	'Khoisan'? →	OROMO
	Langulo/Riangulo	Mijikenda		
	Laa	Giriama, Taita		
	Sanye	Swahili		
	Ndegerre	Duruma		
Okiek	Okiek	Kalenjin	'Khoisan'? → KALENJIN → some MAA and KIKUYU	
	Athi/Asi*	Kikuyu, Meru, Taita		
	Dorobo	Maasai		
	Elmolo	Rendille, Dassenech	'Khoisan'? → E. CUSHITIC → MAA	
Yaaku	Mogogodo	Maasai, Meru	'Khoisan' → E. CUSHITIC → MAA	
?	Noka/Ngulia	Kamba	?	

* The names Athi and Asi are found throughout the northeast and probably are not the name of an ethnic group, but a generalized term for countrymen. The root *thi/si* may well be an earlier form of *chi*, meaning country; thus Athi or Asi merely means 'people of the country', much like *wananchi* today.

Most hunter-gatherers followed many of the cultural practices of their dominant neighbours. From the 16th to the early 19th century Waata interacted closely with Oromo. Today they speak Oromo and have similar clans and age sets. Okiek speak Kalenjin and Yaaku speak an Eastern Cushitic language, but both have Maasai-type age sets and many now speak Maa. The Elmolo fishermen of southern Lake Turkana formerly spoke an Eastern Cushitic language, but now speak Maa and have Samburu style age sets and clans.

The hunter-gatherers thus had their own distinctive cultures while also sharing a great deal in common with their pastoral or agricultural neighbours. Two explanations have been given for this phenomenon. The first sees the hunter-gatherers as pariah, outcaste elements of the locally dominant culture, collections of poverty striken, anti-social people forced to flee during famines or conflict to the forests to take up a marginal form of subsistence. This was frequently the view of the dominant culture. Oromo considered Waata a low caste and refused to socialize with them. Maasai considered people who hunted and ate wild meat as sub-human. What distinguished the hunter-gatherers, then, was their separate mode of production; their culture was largely that of the dominant culture. They spoke the dominant language and followed the dominant pattern of social organization.

The second explanation sees the hunter-gatherers as the direct descendants of the hunter-gatherers who roamed eastern Africa before the development of pastoralism and agriculture. With the gradual loss of the open savanna to the food producers from the last millennium BC, the hunter-gatherers retreated to obscure ecological niches where they could pursue their way of life unchallenged by the more numerous food producers. The fact that the Hatsa of Tanzania still speak a 'Khoisan' language commonly associated with earlier hunter-gatherers, that the Aweera, Dahalo, and Yaaku still carry some evidence of having previously spoken one, that most hunter-gatherers are physically distinguished by their small stature and eye folds, that they still follow a hunting-gathering way of life characteristic of late Wilton times, and that hunter-gatherers have determinedly defended their existence by refusing to mix or marry with others have all been cited in support of this point of view.

The difference between these two explanations is not as great as it would seem; both represent different aspects of what has been a very complex process of historical interaction. On the one hand, the persistence of earlier 'Khoisan' and Southern Cushitic languages among hunter-gatherers is strong evidence of the cultural integrity of these groups and of their ability to maintain their way of life in the face of strong cultural pressure from their neighbours. While many 'Khoisan' speakers were undoubtedly assimilated by Southern Cushitic-speaking people, others persisted in their way of life and only slowly adopted Southern Cushitic speech over more than two thousand years of interaction. Having finally adopted Southern Cushitic speech, they have been equally slow to respond to the pressure of their more numerous Bantu, Maa, Oromo, and Somali-speaking neighbours. On the other hand, we have seen that hunter-gatherers were often closely linked economically and culturally with their neighbours, each providing specialized goods which the other did not produce and playing specialized roles in the other's society. Such close interaction fostered the adoption by the less numerous hunter-gatherers of those aspects of their neighbours' culture, such as language and social structure, which facilitated communication between the two. Maasai pastoralists and Okiek hunter-gatherers who shared the same language, clan, or age set could relate to one another more easily than if they were total strangers. The two thus shared a single interdependent existence. Over the years many hunter-gatherers have found it attractive to adopt herding or farming, and so assimilated fully to their neighbours' way of life. Similarly, many pastoralists and farmers have fled to the forest to settle with their hunter-gatherer clansmen or blood brothers during famines. Thus, hunting-gathering as an adaptive cultural ecology has proved to be highly persistent in the face of the pastoral and agricultural revolutions, but individuals have continued to move back and forth between these different modes.

This process has been explored in great detail by Richard Elphick for the San hunter-gatherers and the Khoikhoi herders of southwestern Africa. The Khoikhoi spoke a San language, but one that was obviously much younger than the more diverse languages spoken by the San themselves. The two were similar in other ways as well. Both shared similar pottery, musical, hunting, and religious traditions, and were genetically similar. Where they differed was that San relied on hunting and gathering for their subsistence, while the Khoikhoi depended on herding and hunting, but the two continued to interact closely with one another. When climatic conditions were favourable to herding, Khoikhoi herds increased and Khoikhoi increasingly came into conflict with San over water rights and pasturage, while San resisted these intrusions and hunted Khoikhoi cattle. As Khoikhoi continued to expand, they formed into powerful social groups under strong military leaders, while San were forced to flee into remote areas or to attach themselves as clients to the dominant Khoikhoi. San clients were initially used by the Khoikhoi as hunters, messengers, herdsmen, and soldiers, but eventually they were given cattle of their own, allowed to intermarry with Khoikhoi, and, thus, became Khoikhoi. During times of cattle disease, famine, or overgrazing, however, the whole process reversed. The large aggregations of Khoikhoi broke down into smaller and smaller groups who were forced to rely more on hunting and gathering for their subsistence, thus becoming San. Having lost their cattle during this phase, the only way in which they could later return to being Khoikhoi was to attach themselves as clients to rich Khoikhoi and repeat the process described above. Thus in the face of the fact that herding did not provide a permanent or secure way of life, the continued existence of hunter-gatherers was assured. This same flexibility and persistence has characterized the hunter-gatherers of Kenya as they continue a tradition as old as mankind itself.

TRADITIONS OF THE EARLIEST FOOD PRODUCERS

There is little in the traditional record relating to the late Stone Age and early Iron Age herders and farmers. This is because traditions relate to the identity of the people who tell them. Since these early peoples have subsequently merged with others and assumed new identities, traditions relating to them have been supplanted by later ones. A few people today, however, do recall earlier farmers and herders who preceded them, though it is difficult to be sure just who these earlier peoples were.

Taita traditions mention that there were two quite different peoples present in the Taita Hills when they first settled there. The first, variously called the Si or Laa, were hunters and gatherers who remained in the hills until the 19th century, contributing to a number of Taita clans as they were slowly absorbed by the Taita. The second group, known as the Bisha, are remembered for their wealth in cattle, their permanent dwellings, their agriculture, and their finely drawn features, and are said to have arrived from Ethiopia long after hunter-gatherers had settled in the area. Whereas the Si hunter-gatherers were able to survive Taita settlement by pursuing a different way of life, the Bisha competed with the Taita and were ultimately defeated and absorbed by them. Traditions about the Bisha are richest in the Mbale area, where there are also numerous stone burial cairns, bao boards, cup marks, and grooves carved into stone, stone circles, and stone terraces, dams, and irrigation works, which the Taita attribute to the Bisha. The traditional description of the Bisha, the archaeological remains, and the fact that both Taita languages (Dawida and Saghala) contain large numbers of Southern Cushitic loan-words suggest that there were late Stone Age food producers and Southern Cushitic speakers in the Taita Hills before the Taita. Elsewhere in Mbale there are also major iron working sites with Maore-ware, similar to that found on Mt. Kilimanjaro and indicative of the early Iron Age, which the Taita also attribute to the Bisha. Since these appear to represent quite a different culture, however, there may well have been a number of different peoples in the Taita Hills before the present Taita emerged.

Another early food-producing people were the Gumba, mentioned in Kikuyu, Cuka, Embu, Okiek, Maasai, and Yaaku traditions. The Gumba are remembered as herders of cattle and sheep and as iron workers who lived in thatched dwellings built over pits dug into the ground. They resisted Kikuyu settlement and were ultimately defeated by the Kikuyu in the 19th century. Kikuyu traditions also relate how they learned iron working from the Gumba and how they adopted Gumba practices of circumcision and clitoridectomy in initiating age sets. Archaeologists digging around the holes allegedly left by the Gumba at Gatung'ang'a have found evidence there of a herding, iron working, and obsidian-using culture with pottery similar to Kwale-ware dating from the 12th–13th century AD. These remains thus indicate a mixture of a late Stone Age food-producing culture and an early Iron Age one. The linguistic evidence is also confused as Kikuyu words for circumcision and clitoridectomy are clearly borrowed from Southern Cushitic languages, whereas iron terminology is Bantu. The most that we can say, then, is that there is evidence for a number of different cultural traditions preceding the Kikuyu in the central highlands.

There is thus a gap between the archaeological evidence relating to the early Iron Age and the linguistic evidence relating to early Bantu speakers, both early in the 1st millenium, and the traditions of the present Bantu-speaking peoples which start no earlier than the 10th–15th century. Perhaps the people responsible for the Kwale, Kilimanjaro, Taita, and Gathung'ang'a sites in the 1st millenium AD were proto-Northeast Coast, proto-Chaga/Taita, proto-Dawida or proto-Saghala, and proto-Thagicu speakers respectively, since these languages were developing about the same time in these areas, but we cannot be sure until more evidence is available. From this rather inconclusive evidence we move now into the more detailed traditional record of the present Bantu-speaking peoples. The period is the 2nd millenium AD.

TRADITIONS OF THE COASTAL BANTU-SPEAKING PEOPLES

One of the earliest traditions of northeastern Bantu origins, and a classic of its kind, is the Singwaya (or Shungwaya) legend related by the Mijikenda, Pokomo, Taita, and Swahili peoples of the coast. The various traditions relate how the Kashur (as they were all known then) once lived along the southern Somali coast as far north as present Brava. There some came into contact with early Arab traders with whom they traded and intermarried, producing the Swahili peoples and language. Sometime later Swahili began to sail south and establish trading centres along the East African coast while the others were driven south of the Juba River and began to split up. There they remained for some time until invaded by the Oromo, who drove them relentlessly down the coast to their present locations. The first to leave settled south of Mombasa as the Digo. Those remaining followed. The Pokomo settled in the Tana River valley, the Taita moved inland up the Galana River to the Taita Hills, while the Mijikenda continued south to settle behind the coast in a number of separate settlements between Malindi and Mombasa.

The Singwaya legend is a particularly valuable one for historians because a large amount of independent evidence exists to confirm its essential veracity and to place it chronologically. First there is the linguistic evidence. All of the Singwaya peoples, except the Taita, speak languages of the Sabaki sub-group of Northeast Coastal Bantu. This sub-group initially developed after its speakers moved away from other Northeast Coast speakers along the

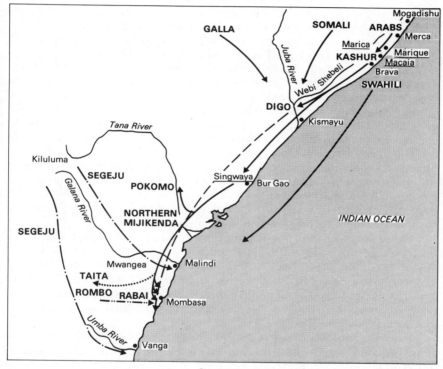

<u>Singwaya</u> = Sabaki names from Lindschoten map, 1596.

Map 3.2 *Coastal traditions*

Kenya–Tanzania border and followed the narrow coastal plain north to settle along the northern Kenyan and Somali coast. Here the initial development of the Sabaki languages took place as some Sabaki speakers settled with Arabic-speaking Shirazi and developed Swahili, a Sabaki language with a large number of Arabic loan-words. Swahili was subsequently dispersed from the 9th century AD as Swahili-speaking traders sailed down the coast and established small trading settlements at various islands and inlets en route, including Tanga, Pemba, Mafia, the Comoros, and Kilwa. The further development of the Sabaki languages occurred as proto-Sabaki speakers continued to disperse at Singwaya and down the coast.

The only discordant note in the linguistic evidence is struck by the Taita. The Taita speak two different languages, Dawida, a member of the Chaga/Taita sub-group, and Saghala, a member of the Saghala/Pare sub-group of Northeast Coast. Since neither is genetically related to the Sabaki sub-group and both are much older languages (see Fig. 2.3), they could not have shared a common origin with Sabaki. Dawida and Saghala speakers must have already been settled in the Taita Hills long before any migrants could have arrived from Singwaya. If some Taita did come from Singwaya, then, they must have settled amongst earlier Dawida and Saghala speakers and adopted their languages. Today different Taita clans claim a number of different origins, including Singwaya; what is obvious is that the Taita Hills have long been a melting-pot of different peoples and cultures.

The different traditions pertaining to Singwaya also cross correlate well, serving to confirm the legend. First are the separate traditions of the Singwaya peoples themselves, all of whom relate essentially the same story. Then there are the independent traditions of the Oromo and Somali, which confirm the early existence of Bantu speakers in the Juba valley and the subsequent Oromo invasion of the Horn. The Oromo invasion has been dated to the mid-16th century by the Ethiopian monk Bahrey. This accords well with the chronology calculated from Mijikenda age sets. The Mijikenda recall seven age sets from the time of their migration to the early 20th century. Since each set lasted approximately fifty years, this places the start of their migration in the mid-16th century. Further dating for the Oromo comes from a number of coastal towns as far south as Gedi raided by the Oromo early in the 17th century and their reported presence along the Kenya coast by Portuguese observers from 1621. Mijikenda had been reported from 1592.

Other points of evidence also confirms the Singwaya legend. For a long time the absence of any firm data actually locating Singwaya has caused people to doubt the legend, yet it appears on a number of 16th- and 17th-century maps located mid-way between the Juba and Tana Rivers. In addition, early Bantu speakers still cultivate in the Juva valley today, Sabaki place names appear all along the coast south of Mogadishu, and Kwale-ware has been found near Brava.

It would thus appear that proto-Sabaki speakers were present around Brava from at least the 9th century, when their languages began to differentiate into the present languages. While Swahili-speaking Shirazi commenced their migrations down the coast from late in the 9th century, other proto-Sabaki speakers remained in Somalia until driven south by Oromo in the mid-16th century, arriving in Kenya late in the century.

What is intriguing about the Singwaya legend is not so much its essential veracity, but what it chooses to omit. One could easily assume from the tradition that the migration from Singwaya was a single movement encompassing all the peoples who today call themselves Mijikenda, Swahili, Taita, and Pokomo, but this was not the case. It is readily apparent in other traditions that substantial numbers of these peoples came from elsewhere. The Rabai while claiming to have come from Singwaya were already present around Mombasa when the Mijikenda entered the area, having previously come from Rombo in Chaga. As a result of close interaction with their Mijikenda neighbours, they adopted the Mijikenda language and so many

Mijikenda customs that they are considered one of the nine Mijikenda peoples today. The Duruma are of diverse origins, but they too have been incorporated as another of the Nine, while we have already examined the likelihood that the earliest Taita pre-dated the Singwaya migration. The same is true for numerous Waata, Kamba, Chaga, and other clans, sub-clans, lineages, and individuals who settled among the Taita, Pokomo, and Mijikenda, adopted their customs, and now claim that they too came from Singwaya. The Segeju also assert that they came from Singwaya, but really came from Thagicu in the Central Highlands. The Segeju spoke a Thagicu language, Daiso, and migrated from the region of the upper Athi River to Usambara and the southern Kenya coast in the 17th century. On the coast they settled among the Digo and slowly adopted their language and customs, including the Singwaya legend.

Why is the legend of a historical journey so important when the facts are so clearly at odds with the legend? The journey itself is not; it merely provides a narrative thread on which to attach a number of significant cultural statements. Mijikenda claim they were forced to leave Singwaya after they had murdered an Oromo for the initiation of their first age-set. They travelled south as separate peoples and settled in separate hilltop villages or *kayas*. The essential magic required for the preservation and prosperity of the people was buried at the centre of the *kaya*. It too had come from Singwaya. The place of the clans within each *kaya* and the order of precedence of the *kayas* themselves was ordered by their respective roles during the migration. Thus all the major institutions of Mijikenda life – its peoples, languages, *kayas*, clans, age-sets, and ritual – derived their legitimacy from their Singwaya origins. Any institution developed subsequently had no formal role in the *kayas*. For the Mijikenda, then, the Singwaya legend is a dramatic symbolic statement encapsulating their cultural identify in a single abstract model. It is little wonder that others who have subsequently become Mijikenda have embraced it so readily. Nor is it surprising that this cultural charter has long survived the demise in the mid-19th century of the *kayas* and other social institutions it describes. It has come to have its own separate reality as a definition of Mijikenda identity.

The legend thus has a number of different levels – narrative, legitimating, and symbolic – all of which are potential historical evidence. By closely examining these various levels we are able to see not just a migration, but the ways a people came to define their core cultural values. As small groups of people moved south under Oromo pressure, they met and interacted with others, settled, and slowly defined their cultures. During this nationalizing process peoples, their cultures, and their myths emerged. Kashur slowly became Pokomo, Giriama, Digo, and Chonyi, just as proto-Sabaki differentiated into separate languages. The Mijikenda, Pokomo, Swahili, and Taita still have a great deal in common today, for they share a single cultural heritage, but they have also developed into distinct peoples and cultures as each has subsequently undergone different experiences and responded to different influences.

THE TRADITIONS OF THE CENTRAL HIGHLANDS BANTU-SPEAKING PEOPLES

The Bantu-speaking peoples who today occupy the central highlands of Kenya east and south of Mt. Kenya and the Nyandarua Ranges have no common origin legend comparable to that of the coastal peoples. And yet these peoples are closely related. All speak closely related Thagicu languages and have similar forms of social organization. Today these people recall three distinct origin traditions.

The people to the south of Mt. Kenya, the Cuka, Embu/Mbeere, Gicugu, Ndia, and Kikuyu, all claim to have migrated from the northern Meru area inhabited today by the Igembe and Tigania. They moved south and then east, curving around the highlands, to Tharaka, Mbeere, and finally into their present locations on the southern slopes of Mt. Kenya and along the Nyandarua Range. In the early stages of the migration these peoples say they were pastoralists and hunters, but upon settling in the higher forest zones they adopted agriculture. From their age sets, Godfrey Muriuki has estimated that Kikuyu and related peoples left Igembe/Tigania in the 15th century and arrived in the northern Kikuyu area early in the 17th century. They then

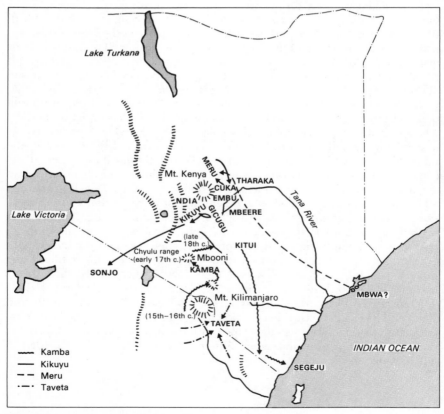

Map 3.3 *Central Highlands traditions*

slowly expanded over the rest of their present range over the next three centuries.

The second set of traditions are those of the Meru-speaking peoples, including the Igembe, Tigania, Imenti, Miutini, Igoji, Mwimbi, Muthambi, and Tharaka, now settled on the northeastern slopes of Mt. Kenya. These peoples claim to have come from an island called 'Mbwa' and migrated up the 'Mbweeni' River and across the 'Maliankanga' or 'Ngaaruni' desert before they split up and settled in their present locations. It is impossible to locate these places with certainty, but Jeffrey Fadiman believes that 'Mbwa' is Manda Island, the 'Mbweeni' River is the Tana, and 'Maliankanga' or 'Ngaaruni' is the arid region south of the bend of the Tana. He has estimated that this migration took place in the first half of the 18th century, long after the Kikuyu, Embu/Mbeere, and Cuka had left the northern Mt. Kenya area.

The third set of traditions are those of the Kamba. Individual Kamba clans and lineages claim a number of different origins, but most agree that the earliest Kamba came from the plains south of Mt. Kilimanjaro, from which they migrated to Chyulu, Kibwezi, and Mbooni. Like the Kikuyu group, the Kamba say they migrated as hunters and pastoralists and only adopted agriculture upon settling in the hills. Kennell Jackson Jr. estimates that the Kamba migration was roughly contemporary with the Kikuyu one, leaving the environs of Mt. Kilimanjaro in the 15th–16th century and arriving in Mbooni in the mid-17th century. After a period of consolidation in Mbooni, Kamba expanded over the rest of Ulu and into Kitui while Daiso speakers later migrated to Pare, Usambasa, and the coast, as we have seen.

Unfortunately, these traditions do not accord well with the linguistic evidence. All these peoples speak languages of the Thagicu sub-group, a highly uniform sub-group which only began to differentiate in the 9th or 10th century (see Fig. 2.3). Proto-Thagicu initially divided into three main sub-groups: proto-West Thagicu, proto-Meru/Tharaka, and proto-Kamba/Daiso. These three sub-groups closely match the three traditional groups: proto-West Thagicu subsequently developed into Kikuyu, Embu/Mbeere, and Cuka; proto-Meru/Tharaka divided into Meru and Tharaka; and proto-Kamba/Daiso differentiated into Kamba and Daiso (the language of the Segeju migrants to the coast). A fourth sub-group developed subsequently with the migration of the Sonjo to west of the Rift Valley. The uniformity and current distribution of Thagicu strongly suggests a dispersion centre for all these languages in the highlands area, thus casting considerable doubt that they could have come from areas as widely separated as Igembe-Tigania, the coast, and Mt. Kilimanjaro, as the traditions assert.

There is also some difficulty in reconciling the traditions with the archaeological evidence. Early Iron Age pottery derivative of Kwale-ware, iron workings, and domestic livestock found at Gathun'ang'a and Chuylu and dated to the 12th to 13th and 15th to 16th centuries indicate that food-producing peoples, possibly Bantu speakers, were present in the highlands before the migrations mentioned in the traditions. Both the linguistic and archaeological evidence, then, indicate that similar peoples have been in the highlands for a much longer period than that claimed by the traditions of the present residents of these areas.

Nor do Meru and Kamba traditions receive much support from the traditions of the surrounding peoples. None of the traditions of the coastal peoples mention Mbwa or a Meru-like people living on Manda Island. Nor do the traditions of the Chaga, Pare, or Taita mention the Kamba migration. Both of these migration traditions, then, appear to have been phrased more in a symbolic idiom than a historical one. Some insight into the symbolic nature of these traditions has been provided by the perceptive analysis of Tigania Meru social structure by Jurg Mahner. Meru clans and generation sets are each divided into two groups. One comprises the religious authorities responsible for managing conflict and restoring harmony and are seen as the 'insiders' or original Meru, while the other exercises political leadership, is responsible for creating conflict, and are considered 'outsiders' or foreigners to Meru. Foreigners are well integrated into Meru society today, and the two groups of generation sets take turns in the roles of 'insider' and 'outsider', but the symbolic division between the two reveals the heterogeneous nature of Meru origins and is probably why the Meru say that they originally came from the left, the side of the 'insiders'. The legend may not relate to a migration at all, therefore, but to the symbolic division of power within Meru society. Thus, although the legends may be at odds with the linguistic and archaeological evidence, they still can tell us much about the nature of the formation of the highlands peoples.

The first is the nature of the ecological adaptation of peoples to the peculiar highland environment of Mt. Kenya and the Nyandarua Range. The highlands areas are sharply differentiated ecologically as one moves up their slopes, with a marked change every 300–600 metres. Only the middle zone, 1 200–1 500 metres in Meru, 1 800–2 100 metres in Kikuyu, and 1 500–2 000 metres in Kamba is suited to agriculture. Below this zone drier woodland suitable for grazing and limited agriculture quickly shades off to arid wasteland, while above it the bracken and forest are useable only for limited root crops, grazing, and hunting-gathering before the ecology becomes too cold, wet, and dense for any activity. The traditions of both the Kikuyu group and the Kamba relate how they practised pastoral and hunting pursuits prior to their migrations and continued to practise these while skirting the highland regions during the course of their migrations. As they began to move up the hillsides into areas more suitable for agriculture, however, they began to cultivate crops. This adaptation is symbolized for the Kikuyu in the granting by God of their present lands to the nine daughters of Gikuyu and Mumbi, thus giving the Kikuyu clans inalienable rights to their lands.

The highlands are also sharply differentiated geographically by deeply cut river beds running down the mountain slopes that divide the area into a series of semi-isolated ridges. These ridges cause the highland peoples to be fragmented into small ridge societies where the most prevalent migration traditions are not the central ones cited above, but those of the countless sub-clans and lineages which relate their movements from ridge to ridge around the mountains in great detail, as each sub-clan or lineage carefully delineates the lands initially cleared or purchased from Okiek hunters by their ancestors. These traditions graphically portray the patterns of migration, settlement, and social development that are lacking in the earlier period of the legends. Godfrey Muriuki and Kennell Jackson Jr. have both written vividly of pioneering individuals among the Kikuyu and Kamba who advanced the frontiers of settlement to clear and settle new land by exploiting the fluid pattern of relationships characteristic of the frontier. They purchased land from Okiek hunters; traded their agricultural produce and livestock with Okiek for the goods of the forest and with Maasai for the goods of the plains below; acquired wives and blood brothers from other areas to extend their influence; and attracted relatives, marriage kin, and landless strangers as clients. In time these informal groups, centred on the personalities of the founders, became institutionalized in formal descent groups in the founders' names with rights in the land they initially established. Disparate groups of individuals were thus welded together into peoples with an ongoing identity and unity. It was no doubt this type of process, characteristic of later Kikuyu and Kamba expansion in the highlands, that was also responsible for the earlier consolidation of peoples and cultures who had long been resident in the central highlands.

A more recent example of this process can be seen in Taveta, a small mountain forest southeast of Mt. Kilimanjaro at the juncture of three major rivers. This secluded oasis was first settled in the late 17th century by peoples fleeing famines and raiding among the surrounding Pare, Shambaa, Chaga, Gweno, Taita, Zigula, and Arusha peoples. Taveta clans today stem from all these peoples. Ann Frontera's study of Taveta traditions reveals how the immigrants entered the forest in small groups and rapidly accommodated to one another, evolving a common culture from the diverse cultural heritages of the immigrants in the context of the historical and environmental circumstances. We will examine such processes of cultural consolidation in the next chapter; what is important here is that in less than three hundred years a single distinct people, speaking its own dialect of Pare, emerged from an amalgam of over half a dozen other peoples.

TRADITIONS OF THE PASTORALISTS

While we already know quite a lot about the farming communities of southeastern Kenya, we know much less about the migratory herders of the northeastern and central areas. Partly this is because historians have only recently started to collect the traditions of these peoples, but it is also because their history is marked by the constant movement of small groups across vast areas, in contrast to the more settled existence of agricultural societies.

The earliest traditional accounts of the area are given by the Rendille camel herders east of Lake Turkana. The Rendille vaguely recall a common origin with the Somali, but so far as they know they have always inhabited northern Kenya. In more recent times, probably in the 19th century, they recall living west of Lake Turkana and being pushed around the southern tip of the lake by advancing Turkana.

The Somali also recall always having inhabited modern Somalia and relate numerous internal migrations dating from the 14th century that were to lead them eventually to spill over into northeastern Kenya. The earliest of these was the migration of the Hawiyya clan family from the southern Ogaden down the Shebelle River to the Benaadir coast, where they were able to gain control of the flow of interior trade to Mogadishu, Merka, and Brava and create the Ajuran state. Later, in the 17th century, another group of Hawiyya, the Gurgate, followed the same route south and overturned the Ajuran, causing the Ajuran and pre-Hawiyya Gurre to flee across the Juba River and into northern Kenya, where they became clients of the Boran Oromo and were subsequently absorbed by them. A number of other clans from the Ogaden subsequently pushed their way into northern Kenya in the second half of the 19th century. These were members of the Hawiyya and Darod clan families who had been forced out of the Ogaden by Ethiopian expansion and by the Muslim holy war of Mohamed Abdille Hassan. They encountered the Oromo

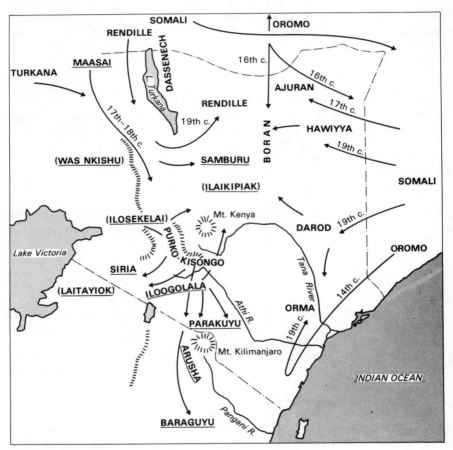

SIRIA – Maa speaking groups, c. 1800 – those in parenthesis absorbed by others during the 19th century.

Map 3.4 *Pastoralist traditions*

in northern Kenya and slowly replaced them as the dominant force east of the Tana River over the following decades.

These historical reconstructions, based on Rendille and Somali traditions, are given greater historical depth by the linguistic evidence. Both

Somali and Rendille are Eastern Cushitic languages originating in southern Ethiopia. The two languages share approximately 50 per cent cognates, placing their initial separation early in the 1st millenium AD. This probably occurred as Rendille speakers moved south into northern Kenya, while Somali speakers moved east into Somalia. Further evidence of these early movements is the fact that the Aweera hunters of the lower Tana speak Somali with subsequent heavy borrowing of Oromo vacabulary, indicating that Somali speakers must have been present in the area prior to the Oromo occupation in the 16th century.

The Oromo-speaking peoples also recall moving from southern Ethiopia during a dramatic series of migrations north into Eritrea, east as far as the Juba River, and south beyond Mombasa, all within less than a century. Today Oromo all speak regional dialects of a single language, indicating that these movements were fairly recent, and we know from the evidence of a 16th-century Ethiopian monk, Bahrey, that their expansion commenced early in that century. In the following decades Oromo advanced down the Juba River, displacing the Sabaki-speaking peoples and pursuing them down the coast as far as Malindi, where they arrived early in the 17th century. Oromo remained in the southern coastal lowlands around the hilltop *kayas* of the Mijikenda until the combined forces of disease, the Somali, and the Maasai conspired to force their withdrawal north of the Tana River from the middle of the 19th century.

It is not known for certain which Oromo sub-groups were involved in the south. Two main Oromo sub-groups inhabit northern Kenya today. The Boran are the larger and live north of the Tana River while the Orma (or Bararetta, Tana, or Wardei) are much smaller and confined to the lower reachers of the Tana. The Orma were probably an offshoot of the Boran initially, but the evidence seems to indicate that it was they who once occupied the hinterland regions further south.

The Oromo migrations are one of the rare instances of rapid mass migration in the history of eastern Africa, comparable in scale to the dramatic expansion of the Zulu and related Nguni peoples from southern Africa in the 19th century. Whereas the Nguni had at their disposal the superior military tactics developed by the Zulu and were able to augment their numbers by assimilating vast numbers of alien peoples, we still do not know how the Oromo were able to achieve their dramatic conquests. Asmaron Legesse has speculated that their expansion was caused by population pressure and the age-set system which the Oromo had at the time. Under this system, all the young men in Oromo society were initiated together into a single set and, once initiated, remained in that set for life, advancing together from warriorhood through elderhood. In order to advance in this way, though, each new set had to prove itself in warfare by raiding previously unraided enemies, leading to progressive expansion as each new set raided successively further and further afield. As the age-sets were initiated every eight years, this expansionary drift could have occurred quite rapidly, as set followed set east into Somalia and south into Kenya.

Maasai traditions of origin also point to northern Kenya and the linguistic evidence for the Eastern Nilotic languages supports this conclusion. They probably began drifting down the Rift Valley in the 17th–18th centuries, displacing earlier Kalenjin and Southern Cushitic-speaking peoples until, by 1800, Maasai sub-groups were well established from Lake Turkana in the north, south to the Maasai steppe in Tanzania. Purko-Kisongo, occupying the grasslands from Lake Nakuru south to Lake Magadi, were at the centre, while arrayed around them were the Laikipiak north of Mt. Kenya, the Samburu southeast of Lake Turkana, the Uas Nkishu and Ilosekelai west of Lake Nakuru, the Siria west of the Mau escarpment, the Iloogolala south of Ngong, and the Parakuyu between lakes Magadi and Manyara.

At this point the traditions become more lively, revealing a series of violent confrontations between various Maasai sub-groups and other peoples as further expansion to the south was halted by powerful neighbours at the same time that Turkana and Pokot continued to push south into the fertile areas of the northern Rift Valley from their rear. The initial stages of this process took place early in the 19th century with Purko-Kisongo raids into Iloogolala territory to the south. The Iloogolala, in turn, were inexorably forced northeast into the Kikuyu, Kamba, and Laikipia, east into the Mijikenda, and south into the Parakuyu, Chaga, and Taveta. By the 1840s the Iloogolala had been overrun and ceased to exist as a people.

But how can a people disappear? Richard Waller has shown that the earlier Maasai expansion had been characterized by successive generations of young warriors raiding beyond their established settlements, seizing cattle to establish their own personal herds, and settling down as married elders in the new territory, thus creating a perpetual drift outwards from established areas into new frontier territories. This drift was halted in the early 19th century, however, as those Maasai sub-groups on the frontiers were turned back by powerful neighbours onto other Maasai behind them, precipitating a series of confrontations among Maasai sub-groups as each sought to continue expanding at the expense of others. Successful groups were able to enlarge their own herds and territories to continue to expand, while unsuccessful ones were forced either to become clients of the victors in order to regain enough cattle to survive or to settle down as farmers on the peripheries of Maasailand. The successful were thus able to further augment their numbers and grow even more rapidly, while the vanquished ceased to exist as identifiable groups.

A further dimension to this process has been added by John Berntsen in his study of Maasai diviners or prophets (*ol oiboni*) and their role in providing a central identity for the various Maasai sub-groups. All Maasai sub-groups shared the same language, way of life, and age-sets. What defined a sub-group and gave it cohesiveness was its shared territory and its hereditary family of diviners who lived apart from other Maasai but provided a number of important religious services. Diviners were responsible for divining and healing sickness, providing protective medicines for the initiation of age-sets, and approving the conduct of raids by the warriors. They thus had considerable power and influence over the major events in Maasai life. In return for their services, they received large payments of cattle which they were able to use to further enhance their prestige by attracting a vast network of clients through loaning or giving cattle and through acquiring wives or paying the bridewealth of others. The most prominent diviners throughout the century were the Nkidongi family of diviners of the Purko-Kisongo, including Supeet, Mbatian, and Lenana.

During one of the Purko-Kisongo raids on the Illoogolala, the Iloogolala diviner and his family fled to Laikipia, depriving the Iloogolala of their ritual leadership and their identity. Individual Iloogolala were left with little alternative but to become followers of other diviners and, hence, to assume the identity of other Maasai sub-groups, or to join other neighbouring peoples. This is exactly what happened as numbers of Iloogolala joined the conquering Purko-Kisongo, further swelling their ranks, while others sought refuge among the Laikipiak, the surrounding agricultural peoples, or by settling down to agriculture themselves, like the Arusha.

With the disappearance of the Iloogolala, the Purko-Kisongo pushed into Parakuyu country, but the Parakuyu were able to withdraw to the south,

Photo 3.1 *Lenana, a Maasai prophet*

retaining their herds and diviner while acquiring new lands on the Maasai steppe. By the 1860s the Purko-Kisongo, swollen by the assimilation of their earlier enemies, turned to the north against the Ilosekelai, Laikipiak, and Uas Nkishu. All were defeated, their cattle and lands seized, their diviners driven into exile in Nandi and Siria, and the people forced to join neighbouring peoples. Thus after nearly a century of continued warfare, many Maasai-speaking people had been dramatically changed, forced to accept new identities among other Maasai or new ways of life among the surrounding agricultural and hunting peoples.

THE QUESTION OF ORIGINS

What has become clear in this discussion of origin traditions is that what the traditions encapsulate in a single, often mythical, moment is really part of a continual historical process of becoming. Peoples and cultures do not emerge fully developed out of a cultural void; whatever they are now, they have developed from something different in the past and will be something different in the future.

Migration is a pervasive image in many of the traditions, but what is being described was more often a pattern of expansionary drift than a long distance trek. Maasai and Oromo warriors of successive age sets continually expanded on earlier conquests, Kamba slowly edged over Ulu and Kitui, while young Kikuyu farmers left older settled ridges to claim new lands on the frontier. Looking back to the earlier movements of Southern Cushitic or Bantu-speaking peoples, we can readily imagine that they expanded in the same way.

The repeated expansion of peoples into and within eastern Africa raises the question of what caused the expansion of these peoples. We can only speculate on possible answers to this problem because there is little hard evidence to guide us, but it seems likely that there has been a steady expansion of population within eastern Africa over the past two to three thousand years. We know, for example, that hunting and gathering activities can only support a fairly light population, while herding can support more people in a given area, and agriculture can support more still. Thus the steady expansion of herding and farming over this period would seem to indicate a growing population. Similarly, the steady expansion of peoples like the Kikuyu, Kamba, and Mijikenda over the past five centuries would also seem to indicate population growth, while the dramatic expansion of the Oromo reveals something more akin to a population explosion.

If population was increasing during this time, then people would have been under pressure to expand their resource base, to intensify their economic activities, or to limit their population. There is little evidence of population control, but much to indicate that people did indeed expand and intensify their economic activities during this period. Expansion is most dramatically seen in the spread of the Bantu-speaking peoples into and throughout eastern Africa, but also in the countless histories of movement traced in the traditions studied above. And economic intensification has been seen in the initial developments of herding and of farming and in the continued development of agriculture as people adopted shorter fallow peiods, irrigation, fertilization, and new crops to increase the yield of their crops. More intensive farming, however, is hard work, requiring greater labour inputs and more complex social arrangements to ensure the greater cooperation among people required for these activities. And here perhaps lies the key to the social and cultural developments during this period. As people were forced to intensify their economic activities, they found it necessary to come together with others to develop more complex forms of social organization. Hunters and gatherers tended to have small-scale social organizations, as we have seen, while herders developed more extensive contacts, based on age-grading, extensive genealogies, and cooperative herding practices, to manage their large herds. Farmers tended to develop social organizations based on descent and locality, as we have seen, to maintain hereditary rights to land use and to ensure cooperation and continuity in working the land over the seasons and through the years. These themes will be explored in greater depth in the following chapter; all that I wish to suggest here is that development of herding and agriculture, the expansion of peoples throughout eastern Africa, and the processes of cultural development over the past five centuries may be seen as linked processes.

Individual founder heroes also figure strongly in origin traditions, and, as we have seen, particular individuals often played decisive roles in defining the loose groups of people who came together in expansionary frontier situations. Maasai sub-groups identified with their diviners and, as diviners rose and fell, sub-groups emerged and disappeared. In Kikuyu and Kamba pioneering frontiersmen attracted diverse followings which, over time, became consolidated into defined lineage groups which have endured to the present day. Individuals were frequently prominent in times of change because it was during just such times that the established rules and institutions were least effective. Prominent individuals rose in their stead, guiding by the force of their own personalities, until new guidelines were established which were appropriate to the changed situation. There is the suggestion in Maasai traditions, for example, that the diviners first rose to prominence prior to the wars of the 19th century. Similarly, it was the agricultural frontiersmen in Kikuyu and Kamba who cleared new lands and gave their names to the institutionalized lineages and clans which followed in their wake.

Finally, origin traditions frequently define a people and their institutions. Thus the Singwaya legend defines each of the Mijikenda peoples, their relations with one another, and their main institutions – *kaya*, clan, and age-set. In actual fact, however, such definitions only emerge slowly as peoples and their cultures change through time. One of the main ways this occurred was when previously separate peoples interacted and slowly merged into one. Thus the Taveta originated as a refugee community, the Taita from the fusion of different peoples in the Taita Hills, the Meru in the merging of 'insiders' and 'outsiders', each Maasai group as the followers of a particular diviner, and the Mijikenda, Kikuyu, and Kamba in the fusion of old and new residents. A number of institutions existed to integrate strangers into a society. In Maasai, for example, a stranger could be initiated into a Maasai age-set, marry a Maasai, or become the client of a respected elder and so be considered part of his lineage. The fact that so many of the traditions of the present peoples of Kenya trace this process back over the past five centuries indicates that this was an unusually fluid period in Kenya's past as both agriculturalists and pastoralists expanded, came into contact with others, and merged with them. Out of this process emerged a number of distinctive sets of institutions, or cultures, combining, for example, the age-grading systems of Southern Cushitic-speaking peoples with the descent groups of Bantu-speaking ones. Peoples were constantly forming and reforming, adapting new cultural expressions in the process of continuing interaction with others and of changing environmental and historical conditions. Thus the present peoples and cultures of Kenya represent merely the latest syntheses in processes which stretch back into antiquity and continue to the present day.

REFERENCES AND SUGGESTIONS FOR FURTHER READING

The classic handbook for traditional history is still Jan Vansina, *Oral Tradition* (London, 1965), as updated in his 'Once Upon a Time: Oral Traditions as History in Africa', *Daedalus*, 100 (1971), pp. 442–468, but the continuing assessment and debate regarding the validity of traditions goes on. An excellent summary and response to the main anthropological critiques is Patrick Pender-Cudlip, 'Oral Traditions and Anthropological Analysis: Some Contemporary Myths', *Azania*, 7 (1972), pp. 3–24, while the definitive study of the dynamics of legends is Joseph Miller, 'The Dynamics of Oral Tradition in Africa', in B. Bernardi (ed.), *Fronti Orali* (Milan, 1978). Further studies of current historical thinking are contained in Joseph Miller (ed.), *The African Past Speaks* (Folkstone, 1980), and T. Spear, 'Oral Traditions: Whose History?', *History in Africa*, 8 (1981). Most of the studies below also contain valuable statements regarding the particular problems posed by the traditional histories of the peoples concerned.

The following specific references are but a few of the vast number of sources on eastern Kenyan traditional history. They represent the most recent and comprehensive studies of tradition, however, and readers are urged to consult the bibliographies in them for earlier references. Additional sources of a primarily anthropological nature are cited in Chapter IV. All American Ph.D. theses are available on microfilm from University Microfilms, Ann Arbor, Michigan.

Earlier syntheses of traditional material include the generally excellent articles contained in the second edition of B. A. Ogot (ed.), *Zamani* (Nairobi, 1973), while a number of recent studies are ably summarized in B. A. Ogot (ed.), *Kenya Before 1900* (Nairobi, 1976), and B. A. Ogot (ed.), *Kenya in the Nineteenth Century* (forthcoming), to which specific references are made below.

Few serious studies have been made of the traditions of the hunting-gathering peoples of Kenya. A major study is the work of R. Blackburn, including 'Honey in Okiek Personality, Culture, and Society' (Ph.D. thesis, Michigan State University, 1971); 'The Okiek and their History', *Azania*, 9 (1974), pp. 139–157; and 'Okiek History' in *Kenya Before 1900*, pp. 53–83, while the debate concerning hunter-gatherer origins is outlined in Roger van Zwanenberg, 'Dorobo Hunting and Gathering: A Way of Life or a Mode of Production?' and Stephen Harvey, 'Comment on the Relationship between the Dorobo and their Neighbours', in *African Economic*

History, 2 (1976), pp. 12–24, and Corinne Kratz, 'Are the Okiek really Maasai? or Kipsiqis? or Kikuyu?' (unpub. paper, African Studies Association, 1978). A valuable comparative study is that by Richard Elphick on the San and Khoikhoi, entitled *Kraal and Castle* (New Haven, 1977).

The most extensive study of the Waata is a sympathetic popular account of their eviction from Tsavo National Park by Dennis Holman, *The Elephant People* (London, 1967). Other evidence comes from the linguistic studies cited in the previous chapter, especially Heine on the Yaaku, and in historical and anthropological studies of neighbouring peoples, such as the Kikuyu, Mijikenda, Oromo, and Samburu cited below.

Limited references to the traditions of the earliest food producers are made in the studies cited of the Taita, Kikuyu, Cuka, Embu, Okiek, Maasai, and Yaaku.

The Singwaya legend of the coastal Bantu has tantalized historians for years. For a recent debate summarizing earlier interpretations and offering a number of new ones, see Frederick Morton, 'The Shungwaya Myth of Mijikenda Origins: A Problem of Late Nineteenth Century Kenya Coastal History', *International Journal of African Historical Studies*, 5 (1973), pp. 397–423; T. Spear 'Traditional Myths and Historians' Myths: Variations on the Singwaya Theme of Mijikenda Origins', *History in Africa*, 1 (1974), pp. 67–84; Thomas Hinnebusch, 'The Shungwaya Hypothesis: A Linguistic Reappraisal' in J. T. Gallagher (ed.), 'East African Culture History' (*Eastern African Studies*, no. 25, Syracuse, 1976); and T. Spear 'Traditional Myths and Linguistic Analysis: Singwaya Revisited', *History in Africa*, 4 (1976), pp. 229–246.

Mijikenda traditional history is detailed in my *The Kaya Complex: A History of the Mijikenda Peoples of the Kenya Coast to 1900* (Nairobi, 1978), as summarized in *Kenya Before 1900*, pp. 262–286 and, for the later periods, Cynthia Brantley, *The Giriama and British Colonialism in Kenya* (forthcoming).

A comprehensive study of Taita traditions is E. Hollis Merritt, 'A History of the Taita of Kenya to 1900' (Ph.D. thesis, Indiana University, 1975), while a recent study is outlined in Stephen Liszka, 'A Preliminary Report on Research on the Origins and Internal Migrations of the Taita People', *Mila*, 4 (1974), pp. 38–64.

The outlines of Pokomo traditions are given in Robert Bunger, 'Islamization among the Upper Pokomo' (*Eastern African Studies*, no. 11, Syracuse, 1973).

Swahili history will be dealt with in detail later, but the basic interpretation followed here is given in H. Neville Chittick, 'The "Shirazi" Colonization of East Africa', *JAH*, 6 (1965), pp. 275–294; James de V. Allen, 'Swahili Culture Reconsidered: Some Historical Implications of the Material Culture of the Northern Kenya Coast in the 18th and 19th Centuries', *Azania*, 9 (1974), pp. 105–138; Randall Pouwels, 'The Medieval Foundations of East African Islam', *International Journal of African Historical Studies*, 11 (1978), pp. 201–227, 393–409; and Esmail Aziz, 'Towards a History of Islam in East Africa', *Kenya Historical Review*, 3 (1975), pp. 147–158. The Singwaya tradition is recorded most completely in E. Cerulli, *Somalia*, vol. 1 (Rome, 1957).

Kikuyu traditions are detailed in Godfrey Muriuki, *A History of the Kikuyu, 1500–1900* (Nairobi, 1974); P. Marvis and A. Somerset, *African Businessmen*

(London, 1971); and P. Rogers, 'The British and the Kikuyu, 1890–1905: A Reassessment', *JAH*, 20 (1979), pp. 255–269. Studies of Embu/Mbeere traditions include Henry Mwaniki, *The Living History of Embu and Mbeere to 1906* (Nairobi, 1973) and *Embu Historical Texts* (Nairobi, 1974), and Satish Saberwal, 'Historical Notes on the Embu of Central Kenya', *JAH*, 8 (1967), pp. 29–38, while Meru traditions are considered by Jeffrey Fadiman in 'The Meru Peoples' in *Kenya Before 1900*, pp. 139–173, and 'Mountain Warriors: The Pre-Colonial Meru of Mt. Kenya' (*Papers in International Studies*, no. 27, Athens, Ohio, 1976).

Kennell Jackson Jr. has written a number of carefully analysed studies based on Kamba traditions, including *The Words of the Past* (forthcoming); '*Ngotho* (the Ivory Armlet): An Emblem of Upper Tier Status among the 19th century Kamba of Kenya, ca. 1830–1880', *Kenya Historical Review*, 5 (1977), pp. 35–69; and 'The Dimensions of Kamba Pre-Colonial History' in *Kenya Before 1900*, pp. 174–261, while Robert Cummings has considered the later periods in 'Aspects of Human Porterage with Special Reference to the Akamba of Kenya' (Ph.D. thesis, University of California at Los Angeles, 1975).

An excellent detailed study of the process of nation building in Taveta is Ann Frontera, *Persistence and Change: A History of Taveta* (Waltham, 1978) and, 'The Taveta Economy in the Pre-Colonial Period', *Kenya Historical Review*, 5 (1977), pp. 107–114.

A number of studies have recently appeared on the Somali. Southern Somali traditions are incisively described and analysed by Lee Cassanelli, 'The Benaadir Past: Essays in Southern Somali History' (Ph.D. thesis, University of Wisconsin, 1973), while the Somali of northern Kenya are considered in Peter Dalleo, 'Trade and Pastoralism: Economic Factors in the History of the Somali of Northeastern Kenya, 1892–1948' (Ph.D. thesis, Syracuse University, 1975) and E. R. Turton, 'The Pastoral Tribes of Northern Kenya, 1800–1916' (Ph.D. thesis, University of London, 1970).

Oromo origins are imaginatively reconstructed in Herbert Lewis, 'Origins of the Galla and Somali', *JAH*, 7 (1966), pp. 27–46, while their movements in Somalia are covered in E. R. Turton, 'Bantu, Galla, and Somali Migrations in the Horn of Africa: A Reassessment of the Juba/Tana Area', *JAH*, 16 (1975), pp. 519–537. I have not been able to see the only study of Kenya Boran traditions, by P. S. G. Goto, 'The Boran of Northern Kenya: Origins, Migration, and Settlement in the 19th Century' (B.A. thesis, University of Nairobi, 1972).

For two excellent recent studies of Maasai history, see John Berntsen, 'Pastoralism, Raiding, and Prophets: Maasailand in the 19th century' (Ph.D. thesis, University of Wisconsin, 1979) and Richard Waller, 'The Lords of East Africa: The Maasai in the mid-Nineteenth Century' (Ph.D. thesis, Cambridge University, 1979). Briefer studies include John Berntsen, 'Maasai Age-Sets and Prophetic Leadership, 1850–1912', *Africa*, 49 (1979) pp. 134–146; Alan Jacobs, 'A Chronology of the Pastoral Maasai', *Hadith*, I (1968), pp. 10–31; and Richard Waller, 'The Maasai and the British, 1895–1905: The Origins of an Alliance', *JAH*, 17 (1976), pp. 529–533.

CHAPTER FOUR

PROCESSES OF CULTURAL DEVELOPMENT
THE ETHNOGRAPHIC RECORD

The period following the settlement of the present peoples of eastern and central Kenya is only vaguely remembered in the traditional record, in contrast to the vivid evocation of legendary heroes of the earlier period and the detailed recall people have of the recent past. Genealogies are sharply telescoped as only a few important ancestors are remembered while most others are unceremoniously forgotten. Individual events are also suppressed. If significant institutions developed in this period, their origins are inevitably transposed back into the period of origins in an updating of the legendary record. What is stressed in this period is the ongoing nature of established institutions. Repetitive processes of life and death, seasonal cycles, the growth and separation of lineages, and the regular initiation of age-groups takes precedence over the distinctive historical events recalled in the earlier traditions as responsible for the establishment of these processes in mythical times.

During the course of the 19th century the peoples of Kenya began to emerge into the written record, as the first European travellers, missionaries and traders traversed the area and recorded what they saw of the peoples at the time. Many of these accounts are catalogues, or ethnographies, which detailed local customs and stressed the same type of repetitive activities discussed in the traditions. Both thus convey an essentially cyclical view of the past, as seasons and generations were seen to come and go with ceaseless unchanging regularity.

Institutions and customs do not simply appear out of a cultural void and continue repetitively through time, as the traditions and ethnographies frequently imply. They are generated out of historical conditions as people adapt their ways to changes in their environment, their mode of production, or their social circumstances. What may have been appropriate behaviour in one set of conditions becomes inappropriate as conditions change. People are always confronting new situations with ideas and modes of behaviour based on earlier ones. There is thus a continual process inherent in history by which people adapt, reform, and transform their cultural structures. It is these processes and structures which we seek to explore here. How did the cultures of the peoples of Kenya develop, and how was their development related to their historical circumstances?

One of the factors that strikes anyone inquiring into eastern and central Kenya during the 17th, 18th, and 19th centuries was the incredible diversity which existed within this fairly small area. The multiplicity of peoples and languages was compounded by the fact that everywhere people made different ecological adaptations and devised unique cultural institutions. Nowhere were there broadly integrated economies or centralized political structures that would impose an easy coherence on the area for the historian. Everything was localized. Most economic, social, and political activity took place in villages, ranging in size from a single family to several hundred people. It is thus difficult to make any statements about specific institutions that hold true for the whole area. Nevertheless, on a more general level, the peoples of eastern Kenya did share a number of basic elements, or structures, and ongoing patterns, or processes, with one another. People may have varied in their methods of farming and crops grown, for example, but all farmers were essentially subsistence producers who grew only enough to feed themselves and to exchange with others to obtain their basic needs. This general pattern had a number of implications for the ways farmers organized their activities. They had to obtain land. They had to live in one place. They had to cooperate with others. And they had to be able to store and distribute food among themselves from one harvest to the next. Let us turn first to examine these general patterns in greater detail.

ECONOMIC STRUCTURES

From the 17th to the early 19th century the peoples of eastern Kenya all followed essentially subsistence modes of economic production. Each individual or family only produced enough food to feed themselves with a small surplus left over to exchange for other basic needs and to insure against

Photo 4.1 *Slash and burn agriculture: uncleared bush*

Photo 4.2 *Slash and burn agriculture: maize growing amongst the burnt bush*

the possibility of production failures in the future. Over time people had carefully adapted their mode of production to the local environment, so that a wide range of specific and localized ecological adaptions were developed. Some were farmers of wet rice in riverine flood plains; others herded camels in the desert, terraced and irrigated mountain sides, hunted wild animals or gathered honey in the forests, practised shifting grain cultivation in the savanna, or fished and traded in coastal entrepots. In every case production was essentially individualistic. Even within a large homestead men and women each farmed their own plots. No one could own the means of production and hence control the activities of others.

Hunting and gathering were the simplest economic activities, requiring the least amount of work to acquire enough food to survive. Hunter-gatherers did not need to invest labour into planting crops or herding animals prior to consuming them; they merely exploited what was readily available in the environment. There was a limit, however, to how much the environment could provide, thus restricting the number of hunter-gatherers who could exploit any one area to small bands able to move easily over the landscape.

Farmers, by contrast, had to make a long-term investment in clearing, planting, weeding, and harvesting the land. Kenyan farmers typically used slash and burn techniques in which the bush was roughly cleared and burned prior to planting, the ash fertilizing the shallow tropical soils. Fields cleared in this way were then used for two or three years before being allowed to revert to bush for long fallow periods of up to twenty years. Farmers thus required access to land greatly in excess of their annual needs in order to maintain such

73

a long fallow cycle. Farmers also required access to different types of land to be able to grow a variety of crops as a hedge against the failure of any one. Thus savanna grain farmers sought bottom lands for rice, bananas, or root crops in addition to higher flat lands for sorghum, millet, or eleusine. Finally, while farming entailed more work to produce a given amount of food than hunting and gathering, it could produce a higher yield per acre and thus support a much denser population living in semi-permanent villages. And as population and villages grew, production could be increased through greater inputs of labour to shorten fallow periods, fertilize and irrigate fields, and stall-feed animals.

Because of unreliable rainfall, limited availability of adequate pastures and water, sporadic epidemic diseases, and uneven production of livestock, herders had to maintain large herds of cattle or camels and goats and sheep to insure adequate food production. Resources were always precarious and the possibility of drought or diseases devastating their stock a constant threat. To insure against these, pastoralists divided their herds, keeping the productive females near the main settlement to provide food, while non-producing cows and bulls were herded at a distance to maximize available fodder and water, and temporarily surplus animals were loaned out to herding partners. They also continually culled their herds, keeping the females who produced milk and reproduced the herd, while slaughtering the males for food or exchanging them with others to maintain social relations. Food production throughout the year was also uneven because female cattle and camels tended to reproduce, and thus lactate, at the same time, encouraging pastoralists to mix large and small stock with different reproductive cycles to exploit fully the total milk, blood, and meat resources of their animals, and to supplement their diets with agricultural produce grown themselves or obtained from nearby farmers. Herding thus rarely produced a self-sufficient economy, and during the frequent droughts and epidemics in northern and central Kenya, pastoralists were forced to abandon herding altogether and seek refuge among neighbouring farmers or hunter-gatherers while they struggled to restore their herds.

SOCIAL AND POLITICAL STRUCTURES

Each mode of production and ecological adaptation was crucial in determining forms of social and political organization and religious beliefs. Farmers, for example, were tied by the need to obtain and maintain sufficient land to produce adequate harvests year after year. This meant that they had to settle in one place and devise a form of social organization that would ensure continuity of personnel from harvest to harvest and from generation to generation. As a consequence farmers normally lived in tightly knit groups of close relatives who were able to cooperate and work together throughout the seasonal cycle and to retain rights of use in land from generation to generation. Hunters and gatherers, on the other hand, felt no such pressure to ensure continuity as they could band together with some for a specific hunt or seasonal activity and then disperse or combine with others for another activity. The hunting band was thus a much smaller and looser form of social organization.

Herders had different social requirements. Each group required a large number of animals and access to extensive pasturage within a day's walk of water without overtaxing the land or restricting their mobility. Small groups clustered around available water in seasonal camps thus became the norm. At the same time, people required ready access to others. This was accomplished in two ways. Each individual was incorporated in an extensive genealogy in which he or she could trace their relationship to anyone else in the society. Thus one could appeal to distant relatives for pasturage or to care for some of one's herd in distant areas. Secondly, each man was also a member of an age or generation group which included all the other males of the same age or generation in the society. Work was allocated on the basis of age. Young boys took care of the settlement herds; young men were warriors, herding and protecting the stock further afield; and married men and elders managed the herds and camp affairs, while maintaining extensive networks of kin, age-mates, and neighbouring farmers and hunter-gatherers as potential herding or trading partners and refuges in times of need. Thus, while herders lived in smaller and more fluid local groups than farmers, they were able to vary their composition and rapidly augment their numbers through widespread links based on kinship and age.

Kinship, residence, and age were thus the three main structures upon which social organization was based. There were no societies with kings, or bureaucrats, or professional armies in eastern or central Kenya. In fact, there were very few with anything more than informal councils of elders to whom disputes were referred because they were the most knowledgeable in customary law. But this is not to say that political activity was not intense as aspiring individuals sought to accumulate large networks of kin, neighbours, and age-mates within which their influence would be felt and which would contribute to their prestige in the larger society.

Descent, alliance and exchange

In most areas the family – a man, his wives, and their children – was the basic economic unit, producing and consuming their own food and other needs. Land and cattle – the basic economic requirements – were usually passed from father to son and thus, over time, a number of descendants of a single man came to farm his ancestral land or to herd his ancestral cattle. This descent group, known as a lineage, was often the largest group of people who cooperated closely in daily activities, while the larger clan – people commonly descended from a more distant ancestor – defined a group which continued through time from the earliest remembered ancestors to the living and those not yet born. All were, or would be, members of the same group.

To reproduce and survive, however, individual descent groups had to establish links with other descent groups. This was commonly achieved through marriage outside one's own lineage or clan. Since marriage was seen as joining not just two individuals but two lineages together, this effectively allied two descent groups with one another. This alliance of two groups was effected by the exchange of valuable goods between the two which accompanied marriage, known as bridewealth, and ultimately by the birth of children which both lineages shared. But alliances between two individuals or lineages could occur in other ways as well. Men who desired to trade with one another often took a blood oath first to treat one another as if they were brothers. Herders loaned portions of their herds to others to obtain their cooperation as partners. Most such alliances were symbolized and given effect by the exchange of valuable wealth, just as in marriage. These valuables were usually commodities in restricted supply, such as cattle, which were valued as much for their potential in welding interpersonal links as for their subsistence value. Exchange, and the alliances between persons that it established, was thus the main means by which people extended their relations to others outside the descent group, and, with descent, defined extended networks of relatives, in-laws and friends to whom one could appeal for assistance. If an individual required land or cattle, for instance, he could appeal to a lineage-mate, a distant clansman, one of his wife's relatives, or a blood-brother. Such networks were commonly mobilized in everyday relations, in disputes, in trade, and during famines or disasters.

But kinship did not merely define one's circle of associates; it was also defined by them. It acted as a pervasive idiom to describe social relations. Two people might have behaved in a certain way with one another because they were brothers or sisters; two unrelated people who behaved in the same way called one another brother or sister. Thus when people used the language of kinship to define their group, they included many people born outside the group within their terms. Kinship, then, defined patterns of behaviour more accurately than it did groups of blood kin. This flexibility of idiom allowed individuals constantly to redefine themselves and to change and adapt their social allegiances through time.

In some societies lineage-mates lived together in a single village and formed a cooperative economic and social unit, but in others lineages were dispersed and each village included members of different lineages. In villages where lineages were localized, however, wives from other lineages were brought in and other outsiders could be accommodated by being adopted within the kinship idiom, while in villages which included a number of different lineages, frequent intermarriage between the lineages over time effectively joined people into complex alliance networks linking everyone in the village.

Age

The peoples of eastern and central Kenya also commonly organized themselves into groups based on age or generation. Periodically, all of the people of the same age or generation were initiated together into a single set and remained members of that set for life. Such sets included people from a number of different descent groups. Membership in a set thus further extended one's relations throughout the society. In age-sets, commonly formed every 10 to 15 years, all the members of the set were roughly the same age and progressed through life, from warriors to married men to elders, together. Greater knowledge, prestige, and responsibility came with age, while political power and religious authority were monopolized by the elders. Youths could only be initiated or advanced in status by petitioning the elders with valuable goods such as cattle. Since the elders themselves controlled these valuable goods, they could, and often did, restrict the young so they themselves could continue to dominate. Conflict between young and old was thus institutionalized. Many societies also had ranked secret societies or associations, which controlled secret knowledge or wielded political power. To join, one had to be sponsored by one's parents, pay a fee to the members, and serve an apprenticeship of service to the members. Like the age-sets, such societies ensured that access to power and authority was controlled by the elders.

Generation-sets also served to maintain the control of the elders, but were more restricted in their operation than age-sets. They were also initiated periodically, but instead of including all the men of the same age, they included all those of the same generation. This was done by including in the

Photo 4.3 *Kikuyu elders*

new set all the sons of a previous generation-set. Whereas brothers of widely differing ages joined different age-sets, they were all included in the same generation-set, and their sons, in turn, would all be members of the same future set. Since a man might have sons over a forty-year period, the differences in age within the following generation-set could be large, and those for successive sets would be even greater as the differences became accentuated over time. Within only a couple of generations the differences could become so great that many men would die before their set was initiated while others who should have belonged to that set were not yet born. Each generation-set thus included men of all ages while failing to include all the men who should have belonged to it. Unlike age-sets, they could neither include all the members of the society, nor could they serve to organize all the men of the same age and status in life into effective corporate groups such as warriors or elders. Like age-sets, however, they asserted the primacy of seniority; the difference being that they stressed genealogical seniority over chronological seniority. A younger man of a senior generation was seen as senior to an older one of a junior generation.

Many societies had both generation-sets and age-sets, with the balance of power and authority between the two alternating over time as the debate over the primacy of age or generation waxed and waned. In expansionary times, age often became dominant because it offered a more efficient military organization, while in times of stability, generation became the dominant principle governing the distribution of power. The conflict between these two principles of seniority as well as the ongoing conflict between seniors and juniors thus provided continuing dynamic elements in these societies as they confronted their changing worlds.

Political action

Descent, alliance, residence, age, and generation were thus complementary alternative principles, providing individuals with extensive ranges of potential personal relations which they could seek to mobilize and manipulate to their own advantage. If one was engaged in a dispute with another, for example, he would seek to mobilize as many kin, relatives by marriage, neighbours, and age or generation-mates as possible to support his case. In the meantime, his opponent would be doing the same thing, and many people would find their support solicited by both parties on the basis of differing allegiances to each. There was thus a continued dynamism to interpersonal relations as people formed and reformed alliances with others according to their daily situation, the most common elements of which included advantageous marriages with locally prominent lineages; laying claims to land or cattle on the basis of kinship, marriage, age, or previous personal contacts; incorporation of others into one's personal following through adoption, blood-brotherhood, or clientship; the splitting of lineages between brothers so that each might command his own personal following; and moving to new areas to seek greater resources in land and personal contacts. The aim behind all of these activities was to amass as large a group of followers – be they wives, children, kin, age-mates, or strangers – as possible. Among societies where everyone had rights to land so that no one could control productive resources and where no centralized political institutions existed, power was a function of one's influence over people. The more extensive one's personal networks, the more people one could mobilize in a dispute, and the larger one's village, the greater prestige and power one enjoyed in village, clan, and societal affairs. Elders who succeeded in amassing a large personal following were widely respected in informal village councils, while those who failed were largely ignored.

The range of possibilities offered by the complementary principles of descent, alliance, residence, age, and generation enabled people to adapt to changes occurring within societies at large. As conditions changed, individuals composing the society could seek to master them by manipulating alternative principles to those normally employed. Thus, in times of warfare people who normally lived in small lineage villages might emphasize alliances or age-groups to join together to establish large, well-fortified multi-lineage settlements, and then reassert the primacy of kinship and disperse again after the danger had passed. Or communal values engendered by lineage settlement on communal land might give way to individual values as land became short and individual lineage members moved elsewhere to establish their own settlements. In either case, the structures were sufficiently flexible to allow individuals and whole societies to master their situations in constructive and innovative ways.

STRUCTURES OF THOUGHT AND BELIEF

In addition to social and economic organization, the peoples of eastern Kenya also shared a number of elements in their thoughts and beliefs about the world and man's role within it. At the centre of these was a fundamental conviction in the unity of the universe. Individual actions, social processes, and natural occurrences were all to be seen within the context of a single interactive system, with human beings standing at the centre in ultimate control. Mankind's moral and social acts could and did have physical consequences. A failure to maintain correct social behaviour, or to observe proper ritual activities could cause misfortune in the form of illness, famine, or natural disaster. Correct social behaviour, on the other hand, promoted abundant harvests, good health, and general prosperity. Thus, whenever misfortune occurred, people immediately sought the personal or social agencies responsible. Who was neglecting his or her responsibilities? Who was promoting social tension? Or who was bewitching someone else? Once the causes could be discovered, remedial action could be taken and misfortune averted.

These were not the irrational and superstitious reactions of scientifically naive peoples. People knew how to avoid sleeping-sickness, how to ensure adequate annual harvests from marginal tropical soils, and how to maintain harmonious social relations. These rules had been discovered by the ancestors through centuries of trial and error and were passed down to the living in the form of obligatory traditions. These traditions were neither irrational nor unchanging. They emerged in the constant interaction between society's heritage and individual experience and were frequently updated to reflect changing conditions. But since ancestral wisdom was usually thought of as unimpeachable, such revisions were, of necessity, assimilated to the ancestral heritage, giving traditions their fixed appearance.

Furthermore, these thoughts and beliefs combined to form eminently logical and coherent systems regulating people's actions with one another and with the natural world. Take witchcraft and witchcraft accusations. All people were thought potentially to harbour the ability unconsciously to harm others. This could occur whenever a potential witch held antisocial views towards a neighbour or lineage mate. The mere entertaining of such views was sufficient for their unconscious powers to be invoked and the person in question to sicken. In the resulting inquest into the causes of the person's illness, it would become known that the individual had had these antisocial thoughts and he or she would be accused of having bewitched the victim. At that point, the accused witch freely confessed, for he or she had indeed been guilty of antisocial behaviour that may well have caused the victim to have become bewitched. Furthermore, the confession of antisocial thoughts by the accused witch, the airing of the social tensions that had previously lain below the surface, and the resolution of the causes for the social conflict were often sufficient to guarantee that the victim recovered from his symptoms. Today we would explain such activity psychologically. The inner tensions within a person forced to repress antisocial thoughts frequently cause physical illness which can be cured when the thoughts are brought to the surface, admitted, and resolved. Whereas Western medicine has concentrated almost exclusively on physical causes of illness, Kenyans have been far more concerned with the psychological causes of why illnesses occurred. Diviners who sought to uncover the causes of illnesses were highly knowledgeable folk psychologists who were intimately aware of the daily tensions within the society in which they lived and thus highly effective therapists.

We have already observed that correct patterns of behaviour were attributed to the ancestors and that those ancestors continued to belong to and influence the behaviour of their lineages long after their death. Thus an even more important cause for misfortune than witchcraft was transgression against the ways established by the ancestors. Ancestors were thought of as spirits who maintained contact with the world after they died. If they became offended in any way, they had the power to cause misfortune among the living until the causes of their grievances were diagnosed and righted. Spirits made their grievances known by communicating these to the living, speaking to them in dreams or possessing them and speaking through them. While people often had dreams or were possessed by spirits, only a few became adept at invoking such communication with the ancestors and communicating it intelligibly to others. These people became diviners or mediums and were called upon to communicate with the spirits whenever misfortune struck. When possessed, mediums entered a trance state in which their eyes went glassy, their limbs twitched irrepressibly, and they spoke in the language of the spirits. Upon emerging from possession, they frequently had no conscious memory of what had occurred, for it was not them acting, but the spirit acting through them. Again, Western psychology is only beginning to understand the nature of possession, but we know that social or personal stress may be felt subconsciously and only expressed when the conscious mind is in a dissociated or trance state. Those possessed by the spirits, then, were expressing deeply felt subconscious anxieties about improper behaviour occurring in their societies.

The ancestral spirits, as guardians of the culture, thus played an important role in preserving its values. They also played a significant role in innovation. If the ways of the ancestors were seen as sacrosanct, then no innovation was possible. But if one could appeal to the ancestral spirits for guidance in times of stress and change, one could receive new ideas from them as revelations. People who communicated with the spirits and revealed new paths are often called prophets, and they were frequently the ones responsible for articulating new ways of doing things. We need not worry whether prophets actually did communicate with the ancestors or merely expressed their own subconscious concern to appreciate the importance of their role. The fact that they were innovators and were believed to have spiritual sanction was enough for them to be effective within the society.

The structures of thought and belief were thus both conservative and radical. Belief in the interrelatedness of the natural and moral worlds and the role of witches and spirits were powerful instruments for social control, restricting as they did both antisocial thoughts and acts. But these same beliefs were also the main ways that new ideas were first received, understood, and eventually accepted. Thus many people when they encountered new influences first spiritualized them in order to bring them within their own conceptual structures. If we can understand this process, we can begin to appreciate how Kenyans themselves perceived and responded to changes in their circumstances.

REGIONAL PATTERNS OF ACTION

The structures which we have considered so far have been mostly those of the individual lineage, clan, and people; it remains to discuss how people speaking different cultural languages were able to interact with one another. The problem is a difficult one, as anyone who has tried to speak with another who does not share his or her language knows, but Kenyans followed a number of practices which made intercultural communication easier. First, many people were bilingual, speaking enough of the language of their near neighbours to make themselves understood. This was particularly true of traders and others who journeyed frequently to other areas, while Swahili came to serve as a common *lingua franca* throughout the area.

Secondly, we have already seen the degree of specialization which occurred within individual economies. Looked at regionally, these individual economies were complementary. Hunters and herders exchanged animal products with farmers for grains. Specialized crafts – baskets, pots, ironwork, weapons, medicines, and charms – were exchanged over wide areas, while many natural products, such as pottery clay, salt, or iron ore, existed in only a few areas and were traded to others. Regional trade was a regular occurrence in balancing individual economies, but it became particularly important in times of drought, famine, or disease, when people were able to avail themselves of the resources of other areas which may not have been affected as badly by disaster.

We have also seen how social relationships could be stretched in a number of directions to include kin, relatives by marriage, neighbours, blood-brothers and age-mates. All of these vehicles were also available to deal with strangers. Intermarriage was common between adjacent peoples, as was blood-brotherhood between traders. Furthermore, certain people had longstanding historical relationships with one another. Along the coast and in the central highlands, farmers and hunters had relationships of gift exchange with each other. Hunters gave the farmers animal products, for which they were later given farm produce. This relationship stemmed from the original settlement of farmers in these areas, when the farmers recognized the hunters as the original inhabitants of the land and thus the guardians of its well-being.

Finally, we have already noted that the peoples of eastern Kenya shared a common world view and were able to incorporate other peoples or new influences by first spiritualizing them. Ritual initiation was also widespread. In the case of the symbiotic hunters and farmers noted above, the hunters as the first settlers and guardians of the land often played an important role in annual fertility rituals and other rituals commemorating the earliest agricultural settlements. Ritual activities and specialists also operated on a regional level. Certain renowned rainmakers, for example, were asked for assistance by others. A few particularly well-known diviners and doctors were visited by patients from distant areas. Medicines and charms were widely traded. And certain rituals were held simultaneously or were linked with those in other areas.

Eastern and central Kenya was thus composed of a number of overlapping economic, social, and religious spheres. In spite of the fact that individual peoples made highly specialized ecological adaptations, spoke different languages, and had different patterns of social organization and of belief, no culture was exclusive. Particular economic spheres might spread out in one direction, while social institutions or ritual practices spread out in others. Ethnicity, the identity of an individual people, could only be relative and situational depending on the nature of the activity. Such identities could, and did, change over time as peoples' allegiances shifted, and declined in intensity as one moved out from the individual and family to the lineage, clan, and area. The peoples of Kenya have, however, always recognized the existence of cultural boundaries, as permeable as these may have been, and reinforced these with legend, language, and behaviour. Let us now look at these individual peoples in the light of the general patterns of structures and processes discussed above to see how they came to develop their own distinctive cultural patterns.

COASTAL FARMERS

The Pokomo: riverine agriculturalists

The narrow flood plain of the Tana River, one to two kilometres either side of the river and stretching inland over 400 km., provided a fertile environment for the agricultural Pokomo in the midst of the otherwise arid savanna woodlands of northeastern Kenya. Flooding twice a year in November–December and May–June, the river deposits a rich layer of silt on the plain in which the Pokomo planted a variety of crops. Wet rice was cultivated in diked fields on the low-lying plain, while coconuts, bananas, and mangoes were grown above flood level around the homesteads, and millet and sorghum were planted inland on flood-deposited silt.

Each Pokomo household of a man, his wives, his sons, and their wives farmed one or more strips of land extending from the river bank inland as far as the dry bush bordering the flood plain. Everyone thus had access to all three kinds of land, enabling them to balance their diet, maintain continual production throughout the year, and balance the risks of any one crop failing. But river-front land was restricted and closely controlled. Each man sub-divided his land and passed it in equal shares to his sons, the eldest son inheriting the plot upriver while younger sons received those downriver. This had two effects. People farming adjacent blocks of land along the river were usually members of the same lineage, closely related descendants of a common ancestor three to five generations back who had originally claimed the land. These localized lineages were the most important groups in managing day-to-day affairs. Lineage-mates farmed adjacent strips of common ancestral land, lived together in villages, and conducted their own political and social affairs. Secondly, as the land was continually sub-divided individual plots soon became too small to be economically viable. Younger sons were forced to move away and obtain land elsewhere, causing the older lineages to split as new ones developed elsewhere.

Related lineages, the descendants of earlier generations of younger sons who had migrated elsewhere to obtain land, were grouped together into clans, based on shared descent from a common ancestor. Clan links were more tenuous than lineage ones, however. Whereas lineage-mates were closely related and interacted with one another daily, clansmen might live at some

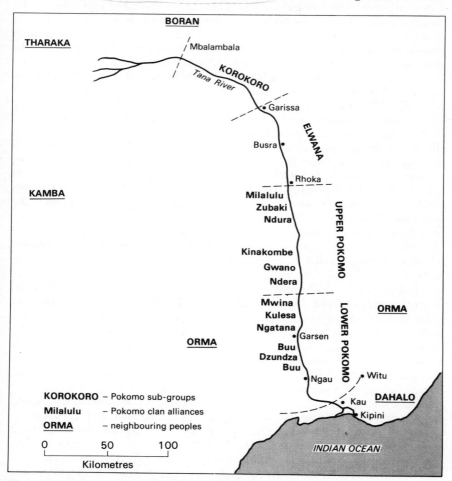

Map 4.1 *Pokomo sub-groups and clan alliances*

distance from one another and the precise descent patterns linking them were only vaguely remembered, if at all. Nevertheless, clansmen recognized a common bond with one another, considered all their lands to be part of a common clan patrimony, and cooperated with one another in major political and religious affairs.

As clansmen were scattered along the river, members of different clans were frequently interspersed with one another. In each area, however, one clan was recognized as senior, based on its claim to be the descendants of the earliest settlers in the area. Clustered around the senior clans were three to eight junior clans living in the same area, constituting a clan alliance. The individual clans of a clan alliance did not recognize any common descent linking them together, but they were closely allied by marriage. Marriage normally occurred outside the clan but within the clan alliance, thus establishing interrelated networks of relations among the different lineages and clans within the alliance. Each clan alliance functioned as a territorial political group. Its members all recognized a common territory, a council of elders composed of influential men drawn from each of the clans, a spokesman chosen by the council, and a senior clan which exercised ritual primacy. In times of severe raids by neighbouring Oromo or Somali all the members of a clan alliance joined together to build a single fortified village, surrounded by impenetrable forest and open only to the river, in which they would together fend off the attack.

Each clan alliance also had its own system of age-sets and its own ritual friction drum whose awesome sound, made by pulling along a rope threaded through its head, signalled the initiation of the young. In Lower Pokomo each alliance was divided into two named sections which alternated in initiating their sets. Section A was the first to initiate its young, followed fifteen years later by section B. These two were followed in turn by the next group of youths from A and then the next group from B. A complete cycle included the initiation of two successive groups from each section, A, B, sons of A, and sons of B, lasting a total of sixty years. The pattern was somewhat simpler in Upper Pokomo where there were no sections or recurrent cycles of sets. Uninitiated youth were simply initiated every fifteen years into a new set and given their own distinctive topical name.

Political action in Pokomo thus revolved around values based on descent, alliance, land, and age. Under ideal circumstances a son acquired land and bridewealth from his father, enabling him to farm and establish his own family within the family's lineage area. If land was short or his harvest poor, however, he would have to go to more distant clansmen or relatives of his mother or wife to obtain land. In either case, he was subject to the control of the elders, and remained so until his age-set had advanced to become elders themselves. Elders thus maintained their control over the young through their control of land and the wealth necessary for young men to marry, become initiated, and acquire secret skills of healing, divining or rainmaking. Many elders sought to monopolize land and wealth for themselves, however, in order to enhance their own prestige and so become influential men within the clan alliance. They achieved this by building up a large following, composed of wives, children, and lineage-mates, as well as making advantageous alliances with one's wives' relatives, partners, and others. A wealthy man could attract landless strangers to his village and adopt them as his own sons or daughters, while a poor man could not even persuade his own sons to remain with him. Wealthy men could also afford to apprentice themselves to established doctors, diviners, or mediums to gain further prestige as men of knowledge and wisdom. Pokomo society was thus a gerontocracy, ruled by wealthy elders who negotiated deftly among their networks of kin, allies, and friends to dominate the politics of consensus.

The clan alliances were the largest cooperative groups in Pokomo. Each was independent of the others. There was, however, a recognition that all shared a common cultural identity as Pokomo. The senior clans of all but one of the clan alliances claimed that they came together from Singwaya late in the 16th century and were the first to settle and clear the land along the river. This was the justification for their ritual seniority. But individual Pokomo also acknowledged a diversity of origins. When the first Pokomo settled along the Tana they encountered hunter-gatherers, many of whom were assimilated as separate clans into developing Pokomo society. Subsequently the Pokomo interacted closely with their neighbours. The Oromo, living on both sides of the river behind the Pokomo, exercised a particularly strong influence on Pokomo culture. The nothern Pokomo, or Korokoro, speak Oromo today, and Oromo loan-words are prevalent in all the Pokomo dialects, indicating that considerable interaction has occured between the two and that substantial numbers of Oromo have been assimilated into Pokomo society. Over the past 400 years, then, the Pokomo have developed a distinctive culture as they became isolated from their Sabaki-speaking cousins, the Mijikenda and Swahili, and interacted with a new riverine environment and the neighbours they found there.

The Mijikenda: the Kaya people

The Mijikenda arrived behind the southern Kenya coast late in the 16th century after leaving the Pokomo on the Tana during their migration from Singwaya. They first settled in six central villages, or *kayas* – Kwale (Digo), Giriama, Ribe, Jibana, Chonyi, and Kambe – while three others were established later as the result of the absorption of other peoples (Rabai and Duruma) and a split in Kaya Ribe (Kauma). Today the nine Mijikenda peoples take their names from these *kayas* and altogether call themselves Makayachenda – The Nine *Kayas* – or the Swahili equivalent Mijikenda.

The *kayas* were the central element in the development of the individual Mijikenda peoples over the 17th and 18th centuries, as each modified their common cultural heritage in distinctive ways. We have already seen how the Singwaya legend provided the basic model for all the major institutions of Mijikenda life. The *kayas* were large circular glades on the hilltops of the coastal ridge and were surrounded by dense forests and high palisades. A *kaya* could only be entered along one of two narrow winding paths, at the end of which were three massive wooden gates carved for the Mijikenda by their Swahili allies in Mombasa. The *kayas* were thus first and foremost defensive fortifications against attack by Oromo who remained on the plains below, and with them the Mijikenda succeeded in steming the Oromo advance south.

Everyone lived within the safety of the *kayas* while daily going out to tend their fields below. The Mijikenda were savanna farmers, raising millet and sorghum along the well-watered coastal ridge. They were few and able to practise extensive forms of shifting cultivation, allowing long fallow periods between crops to restore the fertility of the soil before they again burned the bush, fertilizing the soil with the ash.

Inside, each *kaya* was packed with thatched beehive-shaped dwellings housing up to 1 500 people. Everyone lived within the areas set aside for their clans, the most important descent groups within the *kayas*. The clans had been the original descent groups from Singwaya, and each had its own distinctive role in *kaya* social, political, and ritual life. Each clan possessed its own magical specialties and had designated roles in *kaya* rituals. And influential elders, representing the clans, sat together in the central clearing of the *kaya* to decide *kaya* affairs. Over time the clans split into subsidiary sub-clans and new clans were introduced as strangers were allowed to settle and were adopted by members of the major clans as separate sub-clans. But the sub-clans never

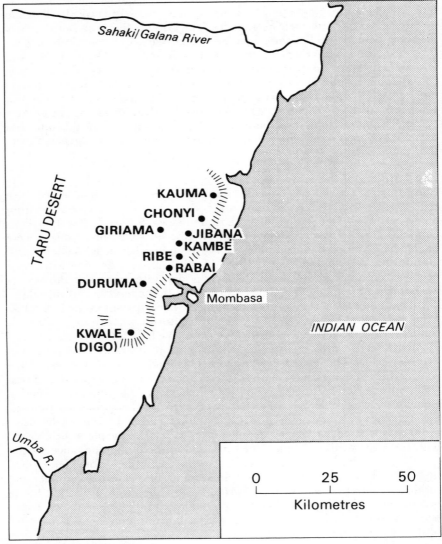

Map 4.2 *Mijikenda Kayas*

Photo 4.4 *Mijikenda elder*

assumed the importance of the clans in *kaya* affairs.

Age-sets cut across the division of the *kaya* into descent groups by uniting all the men of the same age. Those boys coming of age over a three to five year period were initiated into a single sub-set. After thirteen such sub-sets had been formed over a period of approximately fifty years all were corporately

87

initiated as the next age-set, or *rika*. Once initiated, the sub-sets within the *rika* then advanced at intervals to ruling elderhood. Digo sets differed from those of the other Mijikenda, were divided into two sections, and repeated themselves over alternate generations much like those in Lower Pokomo, but the rituals and nomenclature were otherwise similar to those of the other Mijikenda. A further system of grading was based on wealth. Wealthy men were normally men of influence because of their large followings recruited from the offspring and relatives of their many wives and extensive networks of trading partners. The leaders of the age-set were drawn from those who had arranged the extensive payments made to the elders at the time of their initiation and who had paid the fees to join the number of secret societies which controlled special rituals and administered judicial oaths. *Kaya* government was thus dominated by wealthy old men, as Cynthia Brantley has pointed out. The leaders of the senior sub-sets when a *rika* was initiated were already in their sixties and ruled until their death, while those of the junior sub-sets were teenagers at the time of the *rika* initiation and remained permanently junior to the more senior members of the *rika* throughout its life.

Each Mijikenda *kaya* was a cohesive unit, bound together by ties of descent, common residence, intermarriage, and age. But each Mijikenda people also had extensive relations with different peoples in the outside world. From their *kaya* ridge Mijikenda looked out over Mombasa and could easily observe what was going on there. Each *kaya* had a special economic and political relationship with one of the Swahili communities of Mombasa and with the smaller Swahili communities along the coast, as we will see. Individual Mijikenda also maintained relations with individual Oromo or Waata, which were consolidated through intermarriage or blood-brotherhood. Such relations greatly facilitated Mijikenda trade and incorporated them within a wider, intercommunicating cultural world. Mijikenda rapidly became the main agents for trade between the interior and the coast. Foreign seers and doctors frequently traversed the area bringing new knowledge. And foreign spirit possession cults rapidly passed among the various peoples.

The separation of the *kayas*, however, fostered the development of separate cultural variants among the different Mijikenda peoples, just as the common language they spoke developed into separate dialects. Culture, like language, can be divided into its structure, comprising its fundamental rules and values, and its individual cultural traits. Traits, like vocabulary, are easily borrowed across cultures and combined with different elements to convey different meanings, while structure, like grammar, is more persistent. The Mijikenda peoples obviously shared a common structure, while individual cultures developed their own distinctive traits as well as borrowing others from foreigners. The Singwaya legend defined the essence of shared 'Mijikenda-ness', while the diverse traditions of the Rabai, Duruma, and many sub-clans represented some of the variants. By extension, the Mijikenda also shared a cultural heritage with the Pokomo, as shown by their languages, their common descent, formulas, fundamental aspects of village design, and the structure of their age-sets, but each people had subsequently modified that heritage profoundly in response to their different historical circumstances, a situation they shared with the Swahili townsmen of the coast.

COASTAL TOWNSMEN

The Swahili-speaking peoples

We have already seen how the Swahili-speaking peoples emerged from the fusion of early Persian (Shirazi) traders with Sabaki speakers along the southern Somali coast prior to the 9th century. Trade between the East African coast and Asia had been going on at least since Roman times, as documented in *The Periplus of the Erythraen Sea* (2nd century) and Ptolemy's *Geography* (5th century). This was initially coasting trade. Foreign sailors stood off the African coast and exchanged imported iron tools, glass, wheat, and wine for ivory, turtle-shell, rhino horn, coconut oil, gums, and spices from coastal African farmers, herders, and hunters. Permanent coastal trading centres, or entrepots, did not arise until much later. The earliest known town

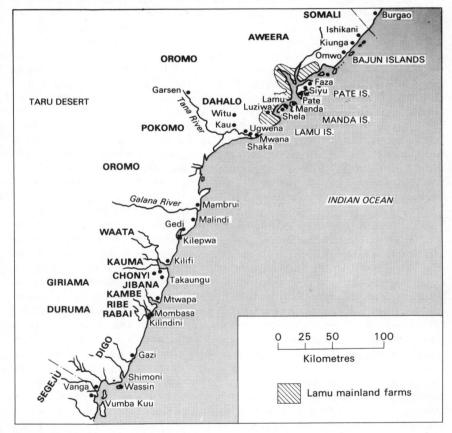

Map 4.3 *Swahili towns of the coast*

sites date from the 9th and 10th centuries, by which time we learn from al-Mas'udi that coastal Africans had kings and priests, cultivated bananas and millet using oxen, and traded ambergris, skins, ivory, rhino horn, tortoise-shell, and gold to Oman, from whence it was traded on to India and

China. The coast still had only a small number of immigrant Muslims, however, and they had intermarried with the local population.

The subsequent development of Swahili culture along the northern coast and its spread southwards to small urban entrepots along the coast owed much to the ecology of Indian Ocean trade. The African coast provided goods in short supply in the Arabian peninsula, Persian Gulf, India, and China. Mangrove poles were needed for building in Arabia, shell and ivory for decorative carvings and bridewealth valuables in India and China, gold for jewellery and coins, and gums, oils, spices, and dyes for cooking and manufactures. Most of these goods could be found all along the African coast, but the weather patterns and sailing characteristics of seafaring dhows favoured the development of the northern ports. The monsoon winds from the northeast bringing traders to East Africa start in November and continue until March, while those from the southwest taking them home again blow from April to August. Both continue at their steadiest along the northern parts of the coast, decreasing as one moves south. Kilwa was the furthest south that traders could expect to reach with time to trade and make the return voyage in the same year; south of Kilwa they arrived too late and had to wait a year to catch the southwesterlies home. The northern ports could thus easily monopolize Indian Ocean trade. Not all the valuable trade goods were available along the northern coast, however, and the most valuable, gold, came largely from the Shona kingdoms of central Africa through the southern port of Sofala. Unable to trade directly with Asian traders, the southern ports were forced to trade with northern merchants, who collected southern goods during local trading expeditions throughout the year in preparation for the annual trading season in the north. Northern towns thus became the main trade centres for the whole coast.

The first area to be settled by Asian merchants was the Benaadir coast of Somalia and the Lamu archipelago of Kenya. By the 10th century Manda, in the Lamu archipelago, had developed as a prosperous trading centre, but the merchants of Mogadishu were able to gain control of the Sofala gold trade and supplant Manda in the 13th century as the most important town along the coast. Mogadishu was eclipsed in turn by the development of Kilwa at the southern extent of annual voyaging in the 14th and 15th centuries, Mombasa in the 15th century, and Pate in the 16th century. These towns and countless others were in constant competition with one another, and none was able to dominate more than a few of the others at a time. Thus coastal politics remained fragmented until Portugal sought to impose its control over the whole coast in the 16th and 17th centuries, but the attempt was never very successful. Portugal was able to maintain its tenuous hold only by manipulating local rivalries within and between the towns and by periodically sending in its fleet to collect annual tribute payments. Frequent rebellions occurred all along the coast, and by the end of the 17th century Portuguese rule was overthrown everywhere along the coast. Thereupon the local towns remained independent until the imposition of Omani rule in the 19th century.

While the towns of the coast were politically independent of one another, they shared much in common culturally. Because of their long written history and their distinctive Muslim culture, conventional histories have viewed the Swahili-speaking peoples as representatives of an alien culture transplanted

Photo 4.5 *Mosque in Lamu*

from the Arabian and Persian gulfs on to African shores by seafaring merchants. They saw the Swahili as members of a literate, urbanized, and Muslim civilization opposed to the illiterate, rural dwelling, pagan cultivators and pastoralists of the interior. Like many earlier views of African history, in assuming a single monolithic origin for the Swahili, this interpretation fails to distinguish properly between race, culture, and language as entities capable of separate development. It has survived because few have explored Swahili culture in depth to analyse its antecedents, little has been known concerning the formative period of Swahili culture late in the 1st millenium, and the relations between Swahili towns and their neighbours have been largely ignored.

Most Swahili towns and villages were small fishing and farming settlements, trading on a small scale with their immediate neighbours and coastal dhow traders. Even the elaborate stone houses of prosperous merchants in the major towns were vastly outnumbered by the mud and wattle houses in which the majority of the population lived, and imported pottery constituted only one per cent of all pottery at Kilwa during the peak of its affluence in the 14th century. Arab influence thus represented only a small aspect of their overall culture. Few Arab or Persian immigrants settled permanently along the coast prior to the 14th century and those settling later were usually dominated by the local elites and quickly assimilated.

If the Swahili were not the outliers of an Arab culture, then, what were they? The best answer is that Swahili culture was a syncretic, or mixed, culture of Afro-Asian origins as nurtured on African soil. The Swahili language is a perfect example. The grammatical structure of Swahili is Bantu and closely related to the Sabaki languages now found in coastal Kenya. Its vocabulary,

91

however, has been strongly influenced by Arabic and Persian borrowings, especially in maritime activities, urban crafts, and religion, where Asian influence was greatest. East African Islam was also a synthesis of Asian and African religions, as African social patterns, festivals, and spirit possession cults fused with Islamic practices. In spite of periodic purification movements to bring such deviations into line with classical Islam, popular East African Islam remains a highly syncretic religion today. Even the distinctive building styles of the Swahili towns owed as much to local innovation as to eastern inspiration. Finally, the Swahili were physically indistinguishable from other Africans, a point first noted by ibn Battuta in 1329.

James deVere Allen has pointed out that what distinguished Swahili culture from that of its interior neighbours was not its alien nature but the fact that it was a specialized urban culture adapted to maritime activities and trade. The Swahili towns, rarely self-sufficient in food supplies or trade goods, were forced to rely extensively on trade with their agricultural and hunting neighbours to fulfill their needs. They thus became more internally specialized than other societies. Individual craftsmen practised weaving, iron and copper work, and bone and ivory carving for inland trade, while others farmed, fished, or collected mangrove poles, ambergris, orchilla weed, and other products for overseas trade. At the apex of Swahili society were the merchants able to exploit their position as middlemen to exchange imported trade goods for the export commodities of the interior. Social stratification accompanied such economic specialization as the prosperous classes re-enforced their economic supremacy with an Arab–Islamic ideology which divided the town populations into freeborn and client or slave, land-owning and landless, foreign and indigenous, religious and secular. These categories were combined in different patterns in the different towns into endogamous castes to restrict the low born from marrying up in status and thus upsetting the prevailing socio-economic class structure. But these specialized and differentiated urban societies were never far removed from their rural roots. With economic decline, a frequent occurrence given the vagaries of inter-town rivalries and trade, even the most prosperous often lapsed into a rural existence. What separated Swahili culture from that of its neighbours, then, was its differentiated international economy, its urban nature, and its maritime links with distant cultures across the Indian Ocean.

These elements can all be seen in the towns of the Lamu archipelago in the detailed study of Margaret Ylvisaker. Each town of the islands was independent of the others, spoke its own dialect of Swahili, and rose to prominence at different times. Manda was the main town in the 9th–10th centuries, Shanga in the 14th century, Lamu in the 15th, Pate intermittently with Siu and Faza in the 16th–17th centuries, and Lamu again in the 19th century.

The different islands of the archipelago varied ecologically, but none could support a dense urban population. Lamu itself is generally unsuited to agriculture and only limited tree crops (coconuts, dates, mango, and tamarind) were grown there. Manda is mostly sand dunes and mangrove swamps, while Pate is much larger and more arable, but had three major towns while lacking an adequate freshwater supply. The Bajun islands stretching up the coast to Kismayu are similarly limited agriculturally. All the towns were thus dependent on the resources of the adjacent mainland for their food supplies and wealth. Lamu's immediate hinterland was unpopulated. Each town had its own area on the mainland where its inhabitants farmed. Most farms were smallholdings, held by individual families, but a few wealthy merchants controlled large plantations worked by landless clients and slaves. The main produce was foodstuffs – millet, sorghum, and rice – consumed locally and traded along the coast. Cotton was also grown to supply the local weaving industry and mangrove poles, cowries, orchilla weed, wild rubber, and salt were collected for export. On the islands themselves weaving, basket-making, and sail-making were major craft industries, while coconuts, mangoes, dates, and tamarind were grown for export.

The people of the islands were divided between an urban population settled in the main towns and a rural agricultural population settled in the lesser villages of the islands and mainland, but even most of the townspeople migrated to the mainland seasonally to grow their crops. The majority of people, townsmen and villagers alike, lived in humble mud and wattle houses, in marked contrast to the elegant stone houses and mosques built by the socio-economic elite in times of unusual prosperity. It was this elite who dominated commerce and were able to maintain their position through an elaborate system of social stratification which ensured that the majority of Lamu's inhabitants remained farmers, craftsmen, and fishermen. The elites appealed to their foreign origins and genealogical descent from the prophet Mohammed to support their position, but Abdul el Zein has shown in dramatic detail how these mythological claims were frequently manipulated to reflect changes in the class structures within the islands. The elites, then, were predominantly local people just like the rest of the island populations, and they strongly opposed newly immigrant Arabs, forcing them to be absorbed into the prevailing cultural categories and stratification patterns.

Recent studies also stress the importance of Lamu's mainland neighbours. Pokomo farmers cultivated the Tana River delta, Dahalo and Aweera hunter-gatherers occupied the forests adjacent to Lamu's mainland farms, and Oromo and, later, Somali pastoralists occupied the dry savanna hinterlands. Each island town maintained important alliances with one or another of these groups and depended on them for trade and for military assistance during frequent inter-town disputes. Pastoralists also frequently raided the mainland farms, forcing their inhabitants to retreat to the islands, and then settled there to farm themselves. But no sooner had they settled than they were in turn forced to flee by other herders. The population of the islands was thus constantly being re-enforced by Pokomo, Aweera, Dahalo, Oromo, and Somali arrivals, effectively reintegrating its cultures with those of the mainland.

While Lamu's culture appeared exotic in the elites' claim to a foreign religious and racial background, it had a firm indigenous base. Its alien appearance was partially due to the fact that it interacted with overseas cultures in addition to African ones, but more substantially to the development of a trade-based economy. The mistake in the past has been to confuse such local socio-economic development with cultural diffusion from abroad. Lamu's language, culture, and subsistence economy were all fundamentally rooted in African soil; it was merely more specialized, more highly urbanized, and wealthier than other East African societies. Alien religious and artistic influences were firmly integrated into prevailing cultural patterns and social stratification. It was, in short, a culture in which neighbouring Pokomo or Oromo could easily feel at home, as they could not in later Indian and European imports.

Moving south along the coast one passes a number of smaller Swahili settlements before coming to Mombasa, the next major Swahili town. According to Berg, Swahili-speaking Shirazi from the Benaadir first settled on Mombasa Island around the 12th century, and soon developed their own dynasty under the legendary Shehe Mvita. Over the succeeding centuries a number of Swahili communities, known as *mataifa*, became established in Mombasa, so that by the 17th century Mombasa was a confederation of twelve *mataifa* organized into two groups, the Nine (*Tisa Taifa*) and the Three (*Thelatha Taifa*), as shown in Fig. 4.1.

Fig. 4.1 *Tensashara Taifa of Mombasa*

Taifa	Origins	Date	Mijikenda allies
Tisa Taifa (settled at Mvita on the north side of Mombasa Island)			
Mvita	Benaadir	*ca*. 12th–16th c.	Giriama and Rabai
	Malindi	1590s	
Jomvu	Benaadir	12th–16th c.	Rabai
Kilifi	Kilifi	early 17th c.	Kauma, Kambe, Ribe
		Oromo raids	
Mtwapa	Mtwapa	early 17th c.	Chonyi, Jibana
		Oromo raids	
Pate	Lamu Archipelago	17th–18th c. wars	none
Shaka	Lamu Archipelago	17th–18th c. wars	none
Faza	Lamu Archipelago	17th–18th c. wars	none
Bajun	Bajun Island	17th–18th c. wars	none
Katawa	Somali	17th–18th c. wars	none
Thalatha Taifa (settled at Kilindini on the south side of Mombasa Island)			
Kilindini	various northern towns	early 17th c.	Digo
Tangana	various northern towns	early 17th c.	none
Changamwe	various northern towns	early 17th c.	Duruma

Two important facts are shown in the diagram. First is the varied composition of Mombasa's population, giving it a range of potential allies along the coast from the Lamu archipelago south as far as Gazi. The second is the network of alliances which existed between the individual communities and the different Mijikenda peoples of the hinterland. It was these two sets of alliances which gave Mombasa its enduring political and economic strength in spite of the vagaries of conquests and trade elsewhere. It alone resisted Portuguese conquest throughout the 16th century until defeated by a combined Portuguese–Malindi–Segeju alliance in 1592. It regained its independence a century later in 1698 and was then the last town to fall to the Busaidi rulers of Oman and Zanzibar in 1837.

Economically, Mombasa had a wide range of trade contacts along the coast and with its Mijikenda neighbours. Mijikenda obtained livestock produce from Oromo and ivory and rhino horn from Waata as well as producing foodstuffs and collecting copal, wild rubber, and orchilla weed for trade to Mombasa. Strong relations existed between the Mijikenda and Mombasa. Each Mijikenda people was allied with a specific Mombasa community, conducted its trade through that community, and received annual tribute payments from them. Mijikenda were invited to the installation of Mombasa Sheikhs and fought along side their Mombasa allies in coastal disputes. With the final defeat of the Portuguese in 1729 by a combined Mijikenda–Mombasa–Omani force, representatives of the Mijikenda accompanied the delegates from Mombasa to Oman to arrange a final settlement. Mijikenda, in turn, received aid and relief in times of famine from their Mombasa allies. Mombasa thus served as a nexus between eastern

Photo 4.6 *Mombasa in the 1880s*

Kenya and the wider world, but if its arms reached out across the Indian Ocean, its economic, political, and cultural feet were firmly planted in Africa.

Moving further south down the coast past dozens of small Swahili and Digo settlements, one comes to Vumba. Vumba was a series of settlements which fluctuated over time, including Vumba Kuu, Vanga, Wassin, and a number of smaller villages all located around the mouth of the Umba River. Vumba was initially settled in the early Shirazi migrations from the Benaadir and continued to receive migrants from other areas along the coast in addition to local Segeju and Digo until these coalesced to form the Vumba diwanate early in the 17th century. William MacKay has detailed the development of a distinctive Vumba identity, the adaption of Shirazi and local culture, and the increasing importance of local alliances which underlie the consolidation of the Vumba as a distinct entity. Vumba maintained close reciprocal relations with neighbouring Digo and Segeju. Digo and Segeju trade provided the basis of the

Vumba economy and migrants from these areas constituted a majority of the Vumba population. Digo and Segeju approved the choice of the Vumba Diwan and attended his installation, at which they were entertained and presented with lavish tribute payments. During a series of succession disputes in the 18th and 19th centuries, Digo and Segeju played decisive roles in their alliances with the competing sections. In return, Vumba assisted Digo agriculture and the Digo were able to avail themselves of the noted Vumba healers and rainmakers.

I have stressed here the indigenous origins of Swahili culture and the ongoing patterns of interdependency with their neighbours for two reasons. First, this is a study of regional patterns of action, and the Swahili played a crucial role as economic and cultural intermediaries between the peoples of eastern Kenya and the outside world. Second, such a stress is necessary to bring earlier views of the alien nature of the coast into balance with the evidence. The evidence itself is quite clear. From an initial Afro-Asian cultural synthesis on the Benaadir coast late in the 1st millenium AD a distinctive African culture emerged that was Muslim, urban, and economically developed. This culture diffused south in the centuries which followed, becoming rooted and localized in dozens of towns and villages along the coast, just as the Swahili language itself developed numerous local dialects. The coast thus developed as a network of interrelated and interdependent entities, each linked to its immediate neighbours, adjacent towns along the coast, and markets abroad.

HIGHLAND FARMERS

The Taita

We have already noted two of the enduring paradoxes of the Taita people: they speak two different languages, Dawida and Saghala, and they recall a range of different origins. How is it, then, that the Taita today identify themselves as a single people?

The Taita occupied the remote upland valleys and slopes of three mountains, Dawida, Saghala, and Kasigau, which rise out of the midst of the arid wasteland of Taru Desert. They produced their food by carefully exploiting the different kinds of land that existed in the highlands. The fertile bottom lands of the river valleys were used for bananas, sugar cane, taro, and yams. These were limited, but could be extended by irrigating the adjacent slopes, while the higher slopes were suitable for dry field-crops such as millet, sorghum, eleusine, and rice. Finally, the highest fields and dry lowland plains were used for grazing cattle. The mountain valleys were both secure and fertile, attracting a steady stream of refugees from famines and political disputes elsewhere.

Taita political and social organization reflected this pattern. The most important social group in Taita society was the neighbourhood, a number of allied lineages living in a single valley. No single lineage claiming original settlement dominated the neighbourhood, as happened in Pokomo and Mijikenda villages; all had come together to exploit equally their valley's resources. Neighbourhoods varied in size, from a few hundred to several

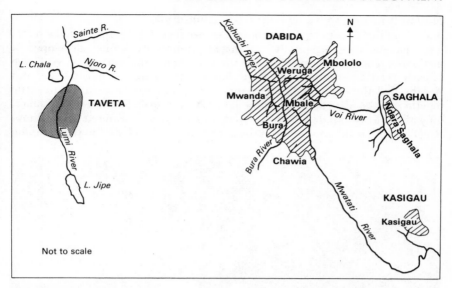

Map 4.4 *Taita and Taveta*

thousand people and were largely self-sufficient. Each lineage controlled sections of bottom land, hillside, and pasture to ensure its own subsistence potential. At the same time, the different lineages within a neighbourhood cooperated socially and politically to consolidate their control over the area. People normally married within the neighbourhood, consolidating social ties and landholdings, and over time distinct local cultural patterns developed.

This is not to say, however, that neighbourhoods were static. Studies by the Harrises of Taita social structure have shown that a variety of means existed whereby neighbourhoods could expand, assimilate strangers, and make alliances with other neighbourhoods, thus integrating foreigners, fostering wider links within Taita, and promoting historical change. Elders sought to accumulate cattle to acquire wives for themselves and their sons from other lineages within the neighbourhood in order to strengthen internal relations and to acquire rights to their wives' lineages' land. But they also made cattle transactions and loans with partners in other neighbourhoods and acquired wives from them to increase their prestige and influence beyond the bounds of the neighbourhood. A man was thus able to build up a personal following from a combination of neighbours, kin, in-laws, and partners elsewhere to achieve social prestige and influence. Through time these activities could also change the composition of the neighbourhood as alliances or intermarriage with adjacent neighbourhoods became sufficiently intense to unite the two. There was thus a continual process of change throughout the mountains as neighbourhoods were redefined or as individuals and lineages expanded and moved from one neighbourhood to another. Over time, then, different immigrant cultures became integrated into a general highlands cultural ecology which defined the Taita as a single people. Even their languages tended to merge together over the years from the intensive interaction and borrowing between their speakers.

Nation building in Taveta: an oasis community

A study of the Taveta by Ann Frontera shows clearly how this could be done. The Taveta were originally a refugee community which developed a distinctive common culture within the last three hundred years. We have already seen how numbers of Pare, Shambaa, Kamba, Taita, Chage, and Arusha fled the endemic famines and raiding of their home areas to settle together in the Taveta forest in the late 17th century. The forest was small, only about forty square kilometres, but sufficiently well watered by the Lumi River and other streams for the earliest migrants to clear individual plots along

Photo 4.7 *A Taveta village*

the rivers to grow yams. As time went on, each of the earliest settlers bequeathed his land to his descendents, and four landholding clans, developed: the Rutu composed of Kamba, Shambaa, and Zigula immigrants, the Ndighiri made up of Taita and Gweno, the Zirai from Pare, and the Menen from Kamba, Zigula, Chaga, and Arusha. All subsequent migrants were incorporated within these four main clans as they became one of the key integrative structures of the Taveta community. With population growth, the Taveta were soon forced to intensify their farming. Bananas were introduced. Irrigation, intercropping, and manuring were started. And plots were cleared in the forest where maize was introduced and grown by shifting cultivation.

The earliest leadership was composed of the leaders of the senior Rutu clan, but during the 18th century a number of central institutions developed to unify the migrants into a single people. One was the *njama*, or elected council of clan heads, age-set leaders, and other wealthy and influential men who met to settle intra-clan and land disputes, to adjudicate violations of customary law, and to conduct the major ritual ceremonies. Another was the *irika*, or age-set system, in which young men were initiated at fifteen-year intervals into the alternating pairs of age-sets similar to the system in Lower Pokomo and Digo. The youngest age-set comprised the warriors while the next older one the *njama*. Power was thus always shared between the two sections in Taveta society. If one section dominated the *njama*, the other was the warrior group. A third centralizing institution was the existence of a single ritual site at Lake Chala at which all Taveta were led by the senior Rutu clan to sacrifice in times of war, famine, disease, or drought. Finally, of course, the adoption of the Pare language by all Taveta, their dense settlement patterns, and increasing intermarriage between the clans over the years all welded them into an increasingly cohesive group.

The process of nation building in Taveta only took about four generations, or a century. The Taveta were solidly formed by the early 19th century, well able to withstand the depredations of trade which upset other societies during that century. It is a remarkable saga and forces us to re-examine earlier assumptions about cultural development. The emphasis among the Pokomo, Mijikenda and Swahili has been on a common culture slowly differentiating over time whereas the Taveta clearly demonstrate that the reverse process could also occur. In the final analysis both processes were usually at work simultaneously as individuals brought their old cultural heritages with them into new situations where common syntheses emerged from dynamic interaction among the constituent elements. Eastern Kenya was a far more volatile cultural situation than most people have believed was possible as individuals continued to move to new areas, peoples were constantly forming and reforming, and cultures maintained a continual process of becoming.

The Kikuyu: peoples of the ridges

We have already seen how the ridges of the central highlands were settled by Kikuyu frontiersmen and their followings of relations, clients, and landless *ahoi* during the 17th and 18th centuries as an expanding population and the requirements of shifting cultivation forced people to move. Such expansion continued through the late 19th century, when Europeans encountered Kikuyu pioneers in the environs of present-day Nairobi, but in the older parts of Metumi, Gaki, Gicugu, and Ndia, Kikuyu culture was already well adapted to life on the ridges.

The descendants of the earliest settlers soon developed into localized lineages with firm claims to the land their ancestors had first cleared or purchased from Okiek hunters. Each ridge was normally composed of several such lineages clustered together in a single fortified settlement on the brow of the ridge surrounded by dense uncleared forest. Such a pattern was particularly prevalent on the frontier to guard against Maasai and 'Gumba' raids, but even in safer areas where settlement was more dispersed local lineages were organized into territorial councils (*kiama*) who mediated disputes and organized common activities along the ridge. Each ridge also initiated its own age-sets (*riika*). The details of their recruitment varied throughout Kikuyu, but the basic pattern included alternate open and closed periods of initiation totalling thirteen to fourteen years before all youths initiated in that period were formally incorporated as an age-set. At this point

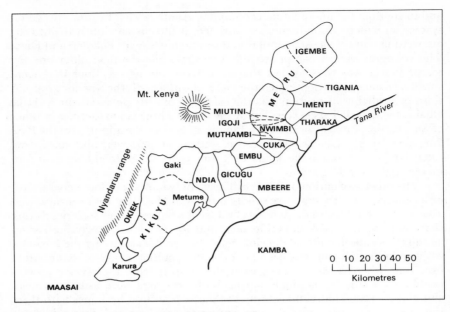

Map 4.5 *Peoples of the Central highlands*

they became junior warriors available for full-time defence of the settlement, while the previous junior warriors advanced to marry and become senior warriors, and the previous senior warriors became elders. It was from the ranks of the latter that the wealthy men who had large followings and who had paid the fees to be initiated into secret knowledge were chosen to sit on the council.

While the ridge was the largest corporate group which consistently acted together, social and economic networks extended into other areas and peoples. Local markets were held at different locations throughout Kikuyu at four-day intervals and were treated as neutral ground where friend and enemy alike could come to exchange surplus agricultural produce as well as specialized craft products, such as iron work, pottery, or basketry. Regional and border markets were also held, where the specialized goods of one region or people were exchanged for those of another. Maasai exchanged livestock produce for Kikuyu foodstuffs and and craft goods, while Okiek traded wild meat and hides for agricultural produce. Such relations were rarely solely economic, however, and Kikuyu and Maasai conducted elaborate mutual oathing ceremonies to establish the peace in between intermittent raids. Intermarriage was common between Maasai and Kikuyu and trade was frequently conducted by women with their relatives on the other side even during times of war. Okiek and Kikuyu had longstanding partnerships, often stemming from the time of original purchase of the land from the Okiek, while blood-brotherhood was made between unrelated individuals wishing to trade. Finally, extensive marriage and social alliances connected various ridges with one another in opposition to other alliances for the conduct of and defence against raids. Inter-ridge raiding for cattle was a common activity and was one means by which a junior warrior could acquire the livestock to enable him to marry and to start his career. All of these types of interchange inevitably led to considerable social mobility among different groups. Maasai frequently sought refuge among their Kikuyu relatives during famines. Kikuyu could and did become Maasai by marrying Maasai, joining Maasai age-sets, or by becoming clients to wealthy Maasai patrons. A number of Kikuyu lineages trace Maasai origins, and the Kikuyu adopted many of the practices of Maasai husbandry, initiation, age-sets, and military organization. Kikuyu culture thus represented an amalgam of local and foreign elements blended in a highland milieu and matured over the generations into a number of distinctive variations.

The Embu and Mbeere: two ecologies, one culture

The Embu and Mbeere claimed common origins, spoke the same language, and shared a common culture. What defined them as two peoples was a difference in ecology. The Embu resided on the fertile and well-watered slopes of Mt. Kenya above 1 200 metres, while the Mbeere lived in the drier savanna below this. As a result, the Embu were able to practise intensive agriculture, while the Mbeere had to farm selectively, growing drought-resistant maize, millet, and sorghum, and were more dependent on cattle. In Embu the population was dense and concentrated; in Mbeere it was scattered and diffuse. In spite of these differences, however, extensive interchange occurred between the two within the context of their common culture. Their economies were complementary and each was able to provide the other with produce they lacked. Famines or diseases in one area were often not shared by the other. Intermarriage and social movement were frequent, facilitating trading partnerships, social intercourse, and military alliances. Contrary to the usual practices in the central highlands, there was very little cattle-raiding between the two, and Embu and Mbeere frequently allied with one another in raids against the Cuka, Gicugu, and others.

The Embu and Mbeere followed typical central highlands cultural patterns in most other respects. Descent structure consisted of dispersed clans and localized lineages, grouped with others into neighbourhoods. Both had age-sets similar to the Kikuyu, while leadership went to those men wealthy in cattle who could amass large followings and join the various secret societies. The Embu and Mbeere were thus part of a broader cultural community going back to the initial dispersion of the Thagicu-speaking peoples among the previous inhabitants of the central highlands from the 15th century, and highlight the role of ecology in their subsequent development.

The Meru, Tharaka, Cuka, and related peoples: insiders and outsiders

The Cuka and Meru-speaking Muthambi, Mwimbi, Igoji, Miutini, and Imenti are highlands farmers occupying adjacent slices of the northeastern slopes of Mt. Kenya between 1 200 and 1 500 metres, while the Meru-speaking Igembe reside at a similar altitude on Nyambene to the north. The Tharaka and Meru-speaking Tigania, however, occupy the lower and drier northeastern and northern plains, where they cultivate drought-resistant grains and herd cattle like the Mbeere.

We have already seen that the evidence regarding the origin of these peoples is ambiguous at best. Linguistically, they are closely related to the Kikuyu and Kamba and yet traditionally they claim to have come from the coast. When we look closely at the structure of Meru society, however, the development of these peoples becomes much clearer. In a study of the Tigania Meru, Jurg Mahner has shown that structural opposition between insiders (original Meru) and outsiders (immigrants) lies at the very roots of Tigania society. Tigania clans, for example, were grouped into red, white, and black groups, each with a different role in Tigania society. The black clans were seen as the descendants of the earliest Meru and were ritually associated with fertility and social harmony, while the red and white clans were known as the descendants of immigrants assimilated into Tigania society and were ritually associated with conflict. Thus immigrant clans were seen as potentially disruptive, while original clans were able to restore harmony. These divisions and ritual roles not only reveal the large-scale assimilation of outsiders by the Tigania and the potential dangers the Tigania saw in doing this, they also show the power of outsiders to influence Tigania society, the dynamic tensions inherent in this process having been formally recognized and institutionalized in Tigania culture.

A second set of oppositions is found in the structure of Tigania generation-sets. The Tigania had a cycle of four generation-sets, divided into two pairs, so that the fathers of one pair formed the initial set lasting 15 years, the fathers of the second pair formed the second set, the sons of the first pair formed the third set, and the sons of the second pair formed the fourth. Political power and ritual authority was divided between the two pairs, the fathers of one pair serving as the ruling elders and their sons as the warriors, while the fathers of the other pair were retired elders and ritual leaders at the same time as their sons were the newly married family men. The pair which dominated political power was known as the right, while the one which had ritual authority was known as the left, as shown in Figure 4.2.

Fig. 4.2 *Tigania generation-sets*

	Left (ritual authority)	Right (political power)
Fathers	Retired elders and titual leaders	Ruling elders
Sons	Married Men	Warriors
	Uninitiated youth	

With the initiation of a new generation and the advancement of each set, these roles and the designations left and right reversed, the ruling elders retiring and becoming the ritual leaders, the married men becoming elders, the warriors becoming married men, and the newly initiated generation becoming warriors. Political leadership and ritual authority thus alternated between the two pairs, while at any one time the two were each dependent on the other. Furthermore, since one was not allowed to marry the daughter of a generation-mate, the two pairs were closely intermarried.

The structural opposition between the generation-sets was parallel to that

Photo 4.8 *Meru* Mugwe

between the clans. The 'right' generations created conflict through the exercise of political power and were equivalent to the red and white clans, the outsiders; while the 'left' generations used their ritual authority to restore harmony and were equivalent to the black clans, the 'insiders'. In both areas, insiders were dependent on the cooperation of outsiders and vice-versa. The essence of 'insideness' was the ritual leader of each of the Meru peoples, the

103

mugwe. Each *mugwe* was associated with the origin tradition of his people and embodied their cultural essence. He alone was morally pure and able to bless major events, to oversee the initiation of the generation-sets, and to administer important sanctions and ritual curses. The *mugwe* was not a political leader; rather he existed as a living link with the past, embodying the essence of group virtues and possessing powers to ensure the continuity of ancient traditions. Naturally enough, the *mugwe* was a retired elder and was thus associated with the black clans, the left generation-sets, and the insiders, the epitome of ritual harmony. The problem of amalgamation of diverse peoples into a single people was thus represented in the deepest structures of Meru societies; the process of becoming Meru was so common it had become a way of life.

The wandering Kamba

The Kamba have long existed apart from their fellow Thagicu speakers. They were separated from them by the dry plains bordering the Athi and Tana rivers and recall southerly rather than northerly origins. But here the remembered histories of the two groups are at odds with the cultural evidence. The Kamba language is closely related to the other Thagicu languages, and Kamba culture was broadly similar. Where it varied from them was a result of their varied experience as they dispersed through Ulu and Kitui.

Kamba history during the 18th and 19th centuries was marked by the same incessant wanderings of small groups in search of land and livelihood that had been characteristic of their legendary migrations from Mt. Kilimanjaro to Mbooni during the 15th and 17th centuries. From Mbooni they spread over the rest of Ulu, crossed the Athi River into Kitui, and dispersed to distant colonies scattered throughout eastern Kenya and northeastern Tanzania. In the process they encountered wide geographic variations and continually had to make new ecological adaptations to survive. Northern Ulu was well-watered highlands, where high-yielding maize and eleusine could be grown in the zone between 1 500 and 2 000 metres and banana and root crops higher, supporting a dense population. This area was characterized by stable settlements as the Kamba intensified their agriculture with irrigation to support an increasing population. In southern Ulu and across the Athi River in Kitui, however, the land became lower and drier. Kamba adapted their economy to cope with these new conditions, growing drought-resistant millets, sorghum, and cassava in the damper areas, shading off into pastoralism in the drier ones, and resorting to hunting along the fringes of Taru Desert.

As a result of such dispersion and variation, clans became hopelessly dispersed across Kamba and even localized lineages were small and lacked a deep association with the land. As in Taita, the neighbourhood group, or *utui*, assumed primary importance. Individuals, families, and lineages living in an area were bound by frequent contact, intermarriage, and oath to cooperate with one another in defence and work. Cooperative cattle sharing and herding were common and youth were bound together as warriors and workers. In keeping with the economic variation, there were enormous differences between *utui*. Some in Ulu were large intensive agricultural settlements, others in Kitui were scattered mixed farms, while still others further east were wide ranging groups of pastoralists. Some *utui* specialized in the production of certain craft items, including iron work, basketry, pottery, medicinal charms, bark cloth, dyes, poisons, and ivory carvings. The variation which existed between individual *utui* led to extensive regional trade as people exchanged their own specialized foodstuffs and crafts and those of other areas.

Authority and leadership were also highly localized as individuals rose to prominence by founding new settlements and attracting to them large personal followings based on their wealth and personal qualities of leadership. The pioneer missionary and explorer Johan Krapf noted in the mid-19th century:

> . . . the head of every family rules the people who belong to him, in accordance with the old customs and usages of the country. Wealth, a ready flow of language, an imposing personal appearance, and, above all, the reputation of being a magician and rainmaker are the surest means by which an Mkamba can attain power and importance, and secure the obedience of his countrymen.

J. L. Krapf, *Travels, Researches and Missionary Labours During an Eighteen Year Residence in Eastern Africa*, p. 355.

The Kamba thus put an emphasis on fluid and flexible social structures which were continually developing in response to new social and economic conditions. These served them well in the varied environments into which they moved and would be a major factor behind their success in the ivory trade in the 19th century, as we will see.

PASTORALISTS OF THE PLAINS

The Boran and Orma Oromo: expansion and contraction

The Oromo impact on eastern Kenya was a dramatic, albeit brief, one. Only three centuries separate the time when they first burst on to the scene to dominate the regions between the Juba River, the Galana River, and the central highlands of Kenya in the late 16th century and their elimination as a vital force in the area by the late 19th century. Little evidence remains from this period, forcing us to rely on recent studies of the Boran Oromo of northern Kenya and southern Ethiopia in an attempt to reconstruct the earlier situation.

The Boran were mainly cattle herders, though they also kept some sheep, inhabiting the lowlands from the Tana River north into Ethiopia. Rainfall in this area varied between 200 and 800 mm annually and is highly variable and undependable, forcing the Boran to move over large areas in search of food and water for their herds. They were not, however, totally dependent on their herds for subsistence, as they traded with Pokomo and Giriama for rice and maize and with Waata hunters for honey.

Boran social structure was characterized by the mobility required to maintain their herds. Cattle camps were temporary affairs, constructed for a season or less, and were composed of both kin and non-relatives. They ranged in size from two to twenty homesteads, associated together on the basis of kinship, marriage, friendship, or membership in the same age- or generation-set. Individuals had a wide range of choices in their selection of where they would live and with whom they would associate, and the composition of the camps varied from season to season. Age- and generation-sets were the only institutions common to all Boran society and even they were effective only within the limits of the homestead and the cattle camp. Generation-sets (known as *luba* in Boran and *gada* elsewhere among the Oromo) were initiated every eight years on the principle that a son could only be initiated into the fifth set following his father's regardless of his age at the time of his initiation. As can be readily imagined, actual generations and the formal generation-sets could rapidly become unsynchronized. If a man continued to have children as long as he was able, the difference in their ages could be as great as thirty to forty years when it became their turn to be initiated. Many of their sons, in turn, would either die before their turn to be initiated or would not yet be born. The age range of each set was thus wide and in time a majority of the male population was excluded from joining any set as they had been born either too early or too late for their set.

The Boran sought to counter this tendency in two ways. The first was to restrict fatherhood to men over the age of forty, thus drastically reducing the possible age differences among a man's sons and the consequent age differences within their generation-set, but significant imbalances between actual generations and the sets still developed. As the newly initiated generation-sets progressively aged in this way they were ineffective as warrior groups and so the Boran had a complementary system of age-sets (*hariyya*) to fulfill the age-related roles of herdsboys, warriors, and elders. The situation thus developed where a small minority of the senior generation of men exercised political power by virtue of being the only ones enrolled in the *luba* system, while the younger men conducted the intermittent raiding that characterized Boran history in the south. There must have been periodic readjustments in the balance of power between the two systems, with the age-sets pre-eminent in times of warfare and expansion, while the principle of generational seniority was reasserted during more stable periods.

The only other structural focus for Boran society was the division of the whole society into two halves, based on descent, each of which was headed by a prophet, or *qallu*. The *qallu* functioned much like the Meru *mugwe* in that his role was more symbolic than practical. The *qallu* was hereditary but was supposed to be born of an unknown father, thus making him the symbolic son of all Boran. He was also supposed to be an only child, marry endogamously within his clan, and not carry arms, protect himself, or own cattle. He was thus proscribed from the very activities by which Boran men acquired the wealth, prestige, and fame which were the prerequisites for leadership and was restricted to a symbolic ceremonial role at *luba* and other rituals.

Boran society was thus extremely decentralized with little enduring corporate activity above the level of the local homestead of a man, his sons and their wives. Nevertheless, their military prowess, exacerbated by the need of successive age-sets to raid further and further afield, was sufficient to enable them to dominate all of Kenya north of the Tana River. The Orma moved at the same time east as far as the Juba River with little opposition, but upon encountering the Somali they were forced south, where they successfully raided the settled Singwaya communities and Swahili towns further along the coast, forcing them south into Kenya. Once in Kenya, however, the Orma were soon contained by the Pokomo in their fortified settlements along the Tana River and by the Mijikenda in their hilltop *kayas*. Others, such as the Swahili of Malindi, were able to appease the Orma by the annual payment of tribute. By the early 19th century the Orma and Boran were both on the defensive. Large-scale Somali migrations from the east, Maasai expansion from the west, and widespread disease and famine caused the Orma to withdraw from south of the Galana River to the lower Tana area, while the Boran were reduced to a small rump in northern Kenya.

The inability of the Orma and Boran to consolidate their domination of the south is highlighted by the comparative experience of the Oromo in Ethiopia, where they were able to adopt settled agriculture and usurp prevailing political authorities, including several kings. Only the Orma and Boran remained nomadic pastoralists, retained the full *gada/luba* system, and failed to consolidate their territorial gains.

Maasai, Samburu, and Rendille: becoming Maasai

We have already seen in the previous chapter how the Maasai peoples formed into their present sub-groups in the course of the wars of the 19th century as they came up against the limits of their southerly expansion into central Kenya and northern Tanzania. Subsequently they developed close relations with neighbouring agriculturalists and hunter-gathers. Many Maasai were virtually pure pastoralists, subsisting on the milk and blood of their cattle. They were thus dependent on their neighbours for supplementary food and other requirements. Trade and intermarriage were common between Maasai and Kikuyu, while the Maasai depended on Okiek for the provision of honey required for all ritual ceremonies, wild animal skins, horns, capes, clubs, bows and arrows, and shields. In times of famine Maasai depended on both hunters and agriculturalists for food and refuge and some Maasai, such as the Baraguyu, required regular grain supplies to supplement their diet. Such interaction was facilitated by relatives and blood partners, while many Okiek and others adopted Maasai age-sets and clans and spoke Maa. Kikuyu clans were often linked with Maasai ones, and traders and residents of border communities frequently spoke both languages.

A classic example of Maasai interaction with their neighbours is the case study by Alan Jacobs of Sonjo–Maasai acculturation at the village of Pagasi in the eastern Rift Valley of Tanzania. Pagasi was located on the escarpment separating the Maasai on the plains below from the agricultural Sonjo on the plateau above. Most of the adults in Pagasi were born in Sonjo, but all claimed to belong to Maasai clans and age-sets, spoke fluent Maasai, and had numerous relatives among the Maasai. While still practising Sonjo irrigation agriculture, most also owned cattle which they placed with their Maasai relations. Jacobs estimates that up to one-quarter of the local Maasai were Sonjo absorbed in this manner. Similar mixed villages existed scattered around the Maasai steppe at Arusha, Taveta, Ngurman (near Pagasi), and Njemps, and greatly facilitated the exchange of peoples and ideas between the Maasai and their neighbours. The point is an important one, because it has frequently been assumed in the past that Nilotic-speaking Maasai pastoralists were utterly different from Bantu-speaking farmers. We now know that people and ideas flowed between the two.

Another classic study of interaction between different peoples is Paul Spencer's study of the Samburu and Rendille, *Nomads in Alliance*. The Samburu are a Maa-speaking people who herded cattle east of Lake Turkana. A lineage's cattle were controlled by the elders who generally exploited the herd to provide more wives and allies for themselves while depriving the warrior *moran* age-set of the right to marry. The Rendille, on the other hand, were Eastern Cushitic-speaking camel herders inhabiting the drier country to the north of the Samburu. In contrast to the Samburu, the Rendille were organized into generation-sets, but both types of sets were synchronized to a common fourteen-year cycle and both peoples initiated their sets at the same time. Like the Oromo, the Rendille sought to control births to keep the sets in synchronization with actual generations. They did this by restricting fatherhood to men in the senior warrior grade and marriage to one wife. A final contrast was the way the two managed their herds. Cattle reproduce rapidly and Samburu readily distributed cattle to in-laws and partners to increase their networks of allies and apportioned their herd equally among their sons as inheritance. Camel herds, by contrast, are small and reproduce slowly. Rendille thus sought to retain the integrity of the herd by restricting distribution to loans and by passing the whole herd intact to the eldest son on a man's death. Younger sons and poor men thus had little chance to acquire their own herds, to marry, and to become influential elders.

Located between the Samburu and the Rendille were the Ariaal, a cultural halfway-house between the two. Most Ariaal were first or second generation Rendille and initially retained Rendille culture, observed Rendille exogamous restrictions, initiated generation-sets with the Rendille, herded camels, and spoke Rendille. Slowly they began to adopt Samburu clans, join Samburu age-sets, acquire cattle, and marry Samburu women. At this point they were truely bicultural. At home they maintained a Rendille wife, herded camels, and passed the whole herd to their eldest son, while in Samburu they maintained a Samburu wife, spoke Samburu, herded cattle, and distributed their herd among their sons, in-laws, and partners. The process was facilitated by the fact that Rendille had a surplus of women because of the restrictions on marriage, while Samburu had a shortage because of extensive polygamy. It was thus relatively easy for a Rendille to marry his daughter to a Samburu and so acquire the initial cattle and in-laws in Samburu necessary to begin the process of transfer. The Rendille and Samburu were thus inextricably linked in a symbiotic relationship because of their complementary cultural ecologies in spite of the fact that the two cultures differed greatly and they were otherwise unrelated.

The Somali: from clientage to independence

The Somali, like the Rendille, herd camels. The earliest Somali clans to migrate into northeastern Kenya were the Ajuran and Gurre at the time of the collapse of the Ajuran state in the mid-17th century. Small in numbers, they quickly became clients of Boran and adopted Boran customs and language. Boran never fully assimilated their clients, however, and Somali continued to be denied equal rights to wells, legal compensation, and marriage. The next migration was much larger and composed of Hawiyya and Darod clans driven out of the Ogaden by Ethiopian expansion in the 19th century. From the middle of the century they slowly drove the Orma from the Juba River until Somali occupied the whole area between the Juba and the Tana, reducing the Orma to a rump on the lower Tana. These Somali successes apparently encouraged the submerged Ajuran and Gurre, who commenced to attack their Boran hosts and by the end of the century they had re-emerged as an independent people and successfully driven the Boran from the northeastern corner of Kenya. Somali were thereafter able to hold their own against the two Oromo peoples and to challenge their access to water-holes and pasturage.

Unlike the Oromo, the Somali were organized primarily by descent and legal (*diyya*) pacts. While Somali lived and herded their camels in small lineage groups, the whole Somali nation was incorporated in a single genealogy embracing every clan family, clan, sub-clan, and lineage. While such genealogies were frequently manipulated to accommodate strangers, they provided a central ideology and potential alliance network for every Somali. Somali were thus able to mobilize considerable forces for individual campaigns by means of appeals to common descent. Individual Somali lineages were also linked in *diyya*-paying pacts. These were local alliances who swore to uphold the group's rights to legal compensation from others who offended against them. Such *diyya*-paying groups were often quite large and able to mobilize their forces quickly against a foreign foe. Somali forces were thus frequently superior to the localized forces of the Oromo, particularly with the large-scale population movements of the 19th century. Earlier, the Ajuran and Gurre had made use of an alternative Somali practice, clientage (*shegat*). When Somali were in a minority they attached themselves as clients to their numerically superior hosts while quietly building up their own numbers by natural increase and adoption until they could successfully challenge their patrons and overthrow them. This tactic was frequently employed in their eastern expansion and accounted for the large number of absorbed peoples within the Southern Somali clans.

CULTURE AS PROCESS

Both traditions and ethnographies commonly assume that cultural processes emerged fully developed during some cataclysmic event in the distant past and have continued unchanged and unchanging every since. But just as we have seen in the previous chapter that change was a gradual process, an ongoing dialogue between traditions and changing circumstances, so continuity is also a constant process of structuring and restructuring as dynamic elements within a culture interact with one another and with external forces. Change and continuity are related parts of a single process of becoming. At any one point in time there are sufficient tensions and contradictions within a society that each individual can and must make choices. Over time, historical circumstances may influence the collective choices of many to skew them in one direction or another and so alter their very nature. Here we have been able to examine a number of the dynamic elements within the cultures of the peoples of Kenya, ranging from modes of production to the values of kinship and marriage, conflicts between young and old, and modes of thought and belief. Within these general categories, we have also seen how the individual peoples of Kenya each employed their own distinctive cultural heritage in the context of their particular historical circumstance to develop new social, economic, political, and intellectual structures. In the absence of a detailed record of events for this period, it has not been possible to write the more usual type of history featuring individuals, peoples, dates, and events, but we have nevertheless been able to examine some of the more fundamental processes and changes which were taking place within the cultural structures of the area. If this has seemed too general to be history, we will now turn to changes where these same processes can be seen in the context of much more specific events during the 19th century.

REFERENCES AND SUGGESTIONS FOR FURTHER READING

The sources for this chapter include those cited in Chapter 3 and the reader who wishes to pursue further the background of specific peoples is advised to consult the more detailed histories there. These have been supplemented by numerous ethnographic and other historical accounts, which are detailed below.

There are few early sources for the Pokomo, but I have relied heavily here on the excellent analysis of their mode of production as it relates to their descent and age structures contained in Norman Townsend, 'Age, Descent, and Elders among the Pokomo', *Africa*, 47 (1977), pp. 386–397. See also Townsend's 'Biased Symbiosis on the Tana River', in W. Weissleder (ed.), *The Nomadic Alternative*, pp. 289–295 (The Hague, 1978).

The Mijikenda, on the other hand, are described in a number of excellent early accounts, including J. L. Krapf, *Travels, Researches, and Missionary Labours during an Eighteen Years' Residence in Eastern Africa* (Boston, 1860); C. New, *Life, Wanderings and Labours in Eastern Africa* (London, 1873); and A. M. Champion, 'The Agiryama of Kenya' (*Royal Anthropological Institute Occasional Papers*, no. 25, London, 1967, – probably written in 1914). Later ethnographic accounts include: Luther Gerlach, 'The Social Organisation of the Digo of Kenya' (Ph.D. thesis, University of London, 1961); David Parkin, *Palms, Wine, and Witnesses* (San Francisco, 1972), 'Medicines and Men of Influence', *Man*, 3 (1968), pp. 424–439, and 'Politics of Ritual Syncretism: Islam among the non-Muslim Giriama of Kenya', *Africa*, 40 (1970), pp. 217–233; and Cynthia Brantley, 'Gerontocratic Government: Age-Sets in Pre-Colonial Giriama', *Africa*, 48 (1978), pp. 248–264, and 'An Historical Perspective of the Giriama and Witchcraft Control', *Africa*, 49 (1979), pp. 112–133.

I have relied primarily on specific studies of the towns of the Swahili coast within the context of the interpretations of Chittick, Allen, Pouwels, and Aziz cited in Chapter III. For the Lamu archipelago these include: Margaret Ylvisaker, 'The Political and Economic Relationship of the Lamu Archipelago to the Adjacent Kenya Coast in the Nineteenth Century' (*African Research Studies*, no. 13, Boston, 1977); Abdul el Zein, *The Sacred Meadows* (Evanston, 1974); and Janet Bujra, 'An Anthropological Study of Political Action in a Bajuni Village in Kenya' (Ph.D. thesis, University of London, 1968). The basic study of Mombasa in this period is F. J. Berg, 'The Swahili Community of Mombasa, 1500–1900', *JAH*, 9 (1968), pp. 35–56; while Vumba is the subject of William MacKay, 'A Precolonial History of the Southern Kenya Coast' (Ph.D. thesis, Boston University, 1975).

Grace and Alfred Harris have written a number of studies of the Taita which summarize and expand upon the earlier accounts. The dynamic relationship between ecology and social structure and the role of exchange is analyzed in Alfred Harris, 'The Social Organization of the Wataita' (Ph.D. thesis, Cambridge University, 1958) while the dynamics of lineage development and alliance networks are covered in Alfred and Grace Harris, 'Property and the Cycle of Domestic Groups in Taita' in P. H. Gulliver (ed.), *The Family Estate in Africa*, pp. 117–153 (London, 1970), and Grace Harris, 'Taita Bridewealth and Affinal Relationships' in M. Fortes (ed.), *Marriage in Tribal Societies*, pp. 55–87 (Cambridge, 1962). Ritual and spirit possession are studied in Grace Harris, *Casting Out Anger: Religion Among the Taita of Kenya* (Cambridge, 1978), 'Possession Hysteria in a Kenya Tribe', *American Anthropologist*, 59 (1957), pp. 1046–1066.

Early accounts of the Kikuyu include W. S. and K. Routledge, *With a Prehistoric People: The Akikuyu of British East Africa* (London, 1910); C. W. Hobley, *Bantu Beliefs and Magic* (London, 1922); and C. Cagnolo, *The Akikuyu* (Nyeri, 1933); while Kikuyu social organization is summarized by Jomo Kenyatta, *Facing Mount Kenya* (London, 1938); H. E. Lambert, *Kikuyu Social and Political Institutions* (London, 1956); and L. S. B. Leakey, *The Southern Kikuyu before 1903* (London, 1978).

Two studies of Embu and Mbeere society are Jack Glazier, 'Generation Classes among the Mbeere of Central Kenya', *Africa*, 46 (1976), pp. 313–326 and Satish Saberwal, *The Traditional Political System of the Embu of Central Kenya* (Nairobi, 1970).

Two incisive analyses of Meru symbolic structures are R. Needham, 'The Left Hand of the Mugwe: An Analytical Note on the Structure of Meru Symbolism', *Africa*, 30 (1960), pp. 20–33 and Jurg Mahner, 'The Outsider and the Insider in Tigania Meru', *Africa*, 45 (1975), pp. 400–409; while Meru society in general is described in B. Bernardi, *The Mugwe: A Failing Prophet* (London, 1959). Tharaka society is summarized in A. M. Champion, 'The Atharaka', *Journal of the Royal Anthropological Institute*, 42 (1912), pp. 68–90.

Early accounts of the Kamba include C. W. Hobley, *Ethnology of Akamba and other East African Tribes* (Cambridge, 1910), and *Bantu Beliefs and Magic* (London, 1922); C. C. F. Dundas, 'History of Kitui', *Journal of the Royal Anthropological Institute*, 43 (1913), pp. 480–549; and Gerhard Lindblom, *The Akamba in British East Africa* (Uppsala, 1920). More recent studies are Donald Jacobs, 'The Culture Themes and Puberty Rites of the Akamba, A Bantu Tribe of East Africa' (Ph.D. thesis, New York University, 1961); K. Ndeti, *Elements of Akamba Life* (Nairobi, 1972); and R. B. Edgerton, *The Individual in Cultural Adaptation* (Berkeley, 1971).

Two major studies of Boran social organization are Paul Baxter, 'The Social Organization of the Galla of Northern Kenya' (Ph.D. thesis, Oxford University, 1954) and Asmaron Legesse, *Gada* (New York, 1973). The latter remains a provocative structural analysis of age and generation-set dynamics in spite of alternative interpretations contained in C. R. Hallpike, 'The Origins of the Borana Gada System', *Africa*, 46 (1976), pp. 48–56 and a number of the studies contained in U. Almagor and P. Baxter (eds.), *Age,*

Generation and Time (Manchester, 1978).

Several excellent studies of Maasai interaction with their neighbours have been written, including Alan Jacobs, 'The Irrigation Agricultural Maasai of Pagasi: A Case of Maasai–Sonjo Acculturation' (*Social Science Research Council Papers*, Section C, Kampala, 1968); John Berntsen, 'The Maasai and their Neighbours: Variables of Interaction', *African Economic History*, 2 (1976), pp. 1–11; and Richard Waller, 'The Maasai and their Neighbours' in *Kenya in the Nineteenth Century*.

An equally important study of Samburu–Rendille interaction is Paul Spencer, *Nomads in Alliance* (London, 1973), while his *The Samburu* (Berkeley, 1968) and 'Opposing streams and the Gerontocratic Ladder: Two models of Age organization in East Africa', *Man*, 11 (1976), pp. 153–175, contain additional material on the Samburu. Somali social structure is the subject of Virginia Luling, 'The Social Structure of Southern Somali Tribes' (Ph.D. thesis, University of London, 1972).

CHAPTER FIVE

TRADE AND SOCIETY IN THE 19TH CENTURY
THE POLITICAL ECONOMY OF CHANGE

Both traditional and conventional historical sources are richer for the 19th century than for the preceding periods. Detailed local traditions recall the exploits of named ancestors in the recent past, reflecting the importance of recent history in lineage politics. Rights in land, the composition of the kin group, the extent of one's relations by marriage, distant partnerships, and the resolution of local disputes were all rooted in the legacy of the recent past. Such traditions emerge slowly in the early decades of the century, but grow more detailed as the century progresses. By the end of the century the events they portray fall within the memory of living men and convey a vivid picture of the past.

Documentary sources develop in a similar fashion as European observers became more closely associated with local realities. Emery's journal of Mombasa in the 1820s is the first sustained reporting of day-to-day life on the coast. His reports were soon supplemented for the interior by the detailed journals of the earliest missionaries. Krapf, Rebmann, Erhardt, New, and Wakefield all settled amongst the Mijikenda in the 1840s to 1850s and conducted extensive expeditions to the surrounding Kamba, Taita, Chaga, and Shambaa. The missionaries were followed in turn by explorers, most notably Guillain and Burton, and by the end of the century, representatives of the Imperial British East Africa Company and colonial administrators. We are thus able to construct a detailed historical narrative of Kenya's past for the first time and to appreciate the diverse actions of individual historical actors within the overall historical drama. The earlier idealized version of the past gives way to a more realistic picture.

The 19th century was a period of numerous and varied changes in eastern and central Kenya. We have already traced some of these from earlier periods. The expansion of the Maasai and the continuing process of definition of individual Maasai groups continued throughout the century, as did the extension of the Kikuyu frontier south towards Nairobi, the dispersal of the Kamba over Ulu and Kitui, and the migration of Somali into northern Kenya, while the earlier Oromo expansion was halted and reversed. Significant new changes were occurring as well. The independent Swahili city-states of the coast were slowly amalgamated into the Zanzibar commercial empire during the course of the century, a process which we will examine in greater detail in the final chapter. The Mijikenda abandoned their *kayas* and many of their centralized institutions during the course of the century to live in dispersed and independent villages. The Kamba, by contrast, reversed their movement into dispersed villages to amalgamate into larger units under the dynamic leadership of influential men. The main causes of these changes were economic.

ECONOMIC PATTERNS IN THE EARLY 19TH CENTURY

The economy of eastern and central Kenya at the opening of the 19th century had altered little from the previous centuries as individual families continued to produce most of their own subsistence needs by farming or herding. During the course of the century, maize gradually replaced sorghum, millet and eleusine as the staple crop grown by savanna grain farmers. Maize could be grown using many of the same production techniques and was capable of producing much higher yields, thus supporting a growing population. But the individual cultural ecologies of eastern Kenya remained distinctive, each with its own technology and raising plant and animal varieties adapted to the local conditions.

Each production routine also represented a careful attempt to balance man's dietary needs against plant and animal needs and the preservation of soil fertility. Farmers exploited varied ecologies to ensure an adequate and balanced diet, as each family sought to have separate fields in bottom lands, on hillsides, and on hilltops, as well as pasturage. Such diversification allowed them to produce legumes, root crops, and meat to supplement staple grains in the diet, as well as to guard against the risk of the possibility of failure of any one crop. Farmers also tended to plant more than their normal needs in order to ensure an adequate harvest in bad years, thus providing what William Allan has termed a 'normal surplus' in good to average years. This normal surplus could then be exchanged with others to supplement or add variety to one's own diet. Finally, farmers practised irrigation, manuring, crop rotation, or intercropping to preserve the fertility of fragile tropical soils. Herders followed similar routines, constantly moving their stock to balance their needs for pasturage and water and splitting their herds among family members and herding partners over as wide an area as possible to guard against the possibility of adverse ecological conditions in any one area.

Local and regional trade enabled individuals to supplement their own production with goods from other areas, as we have seen. Kikuyu exchanged surplus crops together with specialized products, raw materials, and craft products of their own ridge with those of adjacent ridges. Restricted goods found or produced in only one or two highland areas – such as pig iron and iron implements, red ochre, soda, and tobacco – were traded the length and breadth of the highlands, while complementary goods from neighbouring ecologies were exchanged at either border markets or by traders journeying to other areas. Kikuyu exchanged foodstuffs for honey, wild animal skins, and other forest products with the Okiek; foodstuffs, pots, gourds, ironware, ochre, and ivory for skins and livestock with the Maasai; and similar goods for salt, livestock, poisons, medicines, chains, snuff boxes, bows and arrows, and iron ore with the Kamba.

Trade was conducted by local barter, at periodic four-day markets, at special border markets, and by trading expeditions into neighbouring areas. The exchange of foodstuffs and local products occurred at local and four-day markets where people brought their own food surpluses or craft products and exchanged them with those of their neighbours. Such markets were overseen by the elders, while warriors maintained the market peace. Regional trade was conducted at border markets sited between adjacent peoples. The neutrality of such areas was established before trading began by oaths sworn by the two parties. Kikuyu and Maasai each took peace oaths before opening a border market, and Oromo and Giriama sacrificed a goat and swore an oath of friendship before they commenced trading. Trade could thus be conducted by people who were potentially enemies of one another. Regional trade was also

Photo 5.1 *Making blood-brotherhood*

conducted by expeditions journeying to neighbouring areas, but the risks of such expeditions were high. Trading parties could be easily raided and they might find themselves among strangers at their destination with no one willing to trade with them. Kikuyu women frequently travelled to Maasai, but they had relatives among the Maasai with whom they could trade, were led by Maasai guides, and were protected by mutual oaths sworn between the two peoples which remained in force even when the men were fighting one another. If a trader had no relatives in an area, he could either marry locally or establish a trade partnership through swearing an oath of blood-brotherhood with a local trader. Such oaths required the two to treat each other as brothers at all times and was accompanied by each tasting the blood of the other over a sacrifice. Each was then an adopted member of the other's kin group who were responsible for accommodating and protecting the other. Most importantly, one was no longer an unknown stranger, but had a social identity as a member of a local lineage or clan which stood responsible for his behaviour. Trade was thus both a social and an economic enterprise conducted by two people who stood in a familiar relationship to one another.

Food production and exchange of complementary products were both orientated to obtaining subsistence goods required in day-to-day life – food, baskets, pots, weapons, hunting poisons, medicines, and wearing apparel. A separate level of economic activity involved production and trade of market commodities. These were goods not normally used in everyday life – such as ivory, rhino horn, hippo teeth, copal, rubber, copra, mangrove poles, and orchilla weed – but for which a demand existed in India and Arabia.* Trade in these items for Indian cloth, beads, and wire had been conducted at the coast for centuries. Trade was first mentioned in the *Periplus* and Ptolemy's *Geography* in the 2nd and 5th centuries, and the *Kitab al Zanuj* noted that trade had

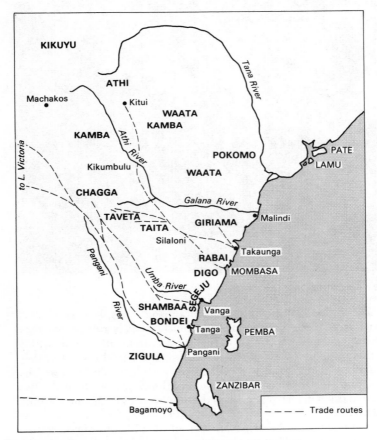

Map 5.1 *Trade and trade routes in the 19th century*

---

* Ivory and hippo teeth were carved for ornaments and jewellery in China and India and were in especially high demand in India where they were used as bridewealth goods. Rhino horn was commonly considered an aphrodisiac in the East. Copal was a gum resin used in varnish, especially for porcelains. Copra was the dried meat of the coconut, from which cooking oils were extracted. Mangrove poles were used as building materials in the Arabian peninsula. And orchilla was a purple dye.

116

occurred at Singwaya between Kashur and the Swahili. Rezende noted similar trade along the Kenya coast in 1634, while Emery reported that Mijikenda came daily to Mombasa to trade in the 1820s. Mijikenda and Swahili were the foremost market traders. Mijikenda channelled African products to the coast where Swahili bulked the goods for Arab and Persian dhows arriving on the northeast monsoon. Mijikenda produced or collected many of these items themselves, including surplus grain, copra, copal, rubber, and orchilla; while they obtained ivory, hippo teeth, and rhino horn in gift exchange from Waata hunters; conducted border markets where they acquired ivory and livestock products from Oromo; and, by the end of the 18th century, led caravans to Kitui to obtain ivory and livestock from Kamba. Similar coast–interior networks linked the Vumba with their Digo and Segeju neighbours; the towns of the Lamu archipelago with the Pokomo, Dahalo, Aweera, and Oromo; and the towns of the Benaadir with the communities of the Juba and Shebelle river valleys.

ECONOMIC EXPANSION DURING THE 19TH CENTURY

Subsistence-oriented production and trade remained the most important part of local economics throughout the 19th century, but market-oriented trade became increasingly important as East Africans responded to increased demand in India, China, Europe, and America for African products. Zanzibar became the headquarters of this trade, and, Zanzibari revenues from exports rose from $50 000 in the 1820s to over $500 000 at the end of the century, while exports themselves rose from $765 000 in 1843 to $4 350 000 in 1878/9.* The value of ivory exported increased over fifty times as exports rose from 18 000 kg to 180 000 kg and the price of ivory increased from $27 to $140 per *frasila* (16 kg) for the highest grade.

Comparable figures are not available for the Kenya coast, but we can safely assume they rose dramatically also. Boteler estimated that Mombasa acquired some $60 000 worth of goods annually from the Mijikenda for its own consumption and export in the 1820s, while Mombasa's exports alone averaged $688 000 by the end of the century and those for the whole Kenya coast exceeded $1 300 000. Kenya's two most important exports by value throughout the century were grain and ivory. Ivory exported from Mombasa remained fairly constant at $50 000–100 000 annually as falling supplies were balanced by rising prices, but the value of grain exported rose steadily to exceed that of ivory in the last two decades.

Mombasa was the dominant town along the Kenya coast at the beginning of the century and was the centre for the export trade for other towns from Pemba to Pate. Local dhows from Mombasa traded up and down the coast throughout the year in preparation for the annual trading season with the ocean-going dhows from Arabia and India. Mombasa's fortunes started to decline from early in the century, however, as Omani influence grew along the coast. The Omanis captured Pemba, Lamu and Pate in the 1820s and Mombasa itself fell in 1837. Mombasa continued to be the most important

---

* The main currency in use throughout the 19th century was Maria Theresa thallers ($), generally worth 4 shillings sterling or 2 rupees.

single town along the Kenya coast for the rest of the century, but it no longer dominated the export trade as the Omanis developed Zanzibar as the main export market.

The relative importance of the different sectors of the Kenya coast can be seen in the following trade figures for the 1890s:

Fig. 5.1 *Exports from the Kenya coast, 1891—1898*

	Average annual duties	Estimated average exports
Mombasa	$21 560	£688 000
Takaungu	3 450	110 000
Mtsanganyiko	6 240	199 000
Malindi	5 580	178 000
Mambrui	2 840	90 700
Vanga and Wassin	2 070	66 000
Comparable figures not available for Lamu		

Source: Hardinge, 'Report', 1898.

Takaungu had been founded by Mombasa in the 1830s as a small plantation settlement, but it developed into a major trading centre following the fall of Mombasa to the Omanis and the exile of some of Mombasa's deposed Mazrui rulers to Takaungu in 1837. Mijikenda trade followed the Mazrui north and Takaungu's outlying trading settlements at Mtsanganyiko and Konjora soon were exporting twice as much grain as Takaungu itself, while the three together easily outpaced Mombasa in grain exports. Malindi and Mambrui, on the other hand, were successfully developed as plantation settlements following their resettlement from Mombasa in 1865, and conducted very little trade with the neighbouring Oromo or Giriama. Vanga and Wassin continued to provide an outlet for the neighbouring Digo and Segeju, while Lamu continued to exploit its own mainland farms and conduct some trade with Pokomo, Oromo, and others.

Mijikenda trade

The increased demand for goods at the coast was rapidly felt in the interior. Mijikenda had already expanded their local trade with Swahili, Waata, and Oromo to forge the first long distance trade routes to Kitui by the beginning of the 19th century, but the majority of their trade continued to be conducted at border markets and with the Swahili of the coastal towns. The Digo were among the earliest market traders. Digo had already moved out of their main *kaya* at Kwale to establish several small market sub-*kayas* along the coast south of Mombasa by 1700. Each sub-*kaya* had its own daily market for subsistence trade and four-day market for market trade with Swahili and other Mijikenda. Digo exchanged sorghum, sesame, copal, and coconuts for fish, cloth, beads, and wire with Swahili, and palm wine for grain with other Mijikenda. The main Mijikenda market throughout the 18th century was the Digo market at Mtawe, on the southern shore of Kilindini Harbour from Mombasa. It was noted as a major source of maize and sesame and continued to operate throughout the 19th century. Digo were also travelling to Bondei and Shambaa to acquire tobacco for trade to the Giriama by the early 19th century, and Vumba–Digo caravans began to pioneer long-distance trade routes from Vanga to Chaga, Taveta, Samburu, and Lake Victoria in the 1830s and 1840s. The Digo did not remain the major traders for long, however, as the above figures for Vanga reveal. Digo had pioneered Mijikenda trade, but the initiative soon passed to the Digo's northern neighbours – the Rabai, Duruma, and Giriama.

The Rabai market at Jomvu had come to rival Mtawe as the most important market around Mombasa by 1800. Jomvu was easily accessible from Mombasa along the local creeks and the Rabai enjoyed close relations with the Jomvu Swahili. Rabai were also closer to Giriama and had begun planting coconut palms late in the 18th century. They were thus able to overtake the Digo as the main suppliers of palm wine to the Giriama and other

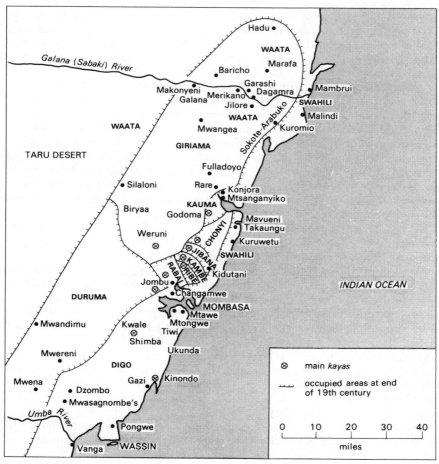

Map 5.2 *Mijikenda in the 19th century*

northern Mijikenda. When the Giriama initiated the caravan trade to Kamba, the Rabai were thus well established to serve as intermediaries between the Giriama and Swahili. And when the Kamba themselves later travelled to the coast, they too sold their ivory at Jomvu. The Rabai were remarkably successful in retaining their trade monopoly with Mombasa; only the well known Kamba trader Kivui was known to be able to bypass Jomvu and trade directly with the Swahili in Mombasa. The Duruma operated a similar market at Changamwe, but it was not as well placed as Jomvu. Duruma never succeeded in capturing the valuable caravan trade from Kamba, though they did act as intermediaries for much of the trade to Taita and Chaga.

Both these markets started to decline by the 1840s as the new Omani rulers of Mombasa allowed their trade partnerships with the Mijikenda to lapse, and the Giriama shifted their trade to Mtsanganyiko and Konjora. Giriama had been the primary suppliers of ivory throughout the 17th and 18th centuries. Giriama acquired ivory locally through hunting, as gifts from Waata partners, and through trade with Oromo. As demand for ivory increased and local supplies ran short towards the end of the 18th century, Giriama pioneered the first caravan routes across Taru and up the Galana and Athi rivers to Taita, Taveta, Chaga, and Kitui. Giriama dominated the caravan trade to the highlands from the 1800s through the 1830s, when Kamba caravans began to supplant them.

The main trade to Kitui was conducted by small groups of independent traders. A party was formed when a knowledgeable traveller announced he was planning a trip to Kitui. Others then gathered their trade goods of cloth, beads, and wire and joined him. The trading party remained together only for the arduous journey across Taru and up the Athi River to Kitui. Once in Kitui the individual members of the party each sought out their own Kamba trading partners, usually blood-brothers, to arrange for the exchange of their trade goods. The party spent several months in Kitui, while their Kamba partners sought out other Kamba with ivory to trade, before they reformed for the return journey to the coast.

The institution of blood-brotherhood was crucial to the whole enterprise. As strangers in Kitui, Giriama had no social or jural standing. No one was responsible for their behaviour or their protection. Nor did they have the social contacts necessary to attract the ivory they needed from the numerous hunters and small traders throughout Kitui who collected it in their individual homesteads. By making blood-brotherhood with prominent Kamba, they entered into kinship relations with specific Kamba groups. These groups were then responsible for their behaviour and protection, and ivory and livestock flowed along its social networks in exchange for the trade goods the Giriama had brought with them. Blood-brotherhood relations endured over successive trading seasons and expanded through time to incorporate whole Kamba and Giriama lineages. Thus successive generations of Giriama traders sought out their fathers' partners, while Kamba journeying to the coast from the 1820s sought out their Giriama partners in turn. By the 1840s Kamba caravans to the coast exceeded those of the Giriama, but Giriama continued to journey to Kamba for ivory and livestock for the rest of the century, and they frequently acted as brokers for their Kamba brothers at the coast.

The second main area of Giriama trade expansion was into Biryaa,

Godoma, and Galana, north of the Mijikenda *kayas*. Oromo and Waata hunters near the *kaya* had long been a major source of ivory for Giriama. With declining local supplies in the early 19th century, however, Giriama were forced to move away from the *kaya* to exploit more distant supplies. Krapf noted a number of prosperous villages in Biryaa in the 1840s. Their inhabitants maintained close relations with Oromo and conducted an annual market at Likoni where they acted as brokers between Oromo, Kamba, and Swahili from Takaungu. They also traded directly with Oromo and Waata as far north as Galana. Trade with the Waata comprised a continuous cycle of gift exchange which had linked Giriama and Waata from the earliest days of Giriama settlement. Waata lived in small groups which followed the elephant herds throughout the coastal area. When a group killed an elephant, they lived off the meat while giving the ivory to a Giriama friend. The Giriama would later reciprocate with gifts of grain, palm wine, livestock, or trade goods. Relations with the Oromo were not so friendly, however, and formal pacts were made annually at Likoni to ensure peace for the duration of the trading season.

Giriama also continued to exchange a wide variety of local products with Swahili, primarily the Mazrui at Takaungu. They collected copal, orchilla, and rubber for sale and disposed of their normal surplus of foodstuffs. The trade in foodstuffs effectively insured Giriama against crop failures as they sold grain at Takaungu in good years and were able to buy it there in bad ones. Giriama were even able to obtain grain during the particularly bad famines which periodically afflicted the coast by borrowing it from the Mazrui, leaving family members as mortgage pawns against future repayment. They then repaid their loans at the next good harvest and reclaimed their pawns. Trade thus supplied the Giriama not only with trade wealth, but also with security against famine.

Giriama conducted most of their trade with Takaungu's two satellite markets at the head of the Kilifi Bay, Mtsanganyiko and Konjora, where two other Mijikenda peoples, the Kauma and Jibana were the main traders. Kauma and Jibana both lived in the environs of Takaungu and probably were responsible for setting up the markets outside Takaungu which contributed so much to its success. Unlike the Giriama, however, the Kauma and Jibana traders found little tolerance in their *kayas* for their activities, and most were forced to move to Mtsanganyiko or Konjora, where they adopted a Swahili life style and converted to Islam.

Kamba and Kikuyu trade

Kamba had begun accompanying their Giriama friends to the coast by the 1820s and soon developed their own flourishing trade terminating at Giriama border markets or at the Rabai market at Jomvu. Such trade was the logical development of previous Kamba trade practices, as detailed by Kennel Jackson Jr. and Robert Cummings. Kamba had spread over the whole of the fertile Mbooni uplands and were begining to move on to the drier lowlands and across the Athi River to Kitui by the early 18th century. These areas were less fertile than Mbooni, and Kamba migrants were forced to adopt more dispersed settlement patterns and more differentiated means of food production to survive. Hunting and pastoralism were pursued along the frontier while various forms of agriculture were practised in the more settled areas. Local trade soon developed as people sought to exploit the varied ecology and different patterns of food production to obtain a wider variety of goods than they could produce themselves. Such trade, known as *kuthuua* ('searching for food'), was commonly conducted by individual family groups exchanging foodstuffs with one another. *Kuthuua* traders were soon wandering the length and breadth of Kitui and some travelled as far as Kikuyu and Embu to exchange Kamba arrows, poison, hides, and craft products for cattle and foodstuffs. Such trade was limited to the small quantities individuals could carry and exchange, however, and extended *kuthuua* trade became increasingly risky as small groups could not provide the necessary security to travel long distances with valuable goods. Elders, warriors, and hunters of local *utui* then began to band together to mount larger, better protected trading parties modelled on the *mwethya* collective working parties. Such parties were able to trade throughout Kikuyu, Embu, Mbeere, and Tharaka as well as to neighbouring Maasai and to expand the volume and range of goods traded to include iron and iron ware, bows and arrows, copper ornaments, poison, and divination apparatus for livestock, foodstuffs and specialized medicines.

The Kitui Kamba had thus already developed an extensive regional trade system based on proliferating networks of descent, trade, and cattle herding partners radiating out from individual *utui* by the time the Giriama arrived in the late 18th century in search of ivory and livestock. Kamba rapidly established partnerships with the Giriama traders and used their trade networks to acquire the ivory and livestock the Giriama required. It was not long before Kamba were organizing their own caravans to the coast. The greater potential of the caravan trade led to the further development of Kamba trading organization. Successful traders were able to expand their networks of kin, in-laws, and neighbours to include other *utui* and trading allies in regional trading organizations capable of mounting caravans of several hundred men to the coast, effectively supplanting the smaller Giriama trading parties. Those trading entrepreneurs with their extensive followings dominated the caravan trade during the 1840s and 1850s, until they too were supplanted in the 1860s by still larger, better financed, and more heavily armed Swahili caravans from the coast. Kitui trading organizations then shrunk back to the scale of the *utui* as Kamba resumed their earlier regional trade patterns.

With the decline of the Kamba entrepreneurs the focus for interior trade shifted to the supply and provisioning of the Swahili caravans from the coast. Unlike previous caravans destined for Kitui, however, Swahili caravans travelled west of Ulu (Machakos) along the modern line of road and rail to Ngong and beyond. The Kitui Kamba were thus relegated to an economic backwater, while trade passed to the Ulu Kamba and Kikuyu. Ulu Kamba and Kikuyu had previously been at the end of the trading chain that stretched from the coast. The dominance of the big Swahili caravans gave them their first opportunity to deal directly with the coastal traders, but few were able to benefit from the new arrangements. Predatory caravan leaders and their Kamba and Kikuyu allies soon found it easier to plunder and steal the provisions and ivory they required than to expend valuable trade goods for them. Many of the early Imperial British East Africa Company caravans and later government punitive expeditions continued to seize goods in this way, and the coming of the Swahili and European caravans ultimately spelled doom to the entire eastern Kenyan trading system as economic initiative slowly passed from African to European hands. By 1910 a railway had replaced the caravan route, and the development of European farming in the central highlands was well under way.

Northern Kenya and the Benaadir

Similar developments were occurring elsewhere along the coast. Lamu replaced Pate as the most important trading centre on the northern Kenya

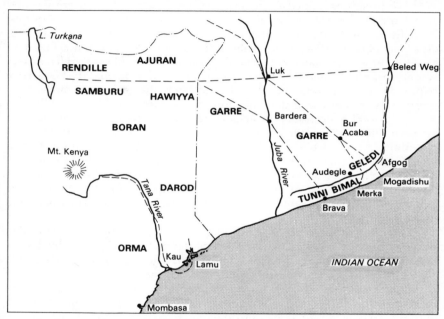

Map 5.3 *Trade routes in the 19th century Benaadir*

coast early in the 19th century. The bulk of Lamu's trade consisted of agricultural produce grown by its inhabitants on the mainland, but Lamu traders at Kau and Kipini travelled up the Tana River in 50-man canoes to trade with Pokomo and Oromo for ivory, hides, and livestock. Other traders journeyed inland from the mainland farms to obtain ivory from Aweera in the adjacent forests.

Further along the coast, the Benaadir towns of Brava, Merka, and Mogadishu were the entrepots for trade networks stretching into southern Ethiopia and extended in the 19th century into northern Kenya as far as Lake Turkana. Geledi, Bimal, and Tunni Somali inhabiting the cultivated Shebelle valley behind the coast produced foodstuffs for the coastal towns as well as acting as brokers for other Somali traders further inland. Caravan routes stretched inland to the market towns of Luk and Bardera on the Juba River and on into Southern Ethiopia and northern Kenya. Somali and Boran traders brought ivory, livestock, and occasional slaves to Luk and Bardera, from which Garre Somali conveyed them to Afgoy, Audegle, and other market towns on the Shebelle before their final trans-shipment to the coast. The Benaadir coast remained the main outlet for this vast inland territory until early in the 20th century when the northern Kenyan trade was redirected to Nairobi and Kismayu.

THE IMPACT OF TRADE ON THE PEOPLES OF EASTERN KENYA

We have already examined the connections between the quest for prestige and power and the control over valuable resources in the 18th and 19th centuries. Wealthy men were able to acquire many wives, to establish partnerships with other men, and to afford the fees for initiation into the most powerful secret societies through exchanges of valuables, usually cattle. These enabled men to acquire large followings who looked to them for leadership and the knowledge required to control supernatural forces and to adjudicate disputes fairly. Such prestige and power was usually the preserve of older men who controlled the restricted wealth necessary to achieve them. Bridewealth was exchanged between elders; ruling elders received the initiation fees paid by the fathers of non-initiates; and partnerships were executed between elders. Thus in Taita a young man's first wife came from the immediate neighbourhood, consolidating local social ties, but only elders could afford to acquire additional wives from distant areas to spread their prestige beyond the neighbourhood. And Samburu elders formally prohibited warriors from marrying at all.

Elders not only controlled the distribution of wealth, they also controlled the acquisition of new wealth. Land and production were allocated by lineage elders and younger men came into control only after their deaths. Mijikenda elders oversaw the acquisition and disposal of ivory and *kaya* elders maintained trade links with the Swahili through official *kaya* agents who conducted the border markets. Similarly, Samburu elders retained control over their whole family herds until they died.

These careful restrictions on wealth began to break down with the expansion of trade in the 19th century. Younger men were able to seize new opportunities to attain wealth and to extend their own social networks. Among the Giriama, for example, the developing caravan trade to Kitui was almost exclusively the preserve of young unmarried men who alone were able to make the arduous journey. A young man was able to establish his own homestead after only a few trips, his prestige enhanced by his worldly knowledge and his following established by the number of wives, age-mates, and Kamba partners who visited him at the coast or joined his homestead during one of the periodic famines in Kitui. These young men usually sought merely to acquire the prestige and power typical of elders, but in time their expansive use of wealth and personal networks so undercut the traditional system that it became radically transformed.

Mijikenda
One of the most dramatic effects of trade was the wholesale abandonment of *kaya* living by the Mijikenda in the second half of the 19th century. We have

already seen how the Digo established a number of small *kayas* near Mombasa and along the coast during the 17th and 18th centuries, but they were merely market villages. None possessed the supreme ritual importance of the main *kaya*; all Digo returned to the main *kaya* for major events; and most Digo continued to live within its boundaries. A few other small sub-*kayas* also appeared in Duruma, Rabai, and Giriama in the early 19th century, but none of these challenged the central importance of the main *kayas*. Almost all Mijikenda still lived within the closely knit societies of their main *kayas* in the 1830s, but in the decades that followed they were to abandon centralized living to expand over the coastal plateau in dispersed settlements. The main traders – the Digo, Rabai, Duruma, and Giriama – were the first to leave as individuals left to pursue trade opportunities elsewhere. The Digo and Duruma moved south down the coast, while the Rabai expanded around Mombasa and the Giriama moved north into Biryaa and Godoma. Other Mijikenda followed in the 1850s, 60s and 70s, but they remained clustered around their original *kayas* until the 1890s when some established detached colonies among the Giriama north of the Galana River.

Traders were thus the main people responsible for clearing and settling the new land west of the *kaya* ridge because they were the only ones who had the need and the resources to do so. Giriama traders, for example, were drawn into the interior regions to supplement the declining stocks of ivory in areas closer to the *kaya*. They had been trading with Waata and Oromo in these areas for years before deciding to settle there. Having established amicable relations with resident Oromo, they were able to purchase land rights from Oromo blood-brothers. The new lands were more heavily wooded than the fertile *kaya* ridge, however, and settlers needed to have enough labour to clear the land and sufficient food stocks to see them through the first harvest. These areas were also drier and could only support dispersed populations. Each settler thus established his own self-contained village, including his family and followers, to clear and farm those new areas. Baba Tora's village of Mikomani in Biryaa, visited by Krapf in 1845, comprised some twenty houses and its inhabitants included a Swahili trader. Baba and his sons farmed, herded cattle, and acquired ivory from neighbouring Oromo for sale in Mombasa. By 1865 Giriama had also settled in Godoma, where Wakefield visited Kazi ya Moyo, the home of Ya wa Medza. Ya spoke Oromo fluently, many Oromo and Waata stayed in his village, and he was known for leading trading parties into Galana to trade with Oromo. By the 1880s Giriama had reached the southern banks of the Galana River and they soon crossed the river to settle as far north as Hadu. The frontier was thus continually being pushed north as elephants were hunted out and succeeding generations of settlers leapfrogged over their elders to clear and settle new land. The genealogies of Giriama elders living in Galana today are replete with stories of their grandfathers' and fathers' successive moves through Biryaa and Godoma to the banks of the Galana River and beyond. Trade thus made it possible for young men to strike out into the drier interior and to establish themselves independently of the elders in the *kaya*.

The most prominent Giriama in the later 19th century was a trader named Ngonyo. Ngonyo's gradfather had come from Digo and settled in Kaya Giriama early in the 19th century. His father, Mwavuo, moved to Rare, near

Mtsanganyiko in about 1850 and developed a flourishing trade with Waata, Oromo, and Swahili in ivory, grain, copal, and rubber. As Mwavuo's wealth grew, he acquired a number of wives and others joined his settlement. Ngonyo followed his father in trade. As a young man he led trading parties to Kamba where he acquired ivory and livestock. He then settled near his father and acquired large tracts of land where he settled hundreds of people fleeing the disastrous famines of the 1880s and 1890s. Ngonyo's village grew to 1 200 people, including Mijikenda, Kamba, Oromo, Waata, and Swahili. Ngonyo assimilated them all to his following. He either married the women himself or arranged for their marriage to others, collecting the bridewealth himself, and he adopted the men as sons and paid their bridewealth for them, thus ensuring that their children would be incorporated within his lineage. He was a model father to his growing family, which grew so rapidly that Ngonyo and his descendants constituted their own sub-clan. Ngonyo's grandfather had been adopted by the Kiza clan when he first came to Giriama; Ngonyo and his descendants became the Hindzano sub-clan of the Kiza, and Ngonyo himself later became the head of the whole Kiza clan.

Ngonyo also forged networks of relations with others. He was blood-brother to several Swahili traders and leaders, as well as to numerous Oromo, Waata and Kamba, and he firmly allied himself with the British after 1895. Ngonyo later settled at Marafa, north of the Galana River, on land obtained from an Oromo blood-brother. As other Giriama moved to Galana, Ngonyo became the acknowledged leader of the area, and he was subsequently appointed a government headman by the British. Ngonyo thus progressed from being the grandson of an alien to being the most powerful man in all Giriama. By the time he moved to Marafa he had acquired all the usual prerequisites of power: he had a large lineage, he was a clan leader, and he was known for his knowledge of customary law and as a ritual expert, diviner, and healer. But he had achieved these attributes in dramatically new ways. Instead of patiently biding his time in the *kaya* raising his own family while apprenticing himself to the elders, Ngonyo had aggresively used his wealth to establish his following and reputation independently of *kaya* elders' control. Ngonyo did not just adopt the occasional stranger; he adopted hundreds until they outnumbered his own descendants, and he had over one hundred wives. While his goals were thus the usual ones of the elders, he so manipulated the means of achieving them that he undercut the power of the *kaya* itself. Ngonyo's personal power provided a viable alternative to declining *kaya* authority, but the alternative was an ephemeral one. There was no one to succeed him after his death and his followers dispersed.

A noted Digo leader was more successful than Ngonyo in this respect. Mwakikonga was the head of a small Digo sub-*kaya* near Vanga in the early 19th century. He grew wealthy trading with the Vumba and was subsequently able to consolidate a number of sub-*kayas* in the area into one large *kaya* at Dzombo. He was then able to monopolise trade with the Vumba and to accede to the symbiotic relationship that had long existed between the two. Digo–Vumba trade was expanded as the two sent joint caravans to Chaga and Taita, and Mwakikonga employed Vumba ritual experts in his court. He also came to dominate Vumba politics during a period when a series of succession disputes divided the Vumba and the contesting parties vied for his support.

Like Ngonyo, Mwakikonga employed his wealth gained in trade to develop personal alliances which enhanced his own following and power. Unlike Ngonyo, however, he also sought to establish a firm institutional base for his rule. Mwakikonga took the title of *kubo* for himself, and six *kubos* succeeded him over three generations. Their rule was so well established that numerous British observers mistakenly assumed that royal rule was the traditional form of Digo government. A contemporary of Mwakikonga, Mtondomera, established a smiliar *kubo*-ship south of the Umba River, and it also endured into the colonial period.

A few leaders even went beyond the bounds of Mijikenda politics to recruit followers among fugitive slaves from the coastal plantations. Mwakikonga's brother, Mwasagnombe, seceded from Dzombo and established his own *kaya* to the south. He adopted a number of fugitive slaves and acquired arms in trade with which he proceeded to raid coastal plantations to free more slaves. His following grew to some 3 000–4 000 people and he was often able to interdict the main Digo trade routes to Bondi and Shambaa. A small group of Giriama traders led by Abe Ngoa also incorporated large numbers of fugitive slaves into their community at Fulladoyo, near Takaungu, but such communities never became a significant force in Mijikenda politics, and predatory raiding and slaving patterns never became established.

While few men became as powerful as Ngonyo or Mwakikonga, the means they assumed became the norms of every Mijikenda household. Dispersed settlement made every Mijikenda homestead dependent on its own resources. A strong patriarch could build a large village; a weak man lost his own sons as they left to establish their own villages elsewhere. The wealth and personality of the village head became of primary importance in determining the collective wealth and security of the village.

Trade and dispersal radically transformed Mijikenda life as the corporate authority of the elders was replaced by the individual power of influential men. The *kayas* themselves had been central symbols in Mijikenda life. They were rooted in the Singwaya tradition and their palisades and surrounding forests had physically bound the people living within them in a single ethnic identity. Even today one does not ask a man who he is, but to which *kaya* he belongs. *Kayas* defined ethnicity; all people born within a *kaya* belonged to that *kaya*. Strangers who were adopted into a *kaya* underwent a ritual rebirth within it. The *kayas* had also defined culture. A man who belonged to Kaya Giriama spoke Giriama, was a member of the Giriama clan, was initiated into Giriama age-sets, and was subject to Giriama spirits. As the *kayas* became abandoned as residences, they ceased to play these central roles in Mijikenda societies. People were born outside the *kayas*, while large numbers of strangers were incorporated into the followings of prominent men. Traders made a virtue out of being multi-lingual and multi-cultural, utilising their associations with other peoples to enhance their own followings and exploiting cultural differences to change prevailing norms.

The clans had been the only recognized descent groups within the *kayas* and played an important part in *kaya* organization and ritual. They too became less important as people left the *kayas* and clans became dispersed, their members too scattered to continue to take corporate action together.

Sub-clans and lineages assumed the most important roles outside the *kayas*. Neither had been formally recognized in the *kaya*, but lineages frequently left the *kaya* and settled together, cleared their own land, and became corporate landholding groups. The more prominent of these lineages grew into sub-clans and these are the largest significant social groups today. Each sub-clan is linked to a specific *kaya* from which its ancestors emigrated. Today it is birth into a sub-clan that defines ethnicity, through the sub-clan's link to a given *kaya*, and sub-clans are the largest groups that commonly assemble together for funerals and other social and ritual occasions, while lineages continue to define the immediate social group concerned with village affairs.

The age-sets by which young men had progressed to become elders also ceased to exist. Dispersal made it increasingly difficult to assemble everyone in the *kaya* for the initiation ceremonies or to consult together, and the devolution of power from the *kambi* elders to individual village heads meant that becoming a *kambi* ceased to have the importance attached to it that it once had. The last Giriama *rika* was initiated about 1870, but its last sub-*rikas* were never properly advanced to *kambi* and no succeeding *rikas* were formed. The formally constituted authority of the *kaya* elders had been supplanted by the informal powers exercised by village leaders with their control over local resources and their detailed knowledge of local land holdings, lineage structure, and ritual.

Kamba

Similar processes were occurring in central Kenya in the later 19th century, particularly in Kitui, as Kamba trade developed from local 'searching for food' to regional trade conducted by *utui* associations of hunters and warriors and ultimately to the caravan trade to the coast conducted by regional associations under the aegis of influential entrepreneurs. Such men are remembered today as *andu anene* ('big men'). The notion of men whose influence and prestige extended far beyond their own *utui* was a category in Kitui thought long before the advent of trading entrepreneurs. These were usually wealthy pastoralists who were able to enlist the assistance of others through the judicious distribution of their cattle in bridewealth payments, gifts, and loans, through feasts and presentations given to their followings, through their knowledge of healing, divining, and tradition, and through their wisdom in adjudicating disputes. The influential trader acted in much the same way, as seen in the life of Kivui Mwenda.

Kivui emerged in the 1820s and 1830s as one of a number of prominent traders in Kitui. He was noted in his early career as a healer who conducted a flourishing trade in amulets and charms. He also began amassing cattle and wives at this time and generously distributed his growing wealth among his wives' relatives and to members of neighbouring *utui*. Thus when Kivui entered into the caravan trade, he already had a large network of partners and clients whom he could recruit as hunters, traders, and caravan porters. While planning a large expedition, Kivui would throw a huge feast and all those attending would be asked to join him. Upon their return, Kivui would distribute the profits among the participants and others who had cooperated in the expedition. Kivui retained little wealth for himself, but he did amass an enormous following of men who looked to him for leadership. Kivui's caravans included as many as three hundred members, and his networks of allies extended throughout Kitui, into Kamba and Embu, and down to Mombasa, where he numbered the Governor, Krapf, and Guillain among his friends. Kivui died on an expedition to Embu in 1851, and his personal network of followers died with him, but other alliances were constantly being mobilized by other traders remembered as *andu anene* in Kamba tradition.

Like Ngonyo, Kivui employed new means to achieve traditional ends. Such means became widely adopted in Kitui by the mid-19th century as all became drawn into the regional associations of *utui* dominated by the *andu anene*. In the early days of the caravan trade small groups of hunters had banded together to carry their own ivory to the coast. As caravans grew to include 200 to 300 porters in the 1840s and 1850s, there was ample opportunity for others to benefit. Young Kamba farmers frequently hired themselves out as porters during the dry season, while pastoral Kamba provided capital and trade goods for the caravans.

With the decline in the Kamba caravan trade from the 1860s, the alliances of the traders naturally withered away and regional trade became organized on an *utui* basis once more. Little had seemingly changed in Kitui society, but such a conclusion is not warranted. A series of prophetic movements in the latter half of the 19th century revealed that changes were occurring deep within Kitui society as people sought to respond to the decline in trade. Such means are common in the history of eastern Kenya. We have seen that traditions were thought to embody the essential and unchanging ways established by God and the earliest ancestors. In such a world view, where knowledge was seen as revealed truth, change could only come through further revelations carrying the authority of the ancestors. Thus times of rapid change were frequently accompanied by outbreaks of spirit possession, wherein spirit mediums and prophets were possessed by the ancestral spirits and spoke on their behalf. The latter half of the 19th century was such a period in Kamba, as the effects of the decline in trade were exacerbated by drought, famine, disease, and raids. The prophets provided a source of new authority which replaced that of the *andu anene*, and they attracted large followings.

Kikuyu

The advent of the caravan trade had less effect elsewhere in the central highlands and dramatic changes were only felt towards the end of the 19th century. The Kikuyu, Embu, Meru, and Ulu Kamba peoples had been involved in trade peripherally throughout the 19th century, as local and regional trade networks were expanded by Kamba expeditions seeking foodstuffs and ivory, but there is little evidence that these caused significant changes in the area. Swahili caravans were the first to intrude directly into the area when large caravans began to open up the route to the west of Ulu in the 1850s and 1860s. These caravans established a number of camping places en route where they sought to trade with local Kamba and Kikuyu for provisions and for ivory. Their needs were enormous. Lugard estimated that a single caravan of 400 men required 800 lbs (360 kg.) of grain a day while encamped in the area and another 19 000 lbs (8 800 kg.) before it could leave Dagoretti for Uganda. And caravans of 1 200–1 500 were not uncommon.

In spite of dramatic increases in agricultural production to meet these needs, prices doubled and tripled as people were unable to meet the demand.

Elders evicted landless clients and put the junior warriors to work to raise production amid increasing tension within Kikuyu society. Initially Swahili and European caravan leaders had depended on their Kikuyu blood-brothers to acquire their goods for them, but later caravans and their local allies took to raiding the countryside when not enough provisions were forthcoming. This led to a period of unprecedented violence in the highlands and the rise in the number of predatory trading chiefs who established their authority through force of arms obtained from Swahili and mercenary armies, easily raised at a time when drought, famine, disease, and raiding were creating widespread uncertainty and insecurity in the highlands. This led in turn to counter raids from the local populace. Such violence continued into the 1890s as I.B.E.A. caravans were forced to prey on the countryside because the company could no longer afford to pay for goods. It was only put down by the notorious punitive expeditions mounted by the colonial authorities using Maasai levies to pacify the area in the late 1890s, though the authorities perpetuated the exploitation of ordinary Kikuyu by self-serving men through the subsequent appointment of their own mercenaries as government chiefs.

The Benaadir
The Geledi and Bimal Somali acted as middlemen for most Benaadir trade. Geledi's economic foundations rested on control of agricultural trade along the riverine plain behind the Benaadir and control of the caravan terminus at Afgoy near Mogadishu. Bimal, on the other hand, controlled the agricultural plain and caravan trade at Audegle behind Merka. Geledi was the centre of a widespread set of clan alliances which included clients settled on Geledi territory, trade partners in Mogadishu, neighbours who paid tribute to Geledi, and distant allies against the Bimal. The Geledi themselves were an alliance of nine lineages dominated by the Gobron, a hereditary lineage of sultans respected for their supernatural powers. The Gobron used their control of trade and wealth to hold their network of allies together, much like the earlier Ajuran state, but the alliance started to collapse in the 1870s. Newly wealthy traders established their own exchange-based networks in competition with the Gobron, thus weakening their control. With a series of defeats by the Bimal in 1878–79, Geledi's trade declined, allies broke away, and tribute payments stopped in a downward spiral of disaggregation of their alliance networks. Bimal's networks correspondingly strengthened and the Bimal–Merka alliance came to dominate Benaadir trade for the remainder of the century.

DYNAMICS OF SOCIO-ECONOMIC CHANGE

We have thus seen a number of ways in which the economic changes of the 19th century fostered cultural change. The most important lesson to be drawn from these is the manner in which people responded to new opportunities within the framework of their existing cultural institutions. Economic change did not suddenly transform society. The impact was far more subtle as a few individuals initially used new opportunities to subvert the social control exercized by the elders through their control of wealth. These were employed by individuals to attain personal prestige and influence through amassing large followings of kin and allies who looked to them for political leadership, judicial decisions, and ritual control. Such followings had previously been composed of one's own descendants acquired by virtue of age, control over lineage wealth, and wisdom. In the expansionary world of the 19th century, however, wealth in trade was available to young men who sought it, and with it came increased contacts and relations with others that could be used in domestic politics. Such wealth was normally used to acquire wives locally, but it could also be used to acquire foreign wives, to attract destitute strangers to one's lineage, and to enlist foreign allies to one's cause. Notable examples can be seen among the Digo, Duruma, and Rabai. All of these peoples followed matrilineal rules of inheritance whereby a man's children inherited their lineage, land, and wealth from their mother's lineage, while his own descent group and wealth continued through his sister's children, making it difficult for a man to accrue a large following through his own efforts. One could acquire foreign wives who had no local matrilineage, however, and so ensure direct inheritance by one's own children. The prevalence of such foreign marriages during the 19th century, especially among the Duruma and Rabai, effectively altered the prevailing mode of inheritance to a bilateral one whereby both lines became equally important.

Men like Ngonyo and Kivui also acquired numerous foreign wives, exploited existing adoptive practices to acquire large numbers of fictional kin, and established extensive networks of trading partners. Today both these men are remembered for their number of wives, their large followings, and for their wisdom, but not for their wealth. The exploitation of such practices effectively subverted the institutionalized modes of descent for a more fluid pattern of alliances centred on big men, whose success rested on how well they mobilized potential allies – kin, in-laws, strangers – through the exchange of valuables.

Such men also seized on cultural alternatives to further their own causes. Aspiring Giriama traders had Oromo, Swahili, and Kamba blood-brothers and frequently spoke their languages, while the Swahili language spread along the trade routes as a *lingua franca*. They adopted new ritual practices to facilitate inter-cultural activities, or incorporated others into their own. New methods of healing and divining, of controlling rainfall, and of spirit possession spread throughout Kenya as individual cultural practices became amalgamated into regional patterns.

While the process of subversion of the old order was thus a slow and subtle one, the process of accommodation to the new one was often abruptly announced in prophetic movements characterized by widespread outbreaks of spirit possession. In the case of the Kamba this occurred with the decline in trade, while among the Giriama similar prophet movements occurred in the early 20th century as people sought to adjust their traditional norms – based on *kaya*, clan and *rika* – to the changed reality of their lives. The changes in the 19th century had been slow and imperceptible, but the disjunction between their results and peoples' perceptions as still articulated in tradition and values forced a fundamental revision of those values. Prophets, speaking for the ancestors, were able to articulate new cultural values in a way no mortal man could, and so fix them into the continual development of tradition.

The patterns of cultural change revealed in the 19th century had their parallels in earlier periods of Kenya's past which we have examined in the preceeding chapters. And since the changes in the 19th century are better documented and known than earlier ones, they provide us with valuable insights into earlier patterns. A major focus of this survey has been to examine the ongoing dynamic of tradition. Often taken to mean a static and 'primitive' past, we have seen instead that tradition has been a vital and dynamic force in Kenyan history. In Chapter 3 we examined the nature of origin traditions and how small clusters of lineages, often formed around a single man or prophet, initially came together, while in Chapter 4 we saw how these groups developed into defined peoples and cultures structured by descent, age, and symbols. In Chapter 5 we have just surveyed a period of extensive change in Kenya where alternative principles of alliance and regional patterns of action altered existing norms in the process of establishing new ones. The twin processes of aggregation and disaggregation thus have an old and established history in Kenya as peoples and cultures have constantly developed, adapted, and changed to meet changing circumstances.

At the same time as these changes were taking place in the interior of Kenya, however, new and ominous changes were taking place at the coast which heralded the decline of eastern Kenya's autonomy and its incorporation within a wider economic, political, and cultural context. This was the intrusion of western mercantile capitalism, which was slowly to subordinate Kenya's development to its own during the course of the 19th century.

REFERENCES AND SUGGESTIONS FOR FURTHER READING

We are only beginning to understand the economic structures of subsistence production. A significant survey of the factors governing subsistence herding and farming is William Allan, *The African Husbandman* (London, 1965), while a crucial foundation for the connection between economic and social structures is established by Claude Meillassoux in '"The Economy" in Agricultural Self-Sustaining Societies: A Preliminary Analysis', in D. Seddon (ed.), *Relations of Production*, pp. 127–157 (London, 1978) and 'On the Mode of Production of the Hunting Band' in P. Alexandre (ed.), *French Perspectives in African Studies*, pp. 187–203 (London, 1973). Equally valuable data for pastoral production is given in Gudrun Dahl and Anders Hjort, *Having Herds* (Stockholm, 1976). A valuable comparative survey of the impact of trade is Richard Gray and David Birmingham (eds.), *Pre-Colonial African Trade* (London, 1970), while comparative studies for East Africa include: Edward Alpers, *Ivory and Slaves in East Central Africa* (London, 1975); Stephen Feierman, *The Shambaa Kingdom* (Madison, Wisconsin, 1974); Isaria Kimambo, *A Political History of the Pare of Tanzania* (Nairobi, 1969); Aylward Shorter, *Chiefship in Western Tanzania* (Oxford, 1972); and Helge Kjekshus, *Ecology Control and Economic Development in East African History* (London, 1977).

I have again relied heavily on the work of others in bringing together the individual case studies discussed here. All are fully referenced in Chapters 3 and 4, but I must mention again Jackson and Cummings on the Kamba; Muriuki, Rogers, and Marris and Somerset on the Kikyuyu, Brantley and myself on the Mijikenda, and Cassanelli on the Benaadir Coast, and introduce R. F. Morton, 'Slaves, Fugitives, and Freedmen on the Kenya Coast, 1873–1907' (Ph.D. thesis, Syracruse University, 1976).

CULTURAL DEVELOPMENT AND ECONOMIC UNDERDEVELOPMENT

So far we have traced how peoples and cultures have developed, interacted and changed since earliest times to produce the present peoples and cultures of eastern and central Kenya. The focus has been on their history with little reference to the outside world. But Kenya's independence was quickly terminated at the end of the 19th century when it became incorporated within the expanding British Empire. Some say the event was precipitous, almost accidental, as the European powers were drawn into a competitive scramble for African colonies. In this view, Kenya was acquired merely to provide access to Uganda. This interpretation takes account of the diplomatic context, but it ignores the fact that Kenyans had been acting within a wider economic context for some time. The time has now come to examine the development of Kenya within that wider context.

Kenyans had participated in Indian Ocean trade for at least two thousand years before the imposition of colonial rule. We have already seen how this led to the development of a syncretic Afro-Asian Swahili culture along the coast, and how peoples in the interior were affected by their participation in the market economy. Compared with other African peoples, however, Kenyans were able to trade without the destructive violence and slaving which frequently accompanied it elsewhere. But even peaceful market trade was not always beneficial to Kenyans. While many were able to obtain cloth, iron, brass, and pottery from Asia and foodstuffs from elsewhere along the coast, Kenyans found themselves adversely affected by market forces that lay beyond their control. The rise and fall of coastal towns, for example, was often related to shifts in supply and demand for certain goods. Kilwa's initial development in the 12th century was founded on the gold trade from Zimbabwe, but it declined as trade dropped in the late 14th century and only recovered with the slave trade in the 18th century. Reliance on trade also produced externally-oriented economies lacking an independent economic base. Africans exported raw materials (ivory, rubber, copal, oils) and imported consumer goods (pottery, cloth, beads) that absorbed potential capital for development. African products were frequently undercut by cheaper imports at the same time. The weaving industries of Kilwa, Lamu, and the Benaadir were severely curtailed by Indian cloth imports, and Kamba iron work was adversely affected by imports. The overall effect was to subordinate the development of African economies to the development of those overseas, even in pre-capitalist times. The unequal exchange of valuable, income producing industrial raw materials for low value manufactured consumer goods effectively transferred economic surpluses from African raw material producers to Asian craft manufacturers and traders, and hence, promoted their further development while African development was stilted and, in many cases, reversed. Emerging mercantile economies were thus able to develop by extracting surplus from others, causing their underdevelopment.

Abdul Sheriff has traced the process of underdevelopment for the East African coast from early in the 1st millenium. During most of this time, however, the volume of trade with Asia was not sufficient to cause significant underdevelopment in East Africa, but by the mid-19th century the increased volume of trade with Europe significantly altered the balance. Sheriff points out, for example, that in 1850 the present less developed countries comprised 75 per cent of world population and produced 65 per cent of world income, while today they produce only 22 per cent. Thus, while the foundations of East Africa's subordination to mercantile capitalism were laid by early Indian Ocean trade, the development of underdevelopment occurred largely during the 19th century as a result of increasing demands for industrial raw materials, capital, and markets by Europe and America.

We have already noted the dramatic increase in market trade during the 19th century, but we must explore the nature of the increase more fully here. The export slave trade had been developed on a commercial scale during the 18th century to supply the French sugar plantation colonies of Bourbon (Reunion) and Ile de France (Mauritius) in the Indian Ocean. Slaves were captured from the regions around Lake Malawi, marched overland to Kilwa, and exported. The acquisition and sale of slaves continued to be centred on Kilwa throughout the 19th century, but the export trade gave way to domestic trade following British attempts to abolish the trade. The slave trade to Mauritius and Reunion was terminated in the aftermath of the British occupation of the islands in 1810, while a series of treaties with Zanzibar increasingly restricted the developing trade to Arabia and India. Trade with India and Christian countries was proscribed by treaty in 1822; trade outside the Sultan of Zanzibar's dominions was made illegal in 1847; trade by sea was proscribed in 1873; and that by land abolished in 1876.

None of these measures was effective in curtailing the overall volume of trade; they merely diverted slaves from the export trade into domestic use. The supply of slaves from northern Mozambique and Malawi remained fairly constant in spite of falling export demand because the political economy of the area had become firmly based on slave raiding. As the supply remained constant while demand dropped, prices fell, and it became more economic to employ slaves as domestic labour and to export the products of their labour. Slaves were thus used to establish clove plantations on Zanzibar and copra and grain plantations along the coast. On the Kenyan coast, coconut plantations were developed north of Mombasa, while grain plantations were established around Takaungu and Malindi. Plantation production centred on these areas accounted for 75 per cent of total grain exports by the end of the century (see Fig. 5.1). Agricultural production employing slave labour was thus developed on a commercial scale for the first time on the Kenyan coast.

Ivory had been exported in limited quantities to India and China at least from the 5th century, but demand for ivory rapidly increased in the early 1800s in the wake of excessive Portuguese taxation of the Mozambique trade and increasing demand from India, Europe and America. Demand constantly exceeded supply during the century, with the result that prices rose from $27

Photo 6.1 *Freed slaves, Magarini plantation*

per *frasila* early in the century to $140 per *frasila* at the close, a fivefold increase. The steady expansion of both demand and price made it highly profitable to open up new sources of supply in central Tanzania, along the Pangani valley, and in central Kenya.

Other industrial raw materials were also in high demand, including copal, hides, orchilla, and rubber. By mid-century East Africa's market had shifted from its traditional Indian Ocean trading partners to Europe. India continued to receive some 40 per cent of East African exports, but at least half of these were destined for re-export to England, while America accounted for 25 per cent of exports, Germany 10 per cent, France 12 per cent, Britain 1 per cent, and West Africa 6 per cent. (The West African market was for cowries exported from East Africa by European traders to finance their trade in West Africa.) Broken down by individual item, direct exports to the west constituted 43 per cent of ivory sold abroad, 96 per cent of oil and seeds, 57 per cent of copal, 84 per cent of orchilla, 92 per cent of hides, and 89 per cent of beeswax. Indian re-exports pushed the figures even higher. East Africa was thus firmly incorporated within the developing world mercantile economy centred on Europe and America. While trade generated a surplus within East Africa, as we have seen, a far greater surplus was accumulated by the European and American traders, which they used in their own capitalist development. Overall, then, East Africans suffered an unequal exchange in trade as surplus was transferred to the developing industrial world, subordinating the East African economy to the mercantile economy and actively preventing its development.

THE RISE OF THE ZANZIBAR COMMERCIAL EMPIRE

The increasing subordination of the East African economy to the developing world economy was expressed locally in the political and economic subordination of the East African coast to the Zanzibari commercial empire established early in the 19th century by the Busaidi rulers of Oman. The analysis is again provided by Abdul Sheriff. Oman became an expansionary maritime power following the recapture of Muscat from Portugal in 1650, challenging Portugal's tenuous control of Indian Ocean trade. By the end of the century the Omanis had allied with Swahili in Pate and Mombasa to overthrow the remnants of Portuguese control of the coast north of Mozambique. Omani trade with East Africa increased during the 18th century. Grain and mangrove poles were carried to the Arabian Gulf, ivory to India, and slaves to Oman. By 1800 the Omanis had captured Kilwa and gained control of the slave trade to the French islands. It was in the 19th century, however, that East African trade increased the most, with the expansion of the ivory trade and the development of commercial plantation crops. During the course of the century, the Busaidi developed Zanzibar as their main trading centre in East Africa and slowly extended their political control along the coast, defeating Kilwa about 1800, Pemba, Lamu, and Pate in the 1820s, and Mombasa in 1837. But Busaidi political control was tenuous at best. Governors were appointed by the Sultan in many of the coastal towns, but they rarely exerted more than nominal control over their territories, rebellions were frequent, and Zanzibar had insufficient troops to maintain continual control. In the 1870s, for example, Zanzibar had only 220 troops in Mombasa, 80 in Pate, 30–40 each in Lamu and Malindi, and no more than 10 elsewhere.

Omani influence was primarily economic, not political. Zanzibar itself was predominantly a commercial enterprise and Sultan Said, the Busaidi ruler for the first half of the 19th century, a merchant prince. Said expropriated large areas of land for his own personal clove plantations, and he produced one-third of all clove exports. He was a major trader in Zanzibar and sponsored trading expeditions to the mainland. The collection of customs was a commercial operation which Said leased to the highest bidder. The army and navy were his personal employees and frequently used in commercial operations. So long as his commercial dominance was assumed, he was content to leave the exercise of political power to others. Said never took the Muslim political-religious title of Iman. He occasionally recruited mercenary forces to put down potential commercial competitors, such as Mombasa in the 1820s and 30s and Pate throughout the century, but he more commonly employed marriage alliances with local authorities and economic incentives to maintain control. Differential tariffs, ranging from $8 per *frasila* of ivory along the Mrima coast opposite Zanzibar to $2 at Lamu and the Benaadir, encouraged the more distant towns to conduct their export trade via Zanzibar. European trading houses all maintained agents on Zanzibar and conducted most of their trade there. At the same time Indian financiers established Zanzibar as the financial centre of East Africa. Indians financed the expansion of plantations and the caravan trade and farmed the customs at Zanzibar. The Busaidi themselves conducted much of the commercial expansion, including the development of clove plantations on Zanzibar and Pemba, grain plantations around Malindi, and caravans into the interior.

The centralization of existing trade on Zanzibar was accompanied by the progressive rationalization of local and regional trading patterns into an integrated trading system. Trade in eastern and central Kenya had been organized sectionally. Kamba collected ivory and sold it to Giriama who then conveyed it to the coast and sold it to Swahili at Mombasa or Takaungu, where it was sold directly to the ocean-going traders from India and Arabia. Each coastal town had its own networks stretching into the interior, along the coast, and across the Indian Ocean. Omani traders, by contrast, organized large caravans from Mombasa which acquired ivory directly from the interior and brought it back to the coast for sale in Zanzibar. Other Omani developed plantations to produce export crops directly for market. These changes profoundly altered trading patterns in Kenya.

Mombasa is a prime example. As a major independent trading centre throughout the 18th century, Mombasa had strong links with the Mijikenda in its hinterland and was the main entrepot for smaller towns along the coast, as we have seen. Mombasa's influence was eroded from early in the 19th century, with the Busaidi conquest of Pemba, raids on Pate, and alliance with Lamu. Mombasa itself was successful in resisting Busaidi attacks, however, until a succession dispute among the ruling Mazrui allowed the Busaidi to intercede and, eventually, to depose the Mazrui in 1837. Mombasa slowly became incorporated as a dependent satellite in the Zanzibari commercial empire in the years which followed. Indian financiers and Omani traders took over Mombasa's development from local Swahili traders. Caravans from Mombasa traded directly with Chaga, Kamba, and as far as Nyanza and Samburu. Initially these were small caravans of independent Swahili traders who shared the trade with Giriama and Kamba caravans, but by the 1860s they were major operations, organized by the governor and other Arab traders, financed by Indians, and employing hundreds of Swahili, Mijikenda, and Kamba as porters.

Mombasa's own agricultural resources were also developed as grain and coconut plantations were established along the northern coast. There was almost no plantation slavery around Mombasa prior to 1830, but in the succeeding decades slaves from Kilwa became increasingly available in the aftermath of British anti-slave trade activity. Slaves were soon employed in the production of grain crops around Takaungu and Malindi and in establishing coconut plantations around Mombasa. The economics of slavery attracted immigrant Arab and Indian investment, as a plantation owner recovered his investment in a slave from a single year's production. Mombasa also became a major trans-shipment port for slaves being shipped further north. An estimated 13 000 slaves moved through Mombasa in 1874, with 500 sold locally and the rest trans-shipped to Takaungu, Malindi, Lamu, and the Benaadir.

Mombasa thus became transformed under Busaidi rule from an independent city of small Swahili traders closely linked with their neighbours in a sectional trading system to a dependent link in an integrated Zanzibari trading system. Immigrant Indian financiers and Arab traders and plantation owners replaced Swahili in trade; direct shipment of ivory from the interior by large caravans supplanted Giriama and Kamba caravans and the Rabai market at Jomvu; and slave production of export crops came to exceed the grain and copra raised by Mijikenda. The effects of these changes were felt almost immediately by the inhabitants of the coast. Mijikenda sensed the new priorities of the Busaidi in the aftermath of the famine of 1836. Mijikenda had been forced to pawn relatives to Swahili traders to obtain grain on credit during the famine. When the Mijikenda went to pay their debts and to reclaim their pawns after the Busaidi takeover in 1837, they discovered to their dismay that the new Busaidi governor had sold many of them as slaves to Arabia in violation of pre-existing practice. The Busaidi also stopped annual tribute payments to the Mijikenda, and allowed the socio-economic links between individual Swahili and Mijikenda peoples to lapse. The Mijikenda were quick to react, shifting their ivory and grain trade to Takaungu where many of their old allies, the Mazrui, had taken refuge. Takaungu and its outlying trading settlements of Mtsanganyiko and Konjora rapidly became the main Mijikenda trading centres for the coast, and Mijikenda and Mazrui remained closely allied until the colonial period. Coastal Swahili no doubt also felt the changes as they became relegated to inferior socio-economic positions. Guillain noted in the 1840s that Arabs and Indians dominated trade, while Swahili were petty traders and hawkers, farmers, fishermen, and mangrove cutters.

While Mombasa tacitly accepted Busaidi control and continued as an important economic centre, the towns of the Lamu archipelago contested Busaidi claims throughout the century. During the 18th century Pate had been the dominant town in the islands, allied with Mombasa, and a wealthy trading centre of its own. But in 1812 a combined Pate–Mombasa army was defeated by Lamu forces at Shela, and the following year Lamu forged an alliance with the Busaidi to ward off possible counterattacks. For the next fifty years the Busaidi–Lamu alliance faced constant opposition from the Nabahani rulers of Pate and their Siyu and Oromo allies in a series of disputes that were reflected in factional struggles within the towns themselves. The Nabahani were eventually forced to flee to Kau and Kipini on the mainland, but were again defeated by the Busaidi and fled inland to Witu in 1862. There they were able to establish a secure existence, however, by giving refuge to slaves fleeing Lamu's mainland plantations and Oromo seeking safety from increasing Somali attacks, by establishing alliances with a number of other escaped slaves and Aweera villages in the forest, and, later in the century, by appealing to Germany to declare the area a protectorate. The Pate ceased to be a commercial force, however, while Lamu developed into a major sesame producer and trader of hides.

The old towns of Malindi and Mambrui had been evacuated in the 1590s when their inhabitants, in alliance with the Segeju and Portuguese, defeated Mombasa and occupied it. They remained unoccupied until the 1850s when Sultan Majid of Zanzibar initiated their resettlement. Malindi was rapidly developed as a major grain and sesame producer. Plantations stretched 10–15 miles inland and were worked by 4 000–5 000 slaves. The prominent landowners were all immigrant Arabs because they were the only ones to whom Majid would loan money to buy land from the Oromo and slaves to work it. Mambrui was settled slightly later as a trading outpost with the Oromo, but little trade was generated and it soon developed along parallel lines with Malindi. Both were thus essentially new towns, established fully on the mid-19th century model of plantation agriculture by immigrant Arabs and slaves. They conducted little trade with the Oromo or Mijikenda and were

Photo 6.2 *Fifteenth-century pillar tomb and modern mosque, Malindi*

developed to produce foodstuffs for Zanzibar and for export.

Takaungu was also settled as a plantation colony, but it developed along different lines from Malindi and Mambrui. Soon after its settlement in the early 1830s it was occupied as a refuge by the ex-Mazrui rulers of Mombasa. (Other Mazrui occupied Gazi south of Mombasa.) Under the Mazrui,

Takaungu soon became a flourishing centre of Swahili-Mijikenda trade, as we have seen. Kauma and Jibana traders established market villages up Kilifi Creek at Mtsanganyiko and Konjora where Giriama traded grain, rubber, copal, and ivory. The Mazrui retained particularly close relations with the Giriama, and especially with Mwavuo and his son Ngonyo, the noted Giriama traders at Rare. Many of the Mazrui leaders were initiated Giriama elders, and Ngonyo was blood-brother with many of them. Takaungu also conducted an extensive trade with the Oromo, whose friendship they secured through periodic payments of tribute. Krapf described vividly the visit of one Oromo leader in 1845:

> When the Sultan of the Gallas (as he is called by the Swahilis) makes his appearance at Takaongo every second or third year, he is accompanied by several hundreds of his savage followers, and he must be received in state and pomp by the Governor of Takaongo, who meets him at the outskirts of the village under a salute of a large volume of firing from the Swahili musketry. When this has been accomplished, the Galla Majesty is placed on a new arm chair and carried by free-born Swahilis in procession through the streets, and at last deposited at an open and large place, where the Governor sits at his side and delivers the presents which consist of the chair (which the Sultan already occupies), of a slave, of a hundred clothes, or a quantity of Tobacco (which the Galla love more than silver and gold, and for which they will readily deliver up their cattle, their copal and their ivory) and some other petty articles. After the Sultan has received these presents, he returns them by giving the Governor a number of cattle and elephants'-teeth. After these transactions a cow is slaughtered by the Muhammedans, and a few bloody parts of the heart are eaten by the Swahilis and the Galla, who both swear in this manner and renew friendship and fidelity to each other. When all these ceremonies have been duely performed, the Galla soldiery is regalled with Tobacco, rice and other eatables. His sable Majesty remains then some ten or twenty days at Takaongo and its vicinity, during which time the Galla sell their goods and buy their commodities from the Swahilis.

J. L. Krapf, 'A Forty Miles Journey to
Takaongo North East of the Island
of Mombasa' (1845).

Takaungu also imported large numbers of slaves, but unlike Lamu and Malindi, these were largely assimilated by the Mazrui to increase their own numbers. Slaves were given land for their own use and allowed to live as free men.

ECONOMICS OF UNDERDEVELOPMENT

Each of the towns of the coast thus became economically subordinated to Zanzibar through direct Omani economic activity, differential tariffs, finance, or the concentration of European demand at Zanzibar. Earlier trade had been based on the interdependence of separate groups within regional networks.

Such trade continued throughout the 19th century, as the example of Mtsanganyiko shows, but most of the expansion of trade occurred in the new Arab caravan and plantation sectors. Thus the initial stage of underdevelopment occurred in the unequal exchange between Zanzibar traders and financiers, on the one hand, and slaves or peoples of the interior, on the other.

The size of the surplus extracted by the traders is unknown, but it must have been over 50 per cent of the $2 million exported annually in the 1850s. We have seen that plantation slaves paid for themselves within a year, while Stanley estimated that profits in the caravan trade were 100–200 per cent after paying 50–70 per cent on finance. Each $3 500 worth of goods purchased in the interior sold for $10 000–14 000 in Zanzibar. Said's personal income from his clove plantations, local taxes, and rent from the customs farm exceeded $400 000 annually, and he owned an estimated 5 000 acres of cloves and 12 000 slaves. His fleet consisted of 16 large commercial and naval vessels of up to 74 guns costing up to $100 000 each and 90 smaller ships of 4–18 guns, and he maintained a regular army of 400 men. His household included 72 wives. Jairam Sewji, the customs master, was probably even wealthier. While Jairam probably made little on the customs itself, he was able to use his position to dominate the export trade. For some time he was a partner of the main American agent and consul, Richard Waters. The figure appears unbelievable, but a French official reported Jairam had $30 million in a Bombay bank, the product of his East African activities.

A large part of the surplus was spent on importing luxury consumer goods – crystal, china, spirits, silk – and arms, while little was invested in industrialization. Said did experiment with ship-building and oil and sugar processing at different times, but the imported machinery quickly broke down and the experiments were abandoned. The balance of the sulplus was exported to India. Even if the figures for Jairam Sewji's bank account are wildly exaggerated, this must have been a considerable amount. Most of the Indians in East Africa represented Indian firms and expatriated their profits for investment there.

The surplus extracted at Zanzibar probably represented only a fraction of the surplus appropriated by the European and American traders, however. They invested minimally in East Africa, maintaining a single agent there at most, and yet must have realized considerable profits which they were able to invest in their own capitalist development. Their imports also displaced local industries. American cloth (called *merikani*) rapidly displaced Indian cottons from the market and further undercut the local industries in Kilwa, Lamu, and the Benaadir. Iron imports soon replaced local pig iron and iron products. Europe also monopolized industrial technology. Said's ships required western captains to sail to Europe and his artillery was useless without French or Turkish gunners. No primary processing industries were started in East Africa. The main imports of beads, cloth, and guns were useless for capitalist development.

With the beginning of colonial rule and the completion of the Uganda Railway to Kisimu in 1901 the focus for underdevelopment shifted to the central highlands where the British had decided on a policy of white settlement to make the railway pay. Excellent studies by E. A. Brett and Colin Leys take up that aspect of the story, but both ignore the pre-colonial roots of Kenya's underdevelopment. The 19th century was only the beginning of that process, but it did anticipate the imposition of colonial rule and underdevelopment that were to follow. Perhaps the ultimate irony was that leading economic sectors in the 18th and 19th century were ignored in colonial development plans as primitive economic backwaters.

Photo 6.3 *Advertisement for Uganda Railway*

CULTURAL DEVELOPMENTS

The economic forces of the 19th century brought about considerable cultural changes in the Swahili towns of the coast, most notably in the influx of new Arab, Indian, slave, and interior populations. Indians seemingly had little impact on the Swahili. Most remained culturally exclusive and few shared the Swahili's Shafi Muslim faith. Arabs could relate more easily to the Afro-Asiatic culture. Some shared the Shafi creed, and many married into African society. Even Said's wives were mostly Africans and his children raised in the harem spoke Swahili. But many Arabs were disdainful of what they perceived as a debased Islamic society, and in spite of extensive local intermarriage, sought to preserve their own cultures. The Busaidi themselves were Ibadi Muslims and remained aloof from local culture. Nevertheless, the Arab influx in the 19th century was the greatest since the 16th century and had the effect of renewing the dialectic between African and Arab synthesized in Swahili culture. Other Africans, slaves from the Lake Malawi region and peoples from the interior, also intruded into Swahili society in large numbers, offering other influences. The total effect was probably the greatest period of interaction and change within Swahili culture since its origins along the Benaadir one thousand years previously.

The Lamu archipelago provides visual evidence of this in the contrast between 18th century Pate architecture and 19th century Lamu building. The styles in Pate are distinctive and indigenous, the product of the development of Swahili culture over the centuries, while the styles in Lamu are predominantly imported. But the change in Lamu was not only visual. As Abdul el Zein has shown in his penetrating study of cultural change in Lamu, profound changes occurred within the deepest structures of the Lamu cultural tradition. Prior to the 19th century Lamu society was divided into four categories of free-born and a fifth of slave. This stratification was based on the tradition of descent of the leading groups from the earliest settlers and the Prophet and was given substance by the rule restricting marriage to members of one's own group, similar rules restricting residence, the recording of precise genealogies in a central book (called the *silwa*), rituals celebrated differently by the various groups, and the structuring of different economic classes within the society. Following the alliance with the Busaidi and the disputes among the islands' towns, new people came into Lamu society and new factions arose which disrupted the social stratification prescribed by tradition. Each faction developed its own line of descent from the Prophet to substantiate its claims to superior status, while Busaidi newcomers insisted on marrying at the highest level. The result was a breakdown in the precise distinctions among the top three groups, amalgamating them into a single generalized class.

Late in the century the situation became even more confused for the status-conscious by the increasing numbers of Arab traders from the Hadhramaut, ex-slaves, and mainland peoples taking up residence within Lamu town, something which had previously been forbidden. Interclass relations with concubines and intermarriage increased to such a degree that the lines of descent became hopelessly confused, and the *silwa* was symbolically thrown into the sea. The ideology of descent was replaced by an egalitarian ethos of the equality of all believers articulated by Hadrami sharifs among the ex-slave and mainland communities. A new tradition emerged and became enshrined in the renowned Muslim college of Lamu. Hadrami sharifs and new African Muslims were responsible for breaking down the pre-existing patterns of stratification embedded in Swahili culture elsewhere along the Kenyan coast and the Benaadir and for introducing a revitalized Islam, including ecstatic possession cults, the veneration of saints, and the Qadiriya, Idrisiya, and Salihiya religious brotherhoods (*tariqas*). Shorn of its cultural specificity East African Islam became more attractive to other Africans and started to spread inland among the Mijikenda (mostly Digo) and Pokomo peoples for the first time.

Photo 6.4 *Rebmann preaching at the Rabai mission*

European culture also began to be felt during the 19th century, but its impact was minimal. Aside from the minor presence of a few British naval officers during the abortive British Establishment at Mombasa from 1824 to 1826, when the Navy came to the aid of the Mazrui in their fight against the Busaidi, the first prolonged European influence in eastern Kenya was that of the missionaries. The first mission in East Africa was established by Krapf and Rebmann for the Church Missionary Society at Rabai in 1846, followed by the United Methodist Free Churches' mission at Ribe in 1862. Neither enjoyed success among the Mijikenda, however, and both soon turned their main efforts to fugitive and recaptured slaves. By 1888 there were more than 1 400 fugitive slaves settled on the mission stations, and at Rabai a distinctive alien, literate, Swahili-speaking Christian community soon emerged along side the local Rabai community.

Changes along the coast thus mirrored those taking place within the interior at the same time, as peoples adapted to economic change within the frameworks of their own cultures and defined regional patterns of action.

CULTURAL DEVELOPMENT AND ECONOMIC UNDERDEVELOPMENT

What was significantly different on the coast was a new dimension of power, and the growing inequality of the groups and economic forces interacting. A wave of subordination was building up which would later crash over Kenya's peoples with the imposition of colonial rule in 1895. Regardless of the inequality, however, many of the same structures and processes would continue to influence Kenyans' perceptions throughout the colonial period, but that is another chapter in the story of Kenya's past.

REFERENCES AND SUGGESTIONS FOR FURTHER READING

The issue of underdevelopment in pre-colonial times is cogently argued by Abdul Sheriff in 'Trade and Underdevelopment: The Role of International Trade in the Economic History of the East African Coast Before the 16th Century', *Hadith*, 5 (1975), pp. 1–23 and 'The Rise of a Commercial Empire: An Aspect of the Economic History of Zanzibar, 1770–1873' (Ph.D.thesis, University of London, 1971), while the colonial period is covered in E. A. Brett, *Colonialism and Underdevelopment in East Africa* (London, 1973) and Colin Leys, *Underdevelopment in Kenya* (London, 1975). The best overview of coastal history is provided by the articles by Neville Chittick and F. J. Berg in *Zamani* (2nd edn). Detailed political history for the 19th century can be found in C. S. Nicholls, *The Swahili Coast* (London, 1971), while the best review of East African Islam in J. S. Trimmingham, *Islam in East Africa* (Oxford, 1964).

One must also take note of some of the more valuable contemporary accounts of the period. The British Establishment in Mombasa (1824–26) is recalled by T. Boteler, *Narrative of a Voyage of Discovery to Africa and Arabia* (London, 1835), W. F. W. Owen, *Narrative of Voyages to Explore the Shores of Africa, Arabia, and Madagascar* (London, 1833), and, most notably, J. B. Emery, 'A Journal of the British Establishment at Mombasa' located in the Public Record Office, London. The first missionaries were also travellers and detailed recorders of the local scene at mid-century. The most detailed accounts are those of J. L. Krapf and J. Rebmann in the Church Missionary Society archives, London, and of Charles New and Thomas Wakefield appearing regularly in the *United Methodist Free Churches' Magazine*. Krapf's memoirs, *Travels, Researches, and Missionary Labours during an Eighteen Years' Residence in Eastern Africa* (Boston, 1860; an abridged translation of the German *Reisen in Ostafrika*), contains a selection from his journals, as do those of Charles New, *Life, Wanderings and Labours in Eastern Africa* (London, 1873). Some extraordinarily observant travellers also visited Kenya in this period, including Richard Burton, *Zanzibar: City, Island and Coast* (London, 1872) and Charles Guillain, *Documents sur l'historie, le géographie et le commerce de l'Afrique Orientale* (Paris, n.d.). Material covering the British consulate and early colonial administration is drawn primarily from the Public Record Office files, London, and the excellent economic survey, W. W. A. Fitzgerald, *Travels in the Coastlands of British East Africa and the Islands of Zanzibar and Pemba* (London, 1898).

For studies of the individual towns of the Kenya coast, see the works cited by Berg, Ylvisaker, el Zein, Bujra, Allen, and MacKay in Chapters 3 and 4, P. L. Koffsky, 'History of Takaungu, East Africa, 1830–1896' (Ph.D.

thesis, University of Wisconsin, 1977), and E. B. Martin, *The History of Malindi* (Nairobi, 1973). A detailed study of slavery in the 19th century is F. J. Cooper, *Plantation Slavery on the East Coast of Africa* (New Haven, 1977).

INDEX

Abe Ngoa, 127
Acheulean Industry, 6, 7–8
age, work of pastoralists allocated
    according to, 75
age-set organization, 76–8, 86, 99, 108
    among hunter-gatherers, 51
    disappearance of, 128
    generation-sets complementary to, 106
    in clan alliances, 84
    linguistic evidence for, 28, 54
    migration caused by, 63
agriculture (*see also* farmers), xvi, xvii
    adaptation to local environment,
        xiv-xivii, xx–xxi, 43–4, 60, 73, 96, 104
    early development, 10–12, 17
    in coastal zone, 82, 85, 92–3
    in highlands, 60, 96, 101, 104
    intensification of, xxii–xxiii, 67
    linguistic evidence for, 28, 31, 32
    mixed, xiv, xv
    peoples engaged in, xv
    production increased to meet needs of
        caravans, 129–30
    shifting, 20, 73–4, 85
    slave labour for on plantations, 134,
        137, 138
    subsistence, 72–3, 114
    techniques, 73–4, 114
Ajuran clan, 108, 109
ancestors, rules for correct social
    behaviour determined by, 79, 80, 129
andu anene, 128, 129
animals, domestication of, 10–11, 17
anthropologists, usefulness of oral
    traditions doubted by, 47–8
antisocial behaviour, 79–80
Arab culture, 143
archaeological data, xii, xviii–xix, 1–21
    traditions conflicting with, 59
archaeological sites, comparisons
    between, 2
Ariaal people, xv, xvii, 108
Australopithecus, 5

Aweera people
    alliances with Swahili, 93
    language, xv, 63
    location, xiv, xv
    traditions, 51

Baba Tora, 125
Bajun Islands, 92
Bantu-speaking peoples, 26, 29–40
    classification, 29, *30*, 33, 35–6
    differentiation of, 37–9
    distribution, *24*, 33, *38*
    interaction with other peoples, 32–3, 43
    spread of, 30–31, 32–3, 37–40
    traditions, 54–61
behaviour
    compared with norms, xxi–xxii, 47
    correct, determined by ancestors, 79,
        80
beliefs, 79–81
    archaeological evidence for 1, 8
    in Neolithic period, 10–11
Benaadir, trade in, 123–4, 130
Benue-Congo languages, 30
bilingualism, 81
Bimal, 130
biologists, archaeological data used
    by, 1
bipedalism, 3
Biryaa, trade and settlement in, 120–21,
    125
Bisha people, 53–4
blood brotherhood, 76, 115, 120
bones, animal, 1
Boran Oromo people
    culture, 105–7
    interaction with Somali, 108–9
    location, xvii, 63
    social and political organization, 105–7
borders, political, xvii–xviii
brain capacity, increase in, 3, 5–6
Brava, 56
    trade in, 123

147